Moira

PLAYS ONE

Moira Buffini trained as an actor and taught drama in
Holloway Prison. The monologue *Jordan,* co-written
with Anna Reynolds, won the Writers Guild Award for
the Best Fringe Play 1992 and a Time Out award for her
performance. She directed her second play, *Blavatsky's
Tower*, on the London Fringe in 1998. *Gabriel*, written
for the Soho Theatre in 1997, won an LWT Plays on
Stage Award and the Meyer Whitworth Award. *Silence*
(1999), winner of the Susan Smith Blackburn Prize,
was commissioned by the National Theatre Studio and
produced by Birmingham Rep and Plymouth Theatre
Royal. In 2001, the RSC produced *Loveplay. Dinner*
was produced at the National Theatre Loft in 2002
and nominated for an Olivier Award for Best Comedy,
transferring to the West End the following year. She has
written and directed three short plays: *The Teacher*,
for the National Theatre's National Headlines series,
The Games Room for the Focus Group at Soho Theatre
and *Doomsday Girl* for the RSC. Her writing for film
includes *Melissa Malone* for the BBC, *Presence* for
Prospect/Film Four and the screenplay of *Gabriel* for
Passion Pictures.

by the same author

DINNER

Introduction

I was in a marquee recently and I was introduced to a man who had just finished writing a novel. He was telling me about it with great pride. When he asked me what I did, I said, 'I write plays.' I don't know what reaction I expected. 'Plays?' He said.

If I wrote novels like him, I would be able to write what happened next (which was nothing much) over four or five pages. I would be able to sketch the physical appearance of both parties, down to the playwright's unfortunate choice of footwear and the muted colours of the spots on the novelist's tie. I would describe the boozy event we were at. I would be able to share the novelist's thoughts as he uttered something sympathetic to the playwright. I would relate over a couple of witty paragraphs how the playwright grew irritated at being condescended to, and how she began to slag off prose. I would express in detail how the novelist smugly began to defend novels at the expense of plays. I would explore the playwright's growing sense of outrage and how it rendered her completely inarticulate. I would be able to explain, without a word of dialogue, exactly how the conversation broke down into mutual resentment and hostility. I would describe how the novelist moved away to find someone more appreciative to talk to. I would be able to linger on a description of his demeanour as he hovered at the edges of the crowd, unable to find anyone who would let him into their conversation. I would express in striking metaphors how the playwright's offence slowly welled up in him. The playwright was clearly drunk. What was she talking about, saying that the novel was a worn out, boring, inferior form? Everyone knew that novels were the pinnacle of literary endeavour. I would be able to give interior voice to his silent brooding. He would dwell upon every bad play he had ever seen. He would feel utterly vindicated at the thought of every tedious night he had spent in the theatre. It's a deathly place to go – a dying art form, surely! There were, he had to admit, *some* good plays, but most of them were written in centuries gone by, before publishing really got off the ground. Yes, that was it. The only good playwright is a dead playwright.

I love plays. I have always loved plays. That is why I write them.

As a playwright (living), the only tools I have to make sense of the world are the words that people say and brief descriptions of the actions that they do. There is only language and spectacle. There is something so inspiring and compelling in this beautiful economy that it has kept me busy for years.

Novelist I'm sorry, what do you do?

Playwright I write plays.

Pause.

Novelist Plays?

I love writing plays for many reasons.

I have never understood human character better than when it has been revealed to me in watching or reading a play.

I have never understood philosophy or faith so well as when I have been enlightened through the journeys of characters in plays.

I have never been so moved and so changed by ideas as when they are dramatically articulated through the action of plays.

I did not know that mere language could make the hair stand up on the back of your neck until I heard it in plays.

I have been made by turns terrified and euphoric, I have been reduced to sobbing and driven to burning rage by plays.

It amazes me how thoroughly a play can be reinvented. Plays are so robust. A good play is endlessly reinterpretable and always relevant.

The text is only the half of it. An alchemy happens when actors, directors, designers and composers apply themselves to a play. It becomes a living thing.

In watching plays – alive, visceral and different every night – I am part of an audience. I like being in an audience, even when I'm angry with everyone in it, even when I am watching something terrible, even on press nights.

You can never do a play on your own. Even a monologue is a collaborative act. We cannot be in isolation when we are involved with plays.

Anywhere that you put a play on is a theatre. They don't have to be dark places, but generally they are. The kind of darkness that you get in a theatre is pregnant with possibility. I find it the most optimistic kind of darkness that there is.

I think plays are very important and I don't think theatre is a dying art form. At least, it won't be, if people continue to write for it – and they are doing, in greater numbers than ever. I think it's going to be a very interesting century for plays, and I think living playwrights, after decades of being marginalised in tiny, black-box spaces are beginning to rediscover their confidence. We are remembering that the stage is a world and not just a room within a room.

The plays in this volume, *Blavatsky's Tower*, *Gabriel*, *Silence* and *Loveplay*, are the first four of mine that got produced. I have a deep and complicated relationship with each one of them and I could – if I was a prose writer – tell long stories about how they came to be written, their journeys towards production and what I think they mean.

But at the end of the day I don't think that would be much use to anyone who actually wanted to put one of them on. As soon as you embark upon transforming a text into a piece of living theatre, it belongs to you. Enough said.

BLAVATSKY'S TOWER

For Ant

Blavatsky's Tower was first performed at the Lion and Unicorn, London, presented by Flying Machine Theatre, on 2 April 1998. The cast was as follows:

Ingrid Josie Ayers
Roland Paul Ebsworth
Blavatsky Richard Evans
Audrey Sarah Malin
Doctor Sam Newman

Director Moira Buffini
Designer Andy Dixon
Lighting Doug Kuhrt
Sound Tom Downs
Assistant Director Patricia Gannon

Characters

Ingrid

Roland

Audrey

Blavatsky

Doctor

Scene One

A large, white room at the top of a block of flats, bright with warm, spring afternoon sunlight. Four antique, straight-backed chairs, and an old television are the only furnishings.

Roland is hunched over his guitar. His awkwardness makes him ugly. The music he plays is classical, passionate. He is watching his sister Ingrid intently. Ingrid is dancing: pale, strange, completely involved in the music. Her movements have an eerie kind of grace. When the music stops, she stays perfectly still, eyes closed. Roland gently tries to kiss her. She punches him. He falls to his knees, winded.

Ingrid Don't.

Ingrid exits to Blavatsky's room. Roland gets up, humiliated. He re-establishes his dignity. He takes his guitar and exits to his room. Pause. A noise, as if the building breathes. Then we hear Audrey and the Doctor outside, and a key turning in the front door.

Audrey (*off*) It's a kind of a penthouse, the only flat on this floor . . .

Doctor (*off*) Oh . . .

Audrey (*off*) The only thing above us is the sky.

Audrey and the Doctor enter, carrying a small, red armchair. Audrey wears shapeless, unfashionable clothes. The Doctor is smartly casual, and wears glasses. They are both exhausted, but the Doctor is in a worse state than Audrey.

Doctor There.

Audrey Thank you. It would have taken me hours, alone.

Doctor How high are we?

Audrey Twenty-five floors; almost three hundred feet.

Doctor Oh . . .

Audrey A long climb, isn't it? Four hundred and six steps, if you include the ones outside the entrance, which I think you should. I often struggle up them with cumbersome things. This is the first time anyone's offered to help me.

Doctor Oh?

Audrey You've been very kind.

Doctor It was nothing.

Audrey Thank you.

Doctor Forget it.

Audrey And now, here we are. (*smiling, shyly*) I've read about the camaraderie of physical exertion.

Doctor I'm sorry?

Audrey Would you mind moving it over here for me, to the light? It's a surprise gift for my father. He's blind. He'll be able to feel the sun on his face here.

The Doctor moves the chair towards the light.

Thank you. (*holding out her hand*) Audrey Blavatsky.

Doctor Oh. Tim Dunn. (*They shake hands.*) Well, I'd better be going.

Audrey Would you like a drink?

Doctor Er, no, I've –

Audrey It's no problem! You can stay for a few minutes, can't you – to recover from your generous exertions?

Doctor Well –

Audrey You're still breathless; you can't possibly go! I'll get you some water.

Doctor Right – OK.

Audrey (*Exits. Immediately re-enters*) Would you like hot or cold?

Doctor Pardon?

Audrey Hot or cold?

Doctor Um, cold.

> *Audrey exits. Roland starts playing the guitar in his bedroom. Music drifts through. The Doctor looks around the strange, empty room, increasingly ill at ease. He sits on a hard-backed chair. It's uncomfortable. Audrey returns with two plastic beakers. He stands.*

Audrey There.

Doctor Thanks.

Audrey It's been boiled.

Doctor Well. Cheers.

Audrey Cheers. (*She clinks his beaker. The guitar music stops.*) You have to let me guess.

Doctor About what?

Audrey You're a doctor, aren't you? Tell me if I'm right.

Doctor (*surprised*) Yes, you're right.

Audrey I thought so.

Doctor How did you know?

Audrey Your glasses.

Doctor Er –

Audrey And your clothes in general. You have the air of a visiting professional. (*She giggles, shyly.*) Actually, the proof came when your jacket swung open.

Doctor What?

Audrey I was able to see your stethoscope.

Doctor Well, I didn't know I looked so obvious.

Audrey (*complimentary*) Oh, you do. Completely obvious.

Doctor Thanks. Have you just moved in?

Audrey We've lived here since the tower was built.

Doctor You don't have much furniture.

Audrey No. My father designed all our interiors.

Doctor I thought you said he was blind.

Audrey Yes.

Doctor Well, that accounts for it, I suppose.

Audrey He says that a simple, clear environment makes for an inspired mind.

Doctor I see. Interesting design idea.

Audrey It is, isn't it? We've never been made complacent by comfort.

Doctor You're lucky living up here, actually. The flats lower down are pretty grim. The one I was visiting in had mould, some kind of black, fungal damp growing all over the walls.

Audrey Oh dear.

Doctor I suppose you must be praying that they demolish this place one day and build you somewhere decent to live.

Audrey I never pray.

Doctor But, what I mean is –

Audrey I know what you mean. You don't like the tower.

Doctor Well, it's a slum, isn't it? (*Guitar music starts again.*) Twenty-five floors high in a little town the size of this? It's an eyesore. Surely you must agree?

Audrey Don't insult it, please. It's a noble building. It's fallen into disrepair because people don't know how to live here. They don't respect it. That's why they have mould. It's as if the walls are weeping.

Doctor Well. (*He glances out of the window.*) Great view, anyway.

Audrey You can see right over the moors on a clear day, to the coal pits in the valleys beyond. The light – that's the beauty of the tower, you see, the light. It changes all year round; the winter sun, the summer evenings – even the darkness has a different quality. Some nights the moon floods in and fills the rooms with such beautiful, steely light that you imagine you're – Well. I won't bore you with what I imagine.

Doctor (*putting his beaker down on a hard-backed chair*) Nice music.

Audrey It's my brother. He plays.

Doctor Oh, he's good, isn't he?

Audrey (*looking down*) Yes. We're very proud.

The music is heartfelt. It suddenly stops.

Doctor Well, it's been nice meeting you, Miss Blatskavy.

Audrey Has it?

Doctor Yes, of course. Well, I'd better be off.

Audrey You can't go.

Doctor I'm afraid I have to.

Audrey I need you!

Doctor What for?

Audrey . . . In your professional capacity.

Doctor Oh.

Audrey It's been part of the excitement of discovering you were a doctor – the possibility that you might be able to help. It's been growing in my mind all the way up the stairs. All the time I've been talking to you I've been thinking, 'Could he? Could he really – '

Doctor Help with what?

Audrey (*stroking the armchair*) My father's devoted his life to suffering and he needs somewhere comfortable to rest in the evenings. I think it's time he had an armchair, don't you?

Doctor Sounds like it.

Audrey He won't reproach me for buying it –

Doctor That's good –

Audrey Because he's dying.

Doctor Oh –

Audrey Yes, he's dying – and I don't know what to do. What shall I do? He's dying, and I don't know what to do.

Doctor Hasn't your doctor been able to help you?

Audrey We haven't got a doctor.

Doctor Surely if your father's blind and elderly, he's got a doctor?

Audrey He won't have them in the house.

Doctor Why not?

Audrey They alleviate suffering.

Doctor Pardon?

Audrey Well, as I've just mentioned, he's devoted his life to suffering. He sees doctors as anathema to his philosophy.

Doctor Are you saying he's actually made a positive decision to suffer?

Audrey Yes.

Doctor Why?

Audrey Only those who live in the shadows can truly appreciate the light.

Doctor Did he say that?

Audrey No, I did. (*Pause.*) My father is trying to discover the truth in things. Truth is painful, therefore he suffers.

Doctor I see.

Audrey Do you?

Doctor Why has he, er . . . What led him to, um, this decision to suffer?

Audrey He was the architect who created this tower.

Doctor Oh.

Audrey He thought it would be beautiful. He never recovered from its ugliness.

Doctor Isn't a life of suffering a bit over-dramatic for one architectural mistake?

Audrey He had high hopes.

Doctor Even so.

Audrey It broke him when they came to nothing. It was his fervour alone that got the tower built, you see. He had a vision of how it would be and . . . when it wasn't like that, he, he decided we would live here to prove it was – a utopia, but – he stopped wanting to look at the world and he shut himself away and – (*She sighs.*) The council wanted a low-level complex with intersecting concrete walkways. That would have been even worse in my opinion.

Doctor How long have you thought he was dying?

Audrey Several weeks.

Doctor (*shocked*) And he's had no medical help?

Audrey He won't allow it! I've agonised over what to do. I've tried everything, exhausted all the healthcare literature I can lay my hands on, and now I'm desperate.

Doctor Where is he?

Audrey (*indicating Blavatsky's room*) In there. It's become his habit to sleep for several hours during the afternoons.

Doctor When can I examine him?

Audrey Now, while he's asleep. I don't want him to know that you're there.

Doctor Why not?

Audrey It would distress him. His feelings about doctors are very strong.

Doctor Supposing he woke?

Audrey He's a deep sleeper, Doctor. I've trimmed his beard without him waking before now.

Doctor But if he were to wake, the shock of seeing me might worsen his condition.

Audrey He wouldn't see you. He's blind.

Doctor Right. (*getting out a notebook*) Tell me about his symptoms.

Audrey The expert on his condition is actually my sister, Ingrid. She watches him. I can't devote as much time to him as I'd like because I'm the breadwinner. (*with shy pride*) I go out to work in an office. The only comfort I can offer, is to read aloud to him in the evenings. He's very fond of Milton, with whom he empathises.

Doctor Yes, but what are his symptoms?

Audrey My father, who is blind . . . sees things.

Doctor What sort of things?

Audrey Things made of light. Visions.

Doctor Oh.

Audrey I don't want you to misunderstand me. He's not mad and he's not senile. Those things lack dignity and Dada's a dignified man. He's had visions since he was young, even before he was blind. It was a vision that inspired him to build the tower.

Doctor A vision of what?

Audrey (*evasive*) Just a vision.

Doctor I see. (*He writes.*) Is he on any medication?

Audrey No. Only herbal tea.

Doctor What about physical symptoms?

Audrey He coughs horribly; he won't eat, convinced that the crushed have contaminated our food supply; his limbs are wasted; and he has trouble with his bowel movements.

Doctor What are the crushed?

Audrey The people who live below – down there.

Doctor OK . . . (*He writes.*) How long has he been blind?

Audrey It came gradually. I don't think he's seen anything for over fifteen years. In his mind, I still have the face of a child.

Doctor And in all this time he's never been to hospital, or seen a specialist?

Audrey Oh no. My father hasn't been out of this flat for as long as we've lived here.

Doctor Not at all? Not even out of the door?

Audrey No.

Doctor Is he agoraphobic?

Audrey Agoraphobia implies fear. He isn't afraid, Doctor. He just won't go out.

Roland (*entering*) Audrey, did you remember to get my – (*He notices the Doctor and crumples in shock and fear.*) Bastard! . . .

Audrey (*consumed with embarrassment*) Roland, this is Dr Tim Dunn. He's come to look at Dada.

Roland, unable to contain his panic, returns to his room.

That was my brother. Roland.

Doctor Is he all right?

Audrey Yes, he's fine.

Doctor He called me a bastard.

Audrey He's not used to strangers, that's all.

Doctor How do you mean?

Audrey Well, he doesn't go out.

Doctor Like your father?

Audrey No; not like my father. My father doesn't go out because he's turned his back on the world. Roland's a little more positive. He's actually made a philosophical decision to stay in.

Doctor Right.

Audrey He says it purifies his thinking if he remains aloof from the rest of the world. You can understand that, can't you?

Doctor I'm not sure.

Audrey Well, his work is delicate, and he feels it would be sullied if he was in constant contact with others, that's all.

Doctor What is his work?

Audrey It's not relevant.

Doctor I'd love to know.

Audrey (*embarrassed*) He's writing a theory of the universe.

Doctor Right.

Audrey You probably think that solitude keeps him out of touch; but he has his means of communication. He endures several hours of television a day and it's given him an intimate knowledge of humanity. He's fighting a brave battle to remain uncorrupted by what he sees, but I'm afraid his language has suffered. That's why he called you a bastard.

Doctor Does anyone ever visit you here?

Audrey Of course. All the time.

Doctor Who?

Audrey We're always getting things through the door. Post, advertisements and things, we've even been invited to enter prize draws for exotic holidays. A constant stream of colourful things fall onto our mat.

Doctor What does your sister do?

Audrey She looks after my father.

Doctor Does she ever go out?

Audrey Why do you ask?

Doctor Just curious. Does she?

Audrey What if she didn't?

Doctor So she doesn't?

Audrey No.

Doctor Is that also the result of a philosophical decision?

Audrey No.

Doctor What keeps her inside?

Audrey Her will.

Doctor Miss Blatskavy, can I ask you: what's your relationship with Social Services?

Audrey Pardon?

Doctor I mean, have they ever visited you? Do they know you're here?

Audrey Why would Social Services be at all interested in us? We're not the crushed.

Doctor No, I just thought that perhaps it might help your brother and sister to talk to someone about their situation.

Audrey In what way does the lifestyle of my brother and sister amount to a 'situation'?

Doctor Well, you have to admit that it's pretty unusual for two young people to spend their lives incarcerated in a top-floor flat.

Audrey No one is incarcerated here. We're all free people.

Doctor Yes, but they don't go out.

Audrey That's their business, Doctor, not yours.

Doctor Yes, but it's quite odd, don't you think?

Audrey Odd?

Doctor Unusual.

Audrey (*pause*) Perhaps you'd better go.

Doctor What?

Audrey I made a mistake in asking you here. Forgive me for wasting your time.

Doctor But what about your father?

Audrey (*opening the door for him*) We'll manage, thank you.

Doctor You just said he was dying!

Audrey Yes. Mortality may take him, but at least we know he won't be removed from us by social workers.

Doctor Miss Blatskavy –

Audrey Blavatsky. I can see what you think of us. You haven't been here half an hour and already you've passed judgement!

Doctor You've totally misinterpreted me –

Audrey We're ordinary people, Doctor, whatever you think; a perfectly ordinary family!

Ingrid (*entering from Blavatsky's room; pale, strange and worried*) Audrey, Dada's – (*She notices the Doctor and crumples with shock and fear.*) Who's he? . . .

Audrey He's just going, darling.

Doctor Hello.

Ingrid What does he want?

Audrey Nothing.

Doctor I'm a doctor.

Ingrid (*straightening up*) Have you come to help Dada?

Doctor Yes.

Ingrid (*approaching him with urgent gratitude*) He's making a funny noise.

Doctor May I see him?

Ingrid (*taking hold of him by the lapels*) Thank you.

Ingrid pulls the Doctor into Blavatsky's room. Audrey cries: deep, heartfelt sobs. She is beginning to recover herself when Roland comes out of his room, with transparently false confidence. He has made a great effort to smarten himself up. He is wearing shoes and he has combed his hair.

Roland Where is he?

Audrey He's seeing Dada. Ingrid's with him.

Roland (*strides over to Blavatsky's door. Stops abruptly*) What's his name?

Audrey I told you. Dr Tim Dunn.

Roland He scared the shit out of me. (*Pause.*) Have you been crying again?

Audrey No.

Roland Twat.

Audrey Roland, when I see you the way that other people see you, it depresses me more than I can say. I'm going to make the tea. Keep out of my way.

Audrey exits to the kitchen. Roland, crestfallen, strides once more to Blavatsky's door. He stands in front of it, but can't muster the confidence to open it. He turns away.

Roland So you're a doctor? Dr Tim Dunn, Tim Dunn, Tim Dunn, Tim Dunn, Dr Timmmmmm Dunn. Yes. I'm Roland Blavatsky. (*Puts out his hand as if to shake.*) Hi! (*Repeats gesture.*) Hi! Welcome to our penthouse home, welcome to Blavatsky's Tower. Bastard.

He exits. Returns almost immediately with a huge manuscript.

Dr Dunn, I presume? I'm Roland Blavatsky. Thanks for coming; thanks awfully for helping with the father. Shit! (*Pause. Briskly*) My father's very ill; dying actually, slowly killing himself. Yes, he's committing suicide and he's a tyrant. My sisters won't tell you that because we have a difference of opinion. They think he's a sweet old man. Only I know what a cruel, magnificent soul he has. Only I know the – My father's had plenty of courage all his life but now it's – The ultimate act of courage is to withstand ridicule. Such acts have their price, of course, and Dada's – To him, the world is total darkness. Despair, Dr Dunn, is Dada's daily diet. Insanity, or truth? (*Puts down his manuscript. Kneels with his ear to the door. Whispers.*) Ingrid! Ingrid . . . (*Kisses the door. Moves away. Sits on one of the chairs.*) Do you watch any of the soaps? I do; I watch them all. They're Real Life Dramas, actually. Real life. I mean if that's real life I'm glad I'm dead. No, I didn't mean that; how disturbing. I especially like *Medics*. Are you like that? Do you have a cavalier bedside manner? Do you struggle against the odds to heal the sick in an underfunded hospital? Perhaps you play golf in your spare time. Doctor, healer, tender of wounds. You stride, valiant against disease, apothecary to the agonised, preserver of life. Is it fun? Or just something to do? Dada. (*Puts his head in his hands, then immediately assumes an air of nonchalance.*) My father. My father and I. He doesn't like me, Doctor. He only tolerates me in the same room as him when I don't speak. I have coped with this fact of life with admirable stoicism, to the point where I can admit it with an air of nonchalance, to an imaginary presence in an empty room. He likes my music. I know I move him because I watch his face slowly change. I watch his blind eyes. Sometimes, Doc, when you're feeling kind of blue, you know, locked in a hideous midnight of your own making, music is the only sanity. It's what the seeing

have in common with the blind – an exquisite light in the
gloom . . . I don't amount to much. That may surprise
you, but I don't amount to very much at all. If I was to
go down and stand sweating and shaking in the street, I
would blow away on the breeze instantly, like a dandelion
clock. But in my room, I'm quite big. How big are you
in your room? Perhaps you amount to quite a lot, out
there on the golf course. May I call you Tim? Of course
your name doesn't matter when you're a doctor. You're
not engaged in an unrelenting struggle with your identity,
like the rest of us. You can wrap your profession around
you like an invisible cloak. Doctor. It's a whole personality
really, like a murderer or a priest. (*Pause.*) Humanity is a
flickering image on a little screen, to me. I have to keep
it far away so I can see it. That's why I disintegrated
when we met. I get overwhelmed, you see, by realness.
Some days, I feel the universe like an egg in my hand –
yet it's blotted out, the whole thing wiped away by even
the thought of someone real standing before me, a
stranger, unafraid, curious even, not unfriendly, who
could reach – over – the – gulf . . . If you were him, if you
were him, I would kiss the hem of your garment. (*Pause.*)
Do you know Dante? Have you read the *Inferno*? I'm
working on a little something myself. (*As he speaks, he
goes to his manuscript and carefully spreads it around
the floor. Bashful*) Yes . . . Oh, about six years. It's for
my father. I know it sounds . . . but if I – Then his life
won't have been in vain. This is my labour and research;
my philosophy. And there are fewer things in heaven and
earth than are dreamt of in my philosophy. Ha! That's
a joke, actually, but even so, it's greater than – I mean
some people have written such bollocks – wasted their
lives on one idea. But when you've opened your mind
to the truth, Doctor, the *truth* . . . The darkness in
everything dazzles me. (*Pause.*) It's a fucking stupid
waste of time, actually. (*frantic*) No it's not!

23

Roland flings himself onto his manuscript. He embraces it. Then he notices the armchair. He examines it. It puzzles him. He panics.

Audrey! . . . Audrey!

Audrey (*off*) I'm busy!

Roland What's this? What is it?

Audrey (*enters with a potato-peeler and a half-peeled potato*) It's an armchair.

Roland What's it doing here?

Audrey It's my surprise gift for Dada. He's old and ill and he needs an armchair.

Roland What a stupid idea!

Audrey It's not a stupid idea. It's a gift of love.

Roland Have you lost your mind? Bringing an armchair into this house, an armchair and a doctor on the same day!

Audrey What's wrong with it?

Roland Bugs, sweat, flakes of crushed skin, grease, filth; it's disgusting!

Audrey It's fully washable, Roland.

Roland You want to drag Dada out of bed and plonk him on that? You'll finish him off!

Audrey It'll do him good.

Roland Bollocks! Oh *shit*! We've got to get rid of it, now, before he knows it's here.

Audrey No.

Roland (*taking the chair*) Quick, out the window! . . .

Audrey (*sitting in it*) Leave it!

Roland Audrey, for fuck's sake!

Audrey If you lay one finger on this chair, you know what will happen.

Roland No, I don't. The future is uncharted territory and can never be accurately predicted by beings confined to linear time.

Audrey I'll cut off your lifeline. There'll be no more library books, no more stationery or music paper, no more welding kits to carry up fifty flights; the next time you want two litres of sulphuric acid or a packet of Jaffa Cakes you can get it yourself! –

Roland All right! (*Pause.*) How did you get it here?

Audrey I dragged it over the wasteland.

Roland Did you use the lift?

Audrey Of course not. The Doctor helped me carry it.

Roland Really?

Audrey Yes, I encountered him on the first floor, coming out of someone's flat. He offered to assist me.

Roland Do you mean to say you've only just met him?

Audrey Yes. He'd been visiting one of the crushed. Someone with mould.

Roland I'm sorry, but I assumed you'd gone to a surgery and made an appointment.

Audrey No, it was a chance encounter; it was fate.

Roland So the man you're trusting to examine Dada is just some fucking bloke you met coming out of a flat?

Audrey Yes.

Roland You stupid, silly cow. He's probably not even a real doctor!

Audrey Of course he is.

Roland How do you know?

Audrey You can tell just by looking at him!

Roland Did you ask for any identification?

Audrey No.

Roland Then he could be anyone!

Audrey He's a *doctor*, Roland.

Roland What's your proof?

Audrey He wears glasses and he has a stethoscope in his pocket.

Roland A real doctor would wear contact lenses and keep his stethoscope in a bag! (*Pause.*) He made you cry, didn't he?

Audrey No.

Roland What did he say?

Audrey Nothing.

Roland He upset you.

Audrey You upset me! You embarrassed me. Everything was fine until you had to slither across the floor and call him a bastard! Why did you do it? He thinks you're a weirdo now.

Roland I'm not a weirdo.

Audrey Yes, you are. You're a total mess. Why can't you just be normal?

Roland I am normal. It's everyone else! . . . (*Pause.*) Audrey, he's in there with Ingrid. Make him go away. Please.

Audrey It's too late.

Roland Dada would never want this.

Audrey Too late.

Blavatsky (*shouts from the bedroom*) Audrey! Audrey!

The Doctor runs from Blavatsky's room, knocking Audrey off her balance. She shrieks.

Doctor Shit! Sorry.

Ingrid (*following the Doctor*) Audrey, he heard the Doctor in the room.

Audrey (*to Doctor*) What's the matter with him?

Doctor I don't know; he just started shouting!

Blavatsky AUDREY!

Audrey I'm here, Dada.

Audrey hurriedly gives the potato and peeler to Roland. She exits to Blavatsky's room.

Doctor (*recovering from his fright*) God.

Ingrid Audrey will calm him; she always does.

Doctor (*laughs*) What happened there?

Ingrid It wasn't your fault.

Doctor No, no, of course not. (*puzzled*) I've never met him before in my life.

Ingrid I know.

The Doctor notices Roland, who is staring at him.

Doctor Hello.

Ingrid This is my brother.

Doctor Yes. (*offering his hand*) Tim Dunn.

Roland (*won't shake*) You're a doctor.

Doctor Yes.

Roland I need some ID.

Doctor What for?

Roland Need it.

Ingrid Leave him alone, Roland.

Doctor It's all right. (*He hands a small card to Roland.*) It's got my title on it. Doctor.

Roland This could be stolen.

Doctor Well, it isn't.

Roland How do I know?

Doctor You'll just have to trust me.

Roland . . . OK. Hi. (*He awkwardly attempts to shake the Doctor's hand. Fails.*)

Ingrid I'm dealing with the Doctor. Why don't you go away?

Roland Golf. It's a microcosm of life.

Doctor Pardon?

Roland I've read the rules. People are handicapped from the beginning.

Doctor Right . . .

Roland Do you play?

Doctor I'm afraid not.

Ingrid Go away!

Roland He's standing on my text!

Doctor (*moving his feet*) Oh, sorry. It that your theory of the universe?

> *Roland looks at the Doctor aghast. Ingrid scoops the manuscript into an untidy pile.*

Yes, your sister was telling me about it. Not this sister, the other one. Sounds great. Good luck with it.

> *Ingrid takes the manuscript to Roland's room and hurls it in. Pause. Ingrid takes hold of Roland and shoves him out. She shuts the door on him.*

Ingrid I think it would be better if you went now.

Doctor I'm sorry if I've caused any trouble.

Ingrid You haven't.

Doctor I'll come back in the morning. I've got nothing with me now, and I want to examine your father more thoroughly, to confirm my diagnosis.

Ingrid You've diagnosed him?

Doctor I think so, yes.

Ingrid How is that possible?

Doctor I'm a doctor. I've been trained to diagnose.

Ingrid Is he going to die?

Doctor Well, he's never had any medical treatment. With proper supervision he could certainly improve. It would help if you and your sister tried to get him used to the idea of seeing me – you know, mention it to him.

Ingrid He despises doctors.

Doctor I realise that, but it's going to be very hard for me to help him if I have to pretend I'm not in the room . . . Look, I'll come back in the morning. You'll be my first port of call – and meanwhile I'll see about admitting him to hospital.

Ingrid (*horrified*) You can't take him to hospital!

Doctor Why not? He obviously needs to go.

Ingrid You can't take him away. The shock would kill him!

Doctor The best place he can be is in hospital.

Ingrid Save him here!

Doctor That's not feasible.

Ingrid It is. I could assist you. He'll never give you permission to take him through that door, never in a million years!

Doctor Well. There's no point deciding anything tonight. Just start to think about it . . .

Ingrid I had a feeling that one day a doctor would come, but I imagined him bald, with a pipe.

Doctor When did you last leave this flat?

Ingrid Prizegiving day at school. I was obliged to attend as I'd won the Geography prize. It was a globe, with a lamp inside.

Doctor Why did you stop going out?

Ingrid The ground's very overrated. You'd feel the same if you lived up here.

Doctor Don't you ever get lonely?

Ingrid (*moving away*) Why should I? I'm surrounded by those who love me.

Doctor Even so.

Ingrid Do you live alone, Doctor?

Doctor Yes.

Ingrid Then what's the difference between your life and mine?

The Doctor laughs.

Don't laugh at me. Why are you laughing? You don't understand me, and you're laughing as if I'm a fool.

Doctor I'm sorry.

Ingrid The human condition is one of aloneness. That's what I'm saying. What's so funny about that?

Doctor Nothing. Sorry.

Ingrid We're discussing Dada. You shouldn't be trying to diagnose me.

Doctor I wouldn't dream of it.

Audrey enters from Blavatsky's room.

Audrey I'm afraid you have to go now.

Doctor I was just saying goodbye to your sister.

Audrey (*showing him out*) Please use the lift.

Doctor I thought the lift wasn't working.

Audrey It is.

Doctor But we lugged the armchair up fifty flights of stairs!

Audrey (*with shaky pride*) The Blavatskys have never used the lift. It's an unnatural displacement of gravity. To ascend over two hundred feet into the air without expending any energy, is shirking our responsibility to endure.

Doctor Right.

Audrey (*holding the door open*) Excuse us, we have to tend to Dada.

Doctor I'm coming back in the morning –

Audrey Thank you –

Doctor (*exiting*) – to examine him more thoroughly and confirm –

Audrey Goodbye.

Doctor – my diagnosis!

Audrey shuts the door on the Doctor.

Audrey What's been going on?

Ingrid Nothing.

Audrey I let you alone with him for five minutes and the whole house is in chaos.

Ingrid Not my fault.

Audrey What did you do?

Ingrid Nothing.

Audrey Dada is not himself.

Ingrid The Doctor examined him; that's all.

Audrey He's terribly disturbed. What happened?

Ingrid Leave me alone!

Audrey You know it doesn't pay to keep things from me. Ingrid, come on. You know what'll happen.

Ingrid Shut up!

Audrey I'll cut off your lifeline. There'll be no more magazines, no bulbs, no cosmetics or seed trays. The next time you want organic mulch or scented candles –

Ingrid All right! (*Sighs.*) The Doctor followed me into Dada's room.

> *As Ingrid describes the scene, the space becomes, with minimum fuss, Blavatsky's gloomy room. We see Blavatsky in his bed, dozing restlessly.*

Dada had been restless. He was sweating and making a horrible noise when he breathed – (*She opens the door and pulls the Doctor in by the lapels.*) but as soon as I brought the Doctor in, he went quiet, serene almost. It was odd. (*to Doctor*) He was making a funny noise.

Doctor I'll just check a few things.

> *The Doctor rapidly examines Blavatsky.*

Ingrid He examined Dada very quickly. He was extremely professional. It was interesting for me, as an amateur carer, to see such an experienced man at work.

Doctor He's blind.

Ingrid I know. I was quiet at first. He was so –

Doctor Heartbeat slightly fast, but steady. Temperature high.

Ingrid I don't remember people being like him, at all.

Doctor Is he incontinent?

Ingrid No. He has the opposite problem.

Blavatsky Put them into the snow . . .

Ingrid takes up an exercise book and pen, and jots down what Blavatsky has said.

Doctor What did he say?

Ingrid He said, 'Put them into the snow.'

Doctor What did he mean?

Ingrid Much of his unconscious imagery refers to differing weather conditions. I write it all down in this book.

Doctor May I see?

Ingrid hands him her book.

Audrey You didn't give it to him!

Ingrid Why shouldn't I? He just glanced at it.

Doctor 'The Dreams and Visions of Hector Blavatsky, Volume 27.' Well. (*He hands it back.*)

Audrey Then what happened?

Ingrid We spoke.

Doctor Do you spend all your time caring for him?

Ingrid No.

Doctor What else do you do?

Ingrid I keep myself amused.

Doctor Up here?

Ingrid Yes.

Doctor Aren't you curious about the outside world?

Ingrid I'm very well acquainted with it.

Doctor Your sister said that you never go out.

Ingrid I go out every evening, when she reads to my father from the classics.

Doctor Where to?

Ingrid We have a roof garden, Doctor. I'm surprised she hasn't told you. She's obviously been so free with all the other intimacies of our family life.

Audrey Huh.

Doctor A roof garden?

Ingrid It's the great outdoors, to me.

Doctor You can't see it from the ground.

Ingrid It's only visible from the sky. It was designed that way.

Doctor What do you do up there? Tell me.

Audrey Don't.

Ingrid I decided to tell him everything. I garden it. My father made it when the tower was new. He loved it. He transported soil, load by load, from the ground to the sky and planted lilies and vines and beautiful, dark roses with petals like lips. The centrepiece was a statue of himself, arms outstretched, eyes gazing up at the sky.

Doctor God.

Ingrid My mother used to sit up there, when she was pregnant with me. She liked the flowers; they reminded her of the ground.

Doctor What happened to her?

Ingrid She died.

Doctor How?

Ingrid In childbirth.

Doctor I'm sorry.

Ingrid For whom? (*Pause.*) Dada boarded the garden up after that, and all through my childhood I never knew it was there. I discovered it one winter afternoon when I was sixteen. I had resolved to end my life and, in order to gain the maximum dramatic effect, I decided to dress nicely and hurl myself off the roof. I broke open the door and pulled myself up into a new world. I was amazed. The garden was all windswept, frosted weeds, roses gone wild, dead blooms still clinging; and the statue, scarred by the weather, had ivy creeping up its face. It looked so beautiful, so unlike Dada, so full of hope. And what was truly fabulous about the place was the air and the sky and the stillness of it all. Freedom.

Doctor Why did you decide to end your life?

Ingrid The usual reasons.

Doctor And they are?

Ingrid You mean you've never tried it?

Doctor No.

Ingrid Then use your imagination.

Audrey What a stupid thing to say.

Ingrid (*pause*) I shouldn't be trusting you, should I?

Doctor Why not? I'm a doctor; I won't betray your confidence in any way.

Ingrid Come here.

Doctor What for?

Ingrid I want to look at you.

Doctor Why?

Ingrid To see if you're sneering behind your eyes.

Doctor My patients usually accept that I'm on their side.

Ingrid I'm not your patient.

The Doctor approaches Ingrid. She looks into his eyes. He finds it difficult to meet her stare.

Doctor (*pause*) Am I, then? Sneering?

Ingrid I can see my reflection. That's odd, isn't it? Your eyes are showing me myself. Roland says I have no thoughts of my own. I'm only capable of imagining other people's. He says I'm blank inside; I have nothing to offer anyone, and ought to go the way of all the crushed. Would you agree?

Audrey (*under her breath*) You've thrown yourself at him! . . .

Ingrid Your eyes are quite deep. What do you see in mine? Apart from yourself. Do you think I'm mad?

Doctor No. I don't.

Audrey I'm sick of this! What happened then?

Ingrid Then –

Blavatsky (*starting to struggle*) Don't leave me! Worms . . . Belial!

Doctor What did he say?

Ingrid (*writing in her book*) He said, 'Don't leave me. Worms. Belial.'

Doctor What did he mean?

Ingrid Don't leave me means don't leave me, worms means worms and Belial is a demon of Hell.

Doctor Right.

Blavatsky Don't leave me! (*He wakes, staring sightlessly around the room.*)

Ingrid It's all right, Dada, I'm here.

Blavatsky Ingrid, something most extraordinary . . . It was real. I want you to write it down.

Ingrid Of course.

Blavatsky Immediately, while the images are fresh in my mind. Are you ready?

Ingrid Yes.

Blavatsky Because this is important, Ingrid. This *must* be written down.

Ingrid Dada began to talk about the dream he'd just had. He was very lucid.

Blavatsky I could see.

Ingrid It was many years in the future. He was walking through the valley, like he used to when he was a young man.

Blavatsky But it was overgrown, full of creeping things . . .

Ingrid When suddenly, he came upon the ruins of the tower.

Blavatsky There it was. I craned my neck backwards and the windows stretched above me, all dark and fractured. It was wounded; cracks gaping in the fabric, naked to the rust. I looked at it and thought: 'This is my child.'

Ingrid He was crying.

Blavatsky So ugly . . . Then I heard a crumbling echo high above me and I knew the tower was about to fall. It was holding itself up with the last, bewildered strength of the dying. So I lay at its feet and waited for it to kill me.

Ingrid Dada, it was just a bad dream.

Blavatsky Write it down!

Ingrid He was most insistent that I wrote it down. I haven't finished it yet, but I will.

Blavatsky I began to float. There, lying on the ground, where I have never felt heavier, I began to float. My body rose up and I saw the end of the tower. The windows shattered as I watched; dust filled the darkness. I heard the lift plunge, roar of bricks and concrete, iron and glass falling. The garden was wild as it fractured, beautiful still to the last. Cascading . . . (*He sighs.*) Oh, it was gone. I was drifting on glittering dust. It was gone and I was floating, the sun on my face so warm. And then, Ingrid, then they came . . . out of nowhere, they were all around me!

Ingrid Who?

Blavatsky It was them, bathing me in light.

Ingrid Oh, Dada!

Blavatsky I was with them! I wanted to look at them, Ingrid, but they hurt my eyes; the very shape of them hurt me. Their light! I would have endured it until they consumed me completely . . . incandescent clarity. But they were gone and I awoke here, in darkness. (*becoming exhausted, fainting*) They're coming, Ingrid. They're going to come to me again. Don't let me sleep . . . (*He sleeps.*)

Doctor Who was he talking about? Who hurt his eyes?

Ingrid The angels. They were too bright.

Doctor Angels? He sees angels?

Ingrid Well, not exactly angels, no.

Doctor Fantastic. Your sister didn't tell me that.

Ingrid She dislikes the term. I call them angels as a kind of a shorthand –

Doctor You see I know about this. I know all about visions of angels. I read a paper on it during my training. They're actually a well documented neurological phenomenon. Recent case histories tend to talk about UFOs or aliens, but all through history there are written testaments of the same thing: visions. Spirits, angels, shimmering Christs . . . But, you see, these psychotic ecstasies are not actually 'visions' at all. They're not planted in the mind by some higher force. They're epileptic, or migrainous manifestations, caused by showers of phosphenes in transit across the visual field –

Audrey (*to herself*) Yes . . .

Doctor Often exacerbated by scotomas, or tumorous pressures in the brain –

Ingrid (*loudly, offended*) What are you talking about?!

Blavatsky suddenly wakes.

Blavatsky Who's there? There's someone in the room!

Ingrid (*motioning the Doctor away*) No, Dada.

Blavatsky Who's there?

Ingrid No one.

Blavatsky I can hear him!

Ingrid You must've heard someone in your dream.

Blavatsky No. I can smell him. Something crushed.

Ingrid There's nobody here.

Blavatsky Who are you?

Ingrid This is nonsense, Dada.

Blavatsky Don't try and hide him.

Ingrid I'm not!

Blavatsky You'd betray me if you could!

Ingrid You have to believe me –

Blavatsky I can smell him!

Ingrid (*flinging her arms round him*) How can you think that I'd lie to you?

Blavatsky (*he calms*) I'm sorry, my little girl.

Ingrid There's no one here, only me and you.

Blavatsky No, no one here. Sit with me. (*He feebly pats the bed beside him.*)

Ingrid You're too ill, Dada.

Blavatsky Sit with me.

Ingrid (*moving away*) No.

Audrey You should have sat with him.

Ingrid Shut up!

Blavatsky Did I tell you of my dream?

Ingrid Yes.

Blavatsky About them, coming back?

Ingrid (*warmly*) Yes . . .

Blavatsky I want to get out of bed.

Ingrid Dada, you can't.

Blavatsky I've got work to do. They're coming back and I must be ready.

Ingrid You're not well enough.

Blavatsky It was like this when they first came. I was walking through the valley one winter night and I saw them in the sky. I put up my hands to shield my eyes and found my face was wet with tears. That is the strongest image of my life.

Ingrid I know.

Blavatsky Such a beautiful thing. I marked the place in the sky where I saw them, and I drew the tower, the tower reaching up. I made them build it, all the little men, I made them. I don't want to die. They're going to come back. I want to be ready.

Ingrid You won't die.

Blavatsky Death is a famine.

Ingrid Shhh . . .

Blavatsky Don't let me die. Save me.

Ingrid I'll save you. I promise.

Blavatsky closes his eyes. Ingrid looks at the Doctor, almost in tears.

He wants me to save him.

Doctor Let me help you.

Blavatsky (*stares right at the Doctor*) I know you. Belial . . . (*Shouts.*) Audrey! Audrey!

The Doctor exits. Ingrid runs to Audrey.

Ingrid He stared straight at him, Audrey, as if he could see! He said he knew him!

Audrey It's all right, darling . . . everything's all right; but listen to me. The Doctor's here to help us, but his help is all we must take. Dada wouldn't want it any other way. It's no good telling him about us; I made that mistake myself. He's from the ground and he doesn't understand. He wanted us to have a social worker.

Ingrid A social worker?

Audrey He – he's superficial, Ingrid. He seems like a man out of a book, all tall and sympathetic, but he's just like they are at work, like they were at school; you give them your trust and they trample it. They laugh at you behind your back.

Ingrid He didn't laugh at me.

Audrey Trust is a black hole, Ingrid. You inch towards it and you get swallowed up in the void. Look at you; he's robbed you of your judgement and your will and now you're left, drowning in his shallows.

Ingrid I'm going out!

Audrey Go on then!

Ingrid I will. He's probably still on the wasteland. I'll find him and –

She opens the front door. A noise, as if the building breathes. She falters.

Audrey Don't think you can go out just like that. It takes courage. Courage I have to muster every day.

Ingrid closes the door, defeated.

It took courage to bring that doctor up here. And I'll deal with him.

Ingrid You're just like Dada! (*She exits.*)

Audrey (*goes to Blavatsky and kneels beside him*) Dada? It's your Audrey. I've got a wonderful surprise for you. Can you imagine? I've bought you an armchair . . .

Scene Two

Late evening of the same day. The room is lit by
moonlight, a reading lamp and the flickering light of the
television. Audrey quietly reads to Blavatsky from book
three of Paradise Lost. *Blavatsky is in the armchair,*
puzzled by its comfort.
    Roland is standing in front of the television, stooped,
fists clenched, scowling with contempt at what he sees.
He wears a pair of old-fashioned headphones. He doesn't
move.

Blavatsky An armchair, a small armchair . . . Who
would have thought an item of furniture would mark my
re-emergence?

    Audrey continues reading Paradise Lost.

There was an armchair where I was a child. It was an
adult's thing. A privilege to sit there. Green. As big and
as restful as the sea . . .

Audrey Yes.

Blavatsky Is this one green?

Audrey Bright, emerald green like a beetle from the
orient.

Blavatsky Audrey, I saw them again in a dream.

Audrey Ingrid told me.

Blavatsky After all this time, to dream of them . . . I was
certain they'd left me. But what if they never did? What
if they've been with me always and I've been blind to
them? What if I was *wrong*? . . .

Audrey I don't know.

Blavatsky I've always ached for the truth in things. But the search is a trail through quicksand. It's like mercury rolling through your hands – beautiful, dangerous and nothing can contain it. It's no more than a word, yet I can feel it, the truth, pressing on my heart. I've been wrong.

Audrey Don't be upset.

Blavatsky Up*set*?

Audrey I'm glad you saw them again.

Blavatsky You don't believe I ever saw them.

Audrey Of course I do.

Blavatsky You think I'm deluded. You always have.

Audrey No.

Blavatsky I'm not angry, Audrey. I've never expected you to understand.

Audrey (*deeply hurt*) No, you never have. (*She reads on.*)

Blavatsky I'm sick of Milton. I want to speak to my son.

Audrey (*amazed*) To Roland?

Blavatsky He is my only son.

Audrey goes to Roland. He takes off his headphones.

Audrey Dada wants to speak to you.

Roland (*panicking*) To me? Why? What have I done?

Audrey I don't know.

Blavatsky Come here.

Roland approaches.

Kneel down. I want to see you.

Roland kneels. Blavatsky examines his face slowly, carefully, with his fingers.

Forgive me.

Roland (*puzzled*) I forgive you. (*Pause*) Would you like me to read you something? Something of my own, just a few pages of –

Blavatsky No, thank you.

Roland I've been writing – it's – I've been – it's my work, Dada –

Blavatsky I said no. I don't wish to hear you read.

Roland Well. I'll – um. Right.

Roland goes back to the television, bewildered, hurt.

Blavatsky Where's Ingrid?

Audrey In her garden.

Blavatsky (*with love*) Her garden . . . Audrey, when I'm gone –

Audrey Shush, Dada. Let's have some more Milton.

Blavatsky Promise me –

Audrey No promises, Dada. You're not going anywhere.

Blavatsky Keep Ingrid away from the crushed. They'll taint her beautiful soul.

Blavatsky closes his eyes. Audrey looks at him with intense anger and bitterness. She reads.

Roland They're putting electronic tags on penguins.

Audrey (*stops reading, irritated*) He's not listening.

Roland How do you know?

Audrey Because if he was, he'd tell you to shut up.

Roland (*turning back to the screen*) It's a dump, the Antarctic. They can melt the fucking place for all I care.

Audrey reads on.

Blavatsky (*stands slowly, as if in a trance*) I can see them.

Audrey What is it, Dada?

Blavatsky They're here.

Audrey Who?

Blavatsky Them.

Audrey Roland!

Blavatsky In the air . . .

Roland runs towards him, pulling his headphones out of the television. Noise blares into the room.

Roland Dada.

Blavatsky Don't touch me! In the air . . .

Audrey Dada, there's nothing there.

Blavatsky's legs give way.

Help me!

Roland I am fucking helping you!

Roland awkwardly helps Audrey to lift Blavatsky on to the armchair.

Blavatsky In the air we shall dwell.

Roland What did he say?

Audrey I don't know.

Roland Oh fuck. Oh God. Dada.

Blavatsky In the air we shall dwell. (*He loses consciousness.*)

Audrey He's dying . . .

Roland Ingrid! INGRID!

Audrey He can't breathe.

Roland Old bastard. Fucking breathe.

They lay him on the floor. Audrey tries to revive him. She puts her head to his chest.

Audrey Turn that thing OFF!

Roland turns the television off. Audrey listens for signs of life.

Nothing. Nothing . . .

Roland and Audrey are silent with shock. They look at one another.

Scene Three

Early next morning. Bright sunshine. There is a strong wind blowing around the tower. The noise of it pervades the scene. Blavatsky has been laid out on the four straight-backed chairs in the middle of the room and covered with a white sheet. Roland and Audrey are wearing black. Audrey is looking anxiously out of the window. Roland is kneeling on the floor, sorting through his bulky manuscript. Ingrid is tied to the armchair, gagged, exhausted and struggling.

Roland He won't come.

Audrey He will.

Roland What if he doesn't?

Audrey He will. He's going to give his diagnosis.

Roland Great.

Ingrid continues to struggle. She makes a noise. Roland looks at her.

Audrey Ignore her; she's attention-seeking.

Roland Do you think we could take the gag off for a while?

Audrey No. She's manipulating you.

Roland She wants to say something.

Audrey She's trying to spoil Dada's death!

Ingrid sinks back in the armchair, exhausted. Roland exits with his manuscript.

Imagine what he'll think when he finds out what you're up to. I wouldn't blame him if he had you committed.

Roland enters with his guitar. He sits close to Ingrid and plays the tune that she danced to in the first scene. This irritates her. Audrey goes over to Blavatsky and folds back the sheet, uncovering his face. Roland stops playing.

Roland What are you doing?

Audrey kisses Blavatsky. Roland puts down the guitar. He stands over Blavatsky.

Hector Blavatsky – architect and visionary.

Audrey Kiss him.

Roland can't. He kisses the air above Blavatsky's lips.

People always look younger when they're dead. Mumma looked younger too. Like a girl. You don't remember, do you?

Roland No.

Audrey Dada said she'd gone into the air to be with them. She was so pale. Then he gave me Ingrid to hold and said he had to get some grown-ups. She still had Mumma's blood on her. I didn't know what to do; she screamed and screamed. (*Whispers.*) Poor little thing . . . You were playing with your bricks on the floor. Right there.

Roland covers Blavatsky with the sheet.

Roland I'd like to recite a short poem about death –

Audrey (*going back to the window, irritated*) Don't.

Roland
Death has flickered over me
With insect wings –

Audrey There he is in the wasteland car park! He's getting out of a red car. His tie's blowing behind him in the wind. Oh!

Ingrid wails. She struggles furiously.

Roland I can't stand this. I'm going to take the gag off.

Audrey All right. I'll do it. I'm head of the household. (*She goes to Ingrid.*) Roland and I would like Dada's death to be a dignified affair so pull yourself together. (*She takes off the gag.*) Stop this madness.

Ingrid I'm not mad. I'm telling the truth.

Audrey I'm warning you.

Ingrid Get me a drink, you cow.

Audrey No.

Roland She wants a drink.

Audrey She'll get one when she asks for it nicely.

Ingrid Don't play these stupid games with me!

Roland Shall I get you one?

Ingrid No, make her. She uses you like a floorcloth; it's unbelievable!

Pause.

Roland (*to Audrey*) She wants you to go.

Audrey Pathetic. (*She goes into the kitchen.*)

Ingrid (*urgently*) Roland, you have to let me go. Everything I said is true. I'm not mad. I can *save* him. Just let me touch him; let me put my hands on his face. Roland, you have to believe me. Let me go!

Audrey (*returns with a beaker of water*) What does she want?

Roland She wants me to let her go.

Audrey Is she still harping on about the same thing?

Roland Yes.

Audrey (*holding out the water*) Here.

Ingrid I don't want it. Let me go!

Audrey throws the water on her. Ingrid shrieks.

Audrey That's for hysterics!

Ingrid I'm not hysterical. I'm speaking the truth!

Audrey Dada is *dead*. How can you hurt us like this?

Ingrid Roland, help me.

Roland I'll get you a towel.

Ingrid I don't want a towel – help me. Don't be such a *weakling*!

Roland I'm not a weakling. You render me powerless; it's a different thing.

Audrey Where's the gag?

Ingrid (*straining towards Blavatsky*) Dada!

Audrey (*snatching the gag*) Give me the gag, Roland. I'm not having this.

Ingrid I'm speaking the truth!

Roland Don't hurt her.

Audrey CO-OPERATE!

Ingrid Get off – Aaaahhhh!

*Audrey tries to tie the gag around Ingrid. She struggles.
There's a knock at the door.*

Roland (*running to the other end of the room*) Oh fuck,
oh fuck, it's the Doctor!

Audrey Let him in.

Roland How can I? Look at us; oh *fuck*!

Audrey Stop struggling! (*She hits Ingrid. Ties gag. To
Roland*) You're so feeble! (*Goes to the door.*) Now,
dignity everybody. We're a united front. Let's greet him
with dignity.

*She opens the door. The Doctor stands on the
threshold, carrying a classic doctor's bag. He's not
wearing his glasses and he looks smarter and more
casual than ever.*

Doctor Miss Blavatsky! I hope I haven't called too early.

Audrey Doctor.

Doctor It's a glorious day; the breeze nearly knocked me
off my feet. It's on days like this that – (*seeing Blavatsky*)
Oh.

Audrey He died during the night. We didn't know what
to do.

Doctor I'm so sorry.

Audrey It's been a desperate time. We're so relieved to
see you.

*The Doctor approaches Blavatsky. Ingrid waits to be
noticed, with dignity.*

Doctor Well, this is terrible. You have my deepest
sympathy.

Audrey You're very kind, very – (*She bursts into tears and turns away. Pause.*)

Roland Where are your glasses?

Doctor Pardon?

Roland You're not wearing glasses.

Doctor No, I've got my contact lenses in today.

Roland Oh.

Doctor It's good for your eyes, to give them a change from time to time.

Roland So, you've arrived with all your equipment?

Doctor Yes.

Roland And you're going to give your diagnosis?

Doctor No, of course not. Not now.

Roland A little *late*, isn't it?

Audrey (*recovering herself*) Doctor, the task of guiding the family through this awful event has fallen upon me, but I feel helpless and distraught and hopeless – and we have no one to ask. Please tell me – what should I do?

Doctor What should you do? You mean in regard to practical matters?

Audrey nods.

Um. Well. Once I've written you a death certificate, you should phone a funeral parlour. That's what I'd do. Undertakers are usually very sympathetic. They'll help you organise whatever you like. They'll probably come to see you, to discuss what kind of coffin, hiring hearses, whether or not you want him embalmed –

Audrey does a horrible sob and turns away in tears once more.

Roland We can't.

Doctor Can't what?

Roland Phone them. We haven't got a phone.

Doctor Oh.

Roland We haven't had any sleep. Audrey doesn't want to go out. She's upset.

Doctor Well. Perhaps I could make a call for you.

Audrey (*in a rush of gratitude*) We want flowers for him. Hundreds of beautiful flowers. And a white memorial stone shaped like a tower, with gold lettering bearing his name and a wonderful epigram.

Doctor Right.

Roland We want a notice in the paper. Those bastards down there should know that they finally killed him. And we want music playing throughout.

Doctor OK, well I'll see what I can do. (*deciding*) Yes, I will. I'll take care of everything. I'll help you.

Audrey (*overcome*) Thank you.

Doctor Where's Ingrid?

The Doctor follows Audrey and Roland's gaze. He turns to see Ingrid, horrified.

What the hell's going on? Why have you tied her up?

Audrey I'm afraid she had a fit, a hysterical fit, so, acting in her best interests and under great emotional duress, we humanely contained her movements.

Roland With the washing line.

Doctor You've gagged her!

Audrey Yes.

Doctor And she's soaking wet!

Audrey I threw a little water on her – to calm her down.

Doctor How long has she been like this?

Audrey Only a few hours.

Doctor A few hours?

Audrey If you'd seen what she was like –

Doctor I'm going to free her, right now.

Audrey No you can't!

Doctor (*taken aback*) Why not? . . . Has she attempted suicide?

Audrey No.

Doctor Then let me take the gag off, at least.

Audrey (*to Ingrid*) Remember what I said. Don't shame me.

Doctor (*kneels in front of Ingrid, takes off her gag*) There.

Ingrid I knew I could trust you. I knew that when you offered your help, you meant it.

Doctor Why have you tied her up?

Audrey (*pause*) Doctor, last night when our father died, Ingrid was in her garden up on the roof. Roland and I coped alone with Dada's last agony. When we could do no more for him, Roland went to find her.

Roland I don't like the roof. I get vertigo.

Ingrid I'd been up there for hours in the fading light, writing down Dada's last dream.

Roland I shouted her name into the darkness again and again, but she didn't answer. It caused me to panic.

Ingrid I'm afraid I'd fainted.

Audrey Naturally, we assumed the worst.

Roland Then she turned up, all covered in soil.

Ingrid I'd come round in a flower bed.

Audrey She seemed feverish but strangely controlled, as if she was in a trance. Then, when I told her the terrible news, she quietly said that she already knew.

Roland It was really weird.

Audrey She took both my hands and said she was going to bring Dada back. She said his death was just a temporary state, an illusion, and that when she touched him he would wake, his sight fully restored.

Ingrid I'd seen the angels.

Audrey I'm trying to protect you.

Ingrid I don't need protecting!

Audrey She's been talking like this all night. It's grief, a delusion.

Ingrid I saw them!

Audrey No! All my life – creatures in the sky . . . (*turning away, upset*) It's not true!

Ingrid I could feel their light, right through my skin.

Doctor You saw angels? Like your father?

Ingrid Yes. It was them.

Doctor What were they like?

Ingrid (*after careful thought*) Light.

Doctor So they weren't winged?

Ingrid Pardon?

Doctor I mean they weren't recognisably human or, um, like the images we'd traditionally associate with angels?

Roland (*under his breath*) Twat.

Ingrid They were light.

Doctor Light as in nebulous, bright, weightless, volatile?

Ingrid (*patiently*) Why don't you just let me tell you what they did?

Doctor Right.

Ingrid Their light, which I'd first seen as an outside thing, began to fill me completely. I stopped looking with my eyes, yet it was so intense, this light, that it started to cause me pain. They began to tell me things, without a voice. Everything fell into place. I knew that Dada was dying, and I knew the moment he was dead. They said it was the sign of a beginning. (*Pause.*) You don't understand, do you?

Doctor . . . How long were they there for?

Ingrid I don't know.

Doctor You must have some idea. How long did it seem?

Ingrid It *seemed* an infinite instant.

Doctor Oh.

Roland Perhaps they operate in a different equation of space and time. Perhaps, for them, time is a three-dimensional paradox, a non-linear –

Ingrid Roland.

Doctor When did you pass into unconsciousness?

Ingrid I don't remember. I came round and found myself lying in the garden. And the first thing, the *only* thing I was conscious of, were these words, beating in my head, in my blood: 'In you is the infinite power of life.'

Doctor As if they'd spoken to you?

Ingrid Yes. 'In you is the infinite power of life.'

Doctor What do you think they meant?

Ingrid Exactly what they said.

Doctor Which is?

Ingrid (*becoming impatient*) I've got the infinite power of life.

Doctor And that's why you believe you can save your father?

Ingrid Absolutely.

Doctor Your power of life will revive him?

Ingrid That's correct.

Audrey (*snapping*) Why are you questioning her in this manner? This isn't the help we want! What about Dada?

Ingrid Yes, what about him? Doctor, you're here for a reason. Your life has led you here, just as our lives have.

Audrey No.

Ingrid This gives a purpose to everything we are: our sadness, our wild imaginings, our isolation. Dada made us ready for them. That was his life's work and I'm not going to see it end!

Audrey You have to stop.

Ingrid Doctor, believe me, I'm telling the truth!

Doctor I believe you.

Roland (*aghast*) Don't lie to her. Why are you lying?

Doctor I'm not lying.

Audrey He's lying to be kind. He's indulging a lunatic.

Roland It's despicable.

Ingrid Believe me! BELIEVE!

Doctor (*touching her*) Ingrid, trust me. I believe you.

Roland (*flabbergasted*) Bastard . . .

Ingrid Untie me.

Roland I'll untie her.

Doctor That's all right. I'm here, I'll do it.

Roland I said I'll untie her. She's my fucking sister!

Doctor (*standing back*) Right, that's fine.

Ingrid I asked the Doctor!

Doctor No, really, it's fine. I have to examine your father anyway, so . . .

Roland moves in front of the Doctor and starts to untie Ingrid.

Ingrid (*to Roland*) You're so immature.

Doctor When you're free we can discuss what's best to do, what takes everyone's, um, wishes into account.

The Doctor pulls back the sheet and starts an examination of Blavatsky.

Audrey (*approaching him*) What are you doing?

Doctor (*confidentially*) I'm confirming that he's dead.

Audrey Why don't you inject her with a sedative?

Doctor I won't inject her with anything unless she medically requires it.

Audrey She does.

Doctor I disagree.

Audrey You're standing by while she walks the path to madness.

Doctor Ingrid's in a state of deep shock. I don't think she's mad. And I don't think you should antagonise her by calling her a lunatic.

Audrey I only want you to stop her.

Doctor If she wants to revive your father, why not let her? She'll try and she'll fail, but at least she'll have tried. What harm can it do? It might even release her grief.

Audrey You know nothing about this family or this place. You're tampering with things you don't understand. I'm not going to let her near him!

Doctor Surely you don't believe she could succeed? (*Pause.*) You *do*, don't you? That's why you tied her up!

Audrey You didn't see her last night.

Doctor My God.

Audrey You didn't hear what she was saying. It was *frightening*! You said yourself that you believed her.

Doctor I was lying.

Audrey She *trusts* you!

Doctor I'm a doctor. Sometimes it's a truth, to lie, when it's for the benefit of our patients.

Audrey She's not your patient. He is – and look what happened to him!

Doctor I can see you're upset, Miss Blavatsky, so I'll let that pass. Your father's dead. What your sister plans is very poetic, but it's a medical and scientific impossibility. It won't happen. Trust me.

Roland (*gently*) I'd like to believe you, Ingrid.

Ingrid Then why don't you?

Roland I always wanted to believe Dada, too. But I never did.

Ingrid (*determined*) I'm going to read you something, Roland. It's at the heart of everything and when you hear it you'll believe. (*She stands, picks up her notebook and slowly walks over to Blavatsky.*)

Doctor How are you?

Ingrid I'm feeling no pain.

Doctor Right. I think it's time for a rational discussion. I think everyone's got something to say and, well, reviving the dead; it's a complex issue. People's feelings should be taken –

Ingrid When I came round in the garden, I discovered I was still holding Dada's book. Following on from the end of his dream, there was a page of new writing, something I didn't recognise. This. I have no memory of writing it.

Audrey Ingrid, if you don't stop and see sense, you'll lose me forever; my friendship, my respect and my care.

Ingrid Listen. (*She reads.*)

'In the air we shall dwell.
Those whose lives have been touched by despair,
Those who have known poverty,
Disease, madness, shame, loneliness, pain,
And have found no meaning,
They shall be healed by the gentle light.
Earthly riches belong to the earth;
We shall return them,
And learn from the wisdom of those who need nothing.
Those who have followed the rules of the petty
Shall trust their own understanding.
The brutal, the ignorant, the aloof –
They will comprehend the pain of the crushed
And compassion will make them the best among us.
We who grieve will find what we have lost;
We will remember what we have long forgotten:
The air beneath our feet
Shall teach our souls to fly.
We will be angels once again.'

Audrey (*pause*) That's very pretty, Ingrid, it's really very lovely and beautiful – but it's got nothing to do with anything.

Ingrid You didn't *listen*! It's got everything to do with everything.

Doctor What does it mean?

Ingrid It means what it says – it's completely clear. Surely I don't have to *explain* it?

Doctor Of course not. But you say you have no memory of writing it?

Ingrid Yes.

Doctor Who wrote it, then?

Ingrid It's in my handwriting, so I suppose I did. (*showing the Doctor*) It was them, writing through me.

Doctor May I borrow it?

Ingrid Of course.

Doctor Thank you.

Roland He doesn't believe a word you've said. Why are you giving him your book?

Ingrid Because I'd like him to read it.

Roland He's so dishonest!

Doctor I am not.

Roland Why can't you show her some respect?

Doctor I've shown her respect since the moment I got here. It wasn't me that tied her to a chair!

Audrey Doctor, stop indulging her; it's so unkind.

Ingrid We're wasting time.

Doctor (*to Ingrid*) What exactly are you going to do?

Ingrid I'm going to lay my hands on him and open myself to the light.

Doctor Right. Well, I can't see any harm in that.

Roland (*quietly*) Neither can I.

Audrey Fools! (*She exits to the kitchen.*)

Ingrid Do you believe me, Roland?

Roland 'In the air we shall dwell.' That was the last thing he said. He was looking at something in the air.

Ingrid He could see them.

Roland And then, twice, he said it.

Ingrid Roland, if he and I both saw them, they must have been there.

Roland But why didn't Audrey and I see them? We were in the same fucking room and we didn't see a thing!

Ingrid Dada never used his eyes and he could see more than all of us. I know you want him back. Be *with* me. Brother.

> *Roland embraces Ingrid. Audrey comes back in with a rolling pin and a potato masher. She stands over Blavatsky.*

Doctor What are you doing with them?

Audrey I am *not* going to let her near him.

Doctor Now look –

Ingrid Audrey, you're making a fool of yourself.

Audrey I'm the only one with any dignity left.

Ingrid Dada will soon be back.

Audrey I don't want him back!

Ingrid Of course you do. We can't go on without Dada.

Audrey We *can.*

Ingrid What about his life's work?

Audrey What about my life's work? What about *me*? I'm glad he's dead!

Ingrid (*deeply shocked*) Audrey.

Audrey We can start again. We can *live.*

Ingrid We're going to live with Dada! When he comes back, it won't be like before –

Audrey Keep back!

Ingrid Everything will be different! It'll be a time of brightness. Dada will be kind to us and Roland will be so handsome.

Audrey I'm fighting for your sanity, can't you see? I'm the only one trying to save you! (*She clings to Blavatsky.*) You will not touch him!

Ingrid (*taking hold of Audrey*) Move away.

Doctor Right, that's enough.

Ingrid Traitor!

Audrey Cripple!

Ingrid (*struggling with Audrey*) Jealous! You're so jealous!

They fight. Roland hides behind the armchair.

Doctor (*attempting to intervene*) This is going to get you nowhere.

Audrey (*shoving him out of her way*) You *quack*!

Ingrid (*shrieking*) Let go!

Audrey The *arrogance*! How *dare* you! You think you're him!

Ingrid I know why you hate me. Audrey, I know . . .

Ingrid pins her down. Audrey struggles.

I killed her! I was born and I killed her! You *hate* me!

Audrey I – don't – hate – you!

Ingrid He loved us, Audrey. He must have another chance . . .

Audrey What chance have we had? Oh, do what you like. Do what you like. I can't bear it.

Audrey cries. Ingrid releases her, then kisses her. She stands, deep in concentration.

Doctor Right. I think we should –

Roland Shut up!

Ingrid slowly kneels down before Blavatsky. She puts her hands on his forehead. Roland half-kneels too. Ingrid closes her eyes. She lets her head fall backwards, as if gathering power. Her concentration is awesome. Long pause. Audrey sits up. She wipes her eyes. Nothing happens. Ingrid's expression momentarily falters.

Ingrid Dada?

Audrey Kiss him.

Ingrid kisses Blavatsky. She gently touches his hair. The tears come. She slumps over him.

Ingrid Where *are* you? (*She sobs with grief.*)

Pause.

Doctor It's released the grief, you see.

Audrey Ingrid. (*She tries to comfort her.*)

Ingrid Don't TOUCH me! (*She runs out.*)

Doctor It'd be best to leave her now. Really it would. It's the kindest thing you could do. After she's cried herself out, I'll give her something to help her sleep. Some kind of –

Audrey exits after Ingrid.

I think that's a big mistake, following her like that, I really do. That kind of grief needs space. I've seen it before and I always try to let the person alone until they're in a fit state – to be seen. It's what we were taught. The release of grief. The first step on the road to recovery. Any bereavement counsellor will tell you the same thing.

Roland Can you hear her crying?

Doctor (*realising*) No.

Roland She's gone up on the roof.

Doctor Oh my God, she'll kill herself!

The Doctor exits in a panic. We hear the wind blowing. Roland's face crumples in pain.

Roland I wanted it to be true. But nothing is. Nothing ever is . . . Dada.

Roland puts his head on Blavatsky's chest. He tries to lift the old man's arms around him.
    He holds him in an embrace. Blavatsky's hand moves. He exhales deeply.
    Roland is paralysed with fear. Blavatsky inhales. He breathes.
    Roland, overcome with panic and terror, grabs the pillow from under Blavatsky's head.
    He smothers him.

Scene Four

The next day. Late afternoon: long shadows and sunset light, giving way to evening. Blavatsky's body, the armchair and one of the chairs have been removed. Roland is seated at a school-type desk, typing on an old machine. He is humming theme tunes from quiz shows. Ingrid enters.

Ingrid (*sleepily*) What time is it?

Roland Almost evening. I couldn't wake you. I moved my work in here so I'd be near. Are you all right?

Ingrid I took the drugs the Doctor gave me.

Roland Why?

Ingrid To see what they'd do.

Roland You should have told me.

Ingrid I couldn't.

Roland Why not?

Ingrid I was asleep.

Roland (*giving Ingrid his chair*) Sit down.

Ingrid (*sitting*) Where's Audrey?

Roland At work.

Ingrid But the Doctor said she wasn't to go! He said she was to give herself time to get over the shock.

Roland I can't believe you listen to that twat. If Audrey and I had listened to him yesterday, you'd have been a splat on the wasteland.

Ingrid He saved me, Roland.

Roland Audrey saved you.

Ingrid It was him.

Roland (*turns away*) Bollocks . . .

Ingrid (*looks at the papers on his desk*) What's this?

Roland I'm going back to the beginning, the beginning of everything, when darkness was on the face of the deep. I had a revelation – last night when I was watching the fire. I've been concentrating too much on the end, because we're living on the edge of it and it's hard not to let that crush you, but, when you think about it, the conditions at the end are precisely those which form the beginning –

Ingrid I actually meant what's this? (*She picks up some leaflets.*)

Roland Oh, they came through the door this morning. You can win a satellite dish. And there's a thing about pizza delivery, I think.

Ingrid 'It's as if the garden lends a hand.' Why have we received this? This is from a garden centre.

Roland Don't know.

Ingrid There's a pull-out order form for next spring's bulbs and tubers. (*She gets up, deeply puzzled by the brochure.*) How did they know we had a garden? We live in a tower block. Who delivered this?

Roland Perhaps a pilot flying overhead in his small but trusty jet noticed the garden, thought, 'I wonder if they've got their bulbs and tubers yet?' and radioed an emergency signal through to a garden centre.

Ingrid Oh yes . . .

Roland (*looking at her*) That's not your dress.

Ingrid It's Mumma's.

Roland (*approaches her, touches the dress*) I remember it.

Ingrid Roland, what are we going to do?

Roland About what?

Ingrid Dada's dead. Something has to change.

Roland Like what?

Ingrid (*pause*) Let's go out.

Roland What?

Ingrid Let's go downstairs.

Roland No way.

Ingrid You and me. Now.

Roland Don't be fucking stupid.

Ingrid Come on, Roland; just down to the wasteland, to feel the ground beneath our feet.

Roland You must be fucking mad!

Ingrid I'm not mad!

Roland There's no way I'm going down there. I'll blow away!

Ingrid Just for five minutes – please!

Roland No!

Ingrid Yes!!

Ingrid pulls the door open. The Doctor is standing on the threshold, just about to knock.

Roland The Saviour.

Doctor Hello.

Roland (*tense, over-friendly*) Hi, Doc. Come on in; make yourself at home.

Doctor (*enters, carrying a plant, some shopping and his bag*) Thank you.

Roland How's things?

Doctor Things are fine. How are you?

Roland Oh, splendid, thanks. Recently bereaved but – on top of the world, really, yes!

Doctor Ingrid.

Ingrid Hello.

Doctor You look much better. (*He holds out the plant.*) Um, this is for your garden. It's an ornamental raspberry bush. They were on offer in the supermarket and I just thought I'd . . .

Ingrid Thank you. (*She takes the plant as if it's very precious.*)

Doctor Sorry I wasn't able to get here until so late. It's been one of those days. I would have phoned to make sure you were OK, but you don't have a phone . . . Anyway, I've got tomorrow and the next day off so I'll call in fairly early to help you deal with the undertakers and I can stay around to help you with anything else that might come up. (*He unpacks his shopping onto Roland's desk.*) I thought perhaps I could cook for you tonight? To save Audrey doing it. (*holding up some fresh pasta*) I bought Italian; do you like it?

Roland No.

Ingrid Yes. We love it. Thank you.

Doctor Where's Audrey?

Roland At work.

Doctor She went to work?

Roland She left this morning with her sandwiches and the complete works of Gerard Manley Hopkins.

Doctor But your father only died yesterday. Why has she gone to work?

Roland She wanted to. Routine is a great anaesthetic, exertion a suppressant of pain. I'm sure you know that.

Doctor Of course I know that; I'm a doctor.

Ingrid Every time I eat a raspberry, I'll think of you.

Doctor Actually, It's ornamental. It doesn't produce fruit.

Ingrid Oh.

Doctor I wish I'd had more of a chance to look at your garden. I only got such a fleeting impression. Amazing. And the statue; much bigger than I thought, quite – imposing. I thought that maybe tomorrow, we could go up there and –

Roland Ingrid spent most of today in a coma. She'd taken those drugs you gave her and I thought she'd gone catatonic.

Doctor They were only sleeping tablets. (*to Ingrid*) I thought they'd give you some peace.

Roland Yes, oblivion is peaceful, isn't it? Ask anyone in a near-death state. (*moving between them*) So how was your ever-so-busy day, then?

Doctor Fine, thank you.

Roland Have you discovered a panacea for all human ills, or were you too busy prescribing psychotropic drugs to the desperate – too busy colluding with giant pharmaceutical companies in their insidious oppression of the crushed?

Ingrid Roland, would you get the Doctor a drink?

Roland I'm only taking an interest in your daily doings, Dr Dunn. Perhaps you were sitting at your desk like me, trying to cope with the fact that the human race is an evolutionary failure?

Doctor Is that the central premise to your 'theory of the universe' – the human race is a failure?

Roland No.

Doctor What is it, then? I'd love to know.

Roland I'm afraid you wouldn't understand it.

Doctor What makes you think that?

Roland You're too stupid.

Ingrid Get him a drink.

Roland Why?

Ingrid Because he wants one.

Doctor Cup of hot water would be great. Thanks.

Roland storms out. Pause.

I read your book. The idea of some unspecified time that the collective human consciousness is yearning to belong to; the idea of returning to, or developing a higher state, a state founded on compassion and – whatever. I mean, if we can imagine such a state, then such a state may certainly exist – on a subconscious level anyway. And the angels – the things you call angels – begin to not exactly make sense, but – in a poetic way – they sort of do make sense, yes. I don't know much about things like this but

I found it – moving. Actually. (*Pause.*) You wrote it, didn't you? Not him. The dream I heard him tell you; you turned it into something so different. It's very good. (*He hands it to her.*)

Ingrid (*deeply moved*) Thank you.

Doctor You're going to laugh at this.

Ingrid What?

Doctor I had a dream about you last night.

> *Roland enters and stands in the doorway with a beaker of hot water, unnoticed.*

Ingrid Was it funny?

Doctor No.

Ingrid Then why should I laugh?

Doctor I don't know.

Ingrid What happened?

Doctor Well, I was on the moors, barefoot, wearing an operating gown, and I saw you walking towards me –

Roland Excuse me.

Doctor What?

Roland Our father has just died. My sister is recovering from a suicide attempt. She's not really interested in your dream. (*He holds out a beaker.*) Drink.

Doctor Thank you.

Roland Cheers.

Doctor (*sips, hurts his mouth*) Well, you'll be glad to hear that I spent this afternoon arranging your father's funeral.

Roland Oh.

Doctor Yes, during my breaks from colluding in the oppression of the crushed, I was working for you. A lot of the people I spoke to remembered your father as a young man. The editor of the *Chronicle* is printing an obituary tomorrow. He said your father was one of the most singular residents the town has ever had; and he asked me if I knew that the tower was going to be listed.

Roland What?

Doctor The tower is going to be made a listed building.

Roland You're joking.

Doctor Apparently it expresses perfectly the architectural ambitions of its time.

Roland Fucking hypocrites! How dare they.

Doctor I thought you'd be pleased.

Roland He despised those bastards and I don't blame him. Listed? What bollocks!

Doctor Well, there you are. I also rang around the undertakers, and got a very reasonable quote from a small firm on the High Street. The details are here. (*Holds out a piece of paper. Neither Roland nor Ingrid takes it.*) I made enquiries about the headstone. A tower shape is difficult; you have to have it specially designed, but they do do a praying angel. How would you feel about that?

Roland Deeply indebted, Dr Dunn, but unfortunately –

Doctor (*becoming terse*) Roland, my name's Tim. Why don't you call me that?

Roland We're awfully grateful for the hard work you've done on our behalf, 'Tim', but I'm afraid it's all been in vain.

Doctor Why?

Roland We organised the funeral ourselves.

Doctor What?

Roland We were worried about Dada's corpse; that it would disturb us and interfere with Ingrid's recovery. So last night, after you'd gone, we held a short memorial service and cremated him on the roof.

Doctor (*appalled*) You did what? . . .

Roland It was my idea. Audrey said it was inspired. When it came down to it, we were most unhappy about his final resting place being down there on the ground amid the dogshit. So we made a great pyre out of his books, his furniture and all the flammables we could find. It consumed him.

Ingrid (*quietly*) All we kept was his wedding ring.

Doctor No.

Roland We used his copy of *Paradise Lost* to start the flames.

Doctor You're not serious.

Roland Are you suggesting we did it as a joke? It was very moving, 'Tim' – a poetic act. It fell upon me, as his only son and head of the household, to light the first match.

Doctor It's not possible.

Roland You underestimate the infinite realms of possibility.

Ingrid The smoke drifted right over the moors, towards the coal pits in the valleys beyond. I've read about people who believe burning releases the spirit of their loved one into the air. Dada would have liked that. We all felt his presence very strongly.

Doctor I can't believe you've done this.

Ingrid Don't you approve?

Doctor It's a disaster.

Roland What do you mean?

Doctor Can't you see?

Roland Perhaps you'd like to enlighten us, 'Tim'.

Doctor I've just spent all day organising your father's funeral, to the point where half the town is expecting it. I'll now have to go round to the undertakers, the council, the local press, the florists, and tell them, sorry, the funeral's off; the deceased's family have burnt his corpse on a bonfire in their garden. What do you suppose they're going to think?

Roland They're going to think you're a pretty stupid bastard for wasting your time.

Doctor (*loses his temper*) That is not the point! The point is, you've broken the law.

Roland What law?

Doctor You can't cremate people in your garden; that's the law! It's a gruesome thing to do and I can tell you now, people will not see it your way.

Ingrid How can it be gruesome? It was done with love.

Doctor Why didn't you tell me you wanted a cremation?

Ingrid We decided last night, as it grew dark. You'd already gone.

Doctor But you didn't have to burn him on the roof! (*hurt*) You should have told me. You could have had it done by experienced professionals.

Roland It wasn't your business, 'Tim'.

Doctor You've committed a criminal act and I'm involved; of course it's my bloody business!

Roland Are you worried that people will blame you?

Doctor My actions have been irreproachable.

Roland Then what's your problem?

Doctor You asked for my help and I gave it in good faith!

Roland Are you trying to tell me you've done all this from motives of pure altruism?

Doctor Of course I have.

Roland You've spent your action-packed day running up and down the High Street for the benefit of a family you barely know?

Doctor That's right.

Roland Bollocks. I know why you've done it, 'Tim'. It's so obvious it's a joke. You want to fuck my sister!

Ingrid goes into the kitchen and slams the door.

Doctor You're lucky I don't pull your head off, you poisonous bastard.

Roland Why don't you try? Come on, fucking try.

Doctor You wouldn't survive five minutes in the real world.

Roland What would you know? You're a fucking cardboard cut-out!

Doctor I'm *warning* you!

Roland And I'm warning Ingrid, so fuck you!

Doctor (*grabbing Roland by the shirt*) You twisted little foetus! You don't know anything about me, or the way I feel.

Roland You've never had a real feeling in your life. You're a fucking hologram. I could put my hand right through you, you're so empty!

Doctor (*shaking him*) Take that back, you piece of shit!

Ingrid comes out of the kitchen with a large pan full of water.

Roland Come on, hit me, Doc, pull my eyes out, blind me!

Ingrid throws the water over them. Roland shrieks. They separate, gasping.

Ingrid That's for hysterics.

Roland, soaked, whimpering, scurries into his room.

Doctor I'm soaked! Shit, my bloody shirt. (*unbuttoning it*) Damn, it's dry-clean only . . .

He notices Ingrid staring at him. He looks at her. Ingrid approaches him.

Ingrid Is it true?

Pause. They are just about to kiss.

Audrey (*off*) Hello, it's me-e-e!

The moment is broken as the front door opens and Audrey enters. She carries a huge bouquet of flowers, shopping and a bag full of library books.

Look at my flowers!

Ingrid Oh Audrey, they're beautiful.

Audrey How are you, my darling?

Ingrid Much better.

Audrey Look what they bought me at work. Not only the flowers, but this beautiful card, saying 'Sorry for your loss.' They were so sympathetic it made me cry. They'd had a whip-around; can you imagine?

Doctor How nice of them.

Audrey Hello, Dr Dunn. Goodness – (*She giggles.*) You're soaking wet.

Ingrid Sit down, Audrey. You must be exhausted after all the stairs.

Audrey Oh, I'm so excited I hardly know how to tell you. I came up in the lift.

Ingrid No . . .

Audrey Hurtling up towards the sky in a dark box! Ingrid, it's amazing – such an exhilarating experience, right on our own doorstep.

Ingrid Weren't you afraid?

Audrey No. (*noticing the plant*) What's that?

Ingrid It's an ornamental raspberry bush. A gift from the Doctor.

Audrey Oh, what a thoughtful idea. We'll be eating raspberries all summer! (*She notices Ingrid's dress.*) That's Mumma's dress.

   Ingrid nods. Audrey hugs her.

Ingrid I didn't imagine them, Audrey. I saw them.

Audrey I know.

Roland enters, drying himself with a towel. He glares at the Doctor.

Doctor I'm sorry, I've got to go. I'm soaking wet.

Audrey (*releasing Ingrid*) But I was going to ask you to stay to tea; I've bought fish fingers. We're all so grateful for what you've done.

Roland He has to go.

Audrey You're *both* soaking wet!

Ingrid I threw water all over them.

Audrey Why?

Ingrid They deserved it.

Roland 'Tim' was very upset. We had quite a tantrum. Apparently, we've broken the law.

Audrey How?

Roland By cremating Dada.

Audrey Oh, oh no . . .

Doctor I'm sorry, Miss Blavatsky. It was an unfortunate thing to do.

Audrey But . . . it was what we wanted. It was private and honourable and true to his spirit.

Doctor Yes, but sadly that's not the way other people will see it. I'm going to have to inform someone.

Audrey Who?

Doctor The police . . . And Social Services.

Audrey Why?

Doctor Because if I didn't, I'd be breaking the law too.

Audrey I brought you up here; I let you in. I strive so hard to do the best thing and it always turns out to be wrong. It's always me; I *ruin* things!

Ingrid That's not true.

Roland We had to cremate our father.

Doctor Why?

Roland (*emphatically*) Because then we knew he was dead.

Doctor (*pause*) I'm sorry. I'm very sorry for you all. I'm sure the authorities will be more than lenient when they hear of your situation up here. It must have been awful.

Roland (You patronising cunt.

Doctor Right. I'm going.

Ingrid Don't.

Doctor Ingrid, I'm sorry.

Roland How he emanates sincerity, how he oozes pain. He could almost convince me he'd got a soul.

Ingrid (*turning on Roland*) You're so jealous!

Roland Jealous, of a tailor's dummy?

Ingrid Of course he's got a soul. It's shining.

Roland What?

Ingrid Nothing's ever damaged him. His eyes are completely clear. He's like snow on the wasteland.

Doctor What do you mean?

Ingrid (*embracing him*) You saved me. I was going to jump. It would have been such a mistake.

The Doctor returns the embrace. Pause. Roland looks away, agonised.

Audrey Roland, stop it. Don't be so weak. (*Pause. She hits him.*)

Ingrid (*breaks off*) I want to go out.

Doctor Now?

Ingrid Yes.

Doctor Right.

Roland You can't.

Audrey Don't you dare take her from here!

Ingrid I want to walk on my own, right the way down.

Audrey She's not going!

Doctor She can go where she likes.

Audrey Then come with me, Ingrid, I'll take you down.

Ingrid I want him!

Audrey He's a stranger; you don't know what you're saying.

Doctor Ingrid, we can do whatever you like.

Roland I'm going to be sick. You think it'll be like letting a dove out of a cage. You think she's never been touched.

Ingrid Ignore him.

Roland Well, let me tell you something –

Ingrid Don't!

Roland You don't know anything about her. What do you think's been going on up here, 'Tim'?

Ingrid (*tries to physically restrain Roland from speaking*) Shut up!

Roland Ingrid and I, all on our own?

Ingrid NO!

Roland It was her idea.

Ingrid NO!!

Roland Doesn't it amaze you that someone like her could do it with a creep like me?

> *Ingrid punches Roland in the stomach. He falls to his knees.*

Ingrid How dare you say that in front of Audrey! How *dare* you! (*approaching Audrey, who is ashen*) Audrey, please. I'm sorry. I'm sorry. I'm sorry. We were so lonely! Please . . . (*Pause. To the Doctor*) I think it would be better if you went now.

Roland (*standing*) And take that fucking plant with you.

Doctor (*picking up her book*) Here's your book. Do you want to bring it?

Ingrid What?

Doctor Come on. Get out of here before it kills you.

Roland (He'll get you down there and when he finds out what a mess you are, he'll have you committed. You're fucked up, Ingrid. You think you're going to be happy? Bollocks. You're too fucking damaged. We all are.

Ingrid (*to the Doctor*) Wait.

> *Ingrid exits to her room. Pause.*

Doctor I won't have her committed and I'm not empty. (*He pulls a small bottle out of his bag.*) Here's some

Arnica; it's a homeopathic remedy for shock. You can't
overdose on it, so I'll leave you the bottle. I suggest
you have one each now, and one before you go to bed.
(*He puts the bottle on the desk.*) Up to you whether you
take it.

Ingrid returns. She has stuffed some clothes in a
school satchel and she carries a globe lamp.

Ingrid I'm not saying goodbye. I'm not even going to
look.

Audrey Ingrid! . . .

Ingrid goes to Audrey. They hug one another tightly.
She goes to Roland. He turns from her.
The Doctor opens the door. A noise, as if the
building breathes.
Ingrid leaves the flat. The Doctor follows.
Roland picks up the ornamental raspberry bush.
He studies it carefully. He puts it down. Then, with
a sudden movement, he pulls it to pieces. He ruins the
Doctor's shopping, mangling the pasta, stamping on the
salad. He crushes the pills under his heel. He goes on
until everything belonging to the Doctor is destroyed.
He tears some of his manuscript. He looks at it and
stops. He is sobbing.
Audrey slowly goes to him. She comforts him.

Roland, don't cry, please. My poor brother. I'm here . . .
I'll never leave you, my darling. I'll never leave you.

GABRIEL

For my dad, John Buffini

Gabriel was first performed at the Soho Theatre, London, on 1 May 1997. The cast in order of appearance was as follows:

Estelle Becquet Gemma Eglinton
Lake Gillian Goodman
Lily Jennifer Scott-Malden
Von Pfunz Philip Fox
Jeanne Becquet Lisa Harrow
Gabriel Stephen Billington

Director Fiona Buffini
Designer Julian McGowan
Lighting Designer Jason Taylor
Assistant Director Alison Newman
German translations Antje Menna

Characters

Jeanne Becquet
a widow

Estelle
her daughter, aged ten

Lily
her daughter-in-law

Lake
a housekeeper

Von Pfunz
a Nazi

Gabriel
a lost man

Setting

An old farmhouse on the island of Guernsey.
February 1943. Hitler's occupying forces have
been on the island for two and a half years.

Everything possible to be believed
is an image of the truth

William Blake

Scene One

*A winter evening. The crumbling kitchen of a very old
farmhouse: stone floors, an old stove. The table is piled
up with boxes of groceries and crates of spirits. All is in
darkness. Estelle, a child of ten, is lit by a single candle.
She is drawing a chalk square around a flagstone. When
it's finished, she makes some strange gestures with her
hands. She puts her ear to the ground in the middle of
the square, and listens.*

Estelle Don't let them come any nearer. Keep them away,
  please keep them away . . .
  I send my wish crashing through the rocks
  that everything'll fall on them,
  in the sky that their planes will crash in flames,
  that the sea will roar with storms
  and I say drown them all; destroy them all,
  fling them to pieces for taking our house –
  and let my brother come like a bright angel
  to save me. Save me.

  Lake, a housekeeper, enters carrying a lamp.

Lake What are you doing?

Estelle Nothing.

Lake Well, get up then. (*Puts the lamp on the table.*)
And blow that candle out. I shouldn't think we'll get
power back 'til morning now.

Estelle I'm afraid I can't move just yet, Mrs Lake.

Lake Why not?

Estelle I'm involved in something.

Lake You were going to help me with these orders.

Estelle Sorry.

Lake Well, suit yourself. (*Sorting through boxes of groceries.*) Everything in at once and nowhere to blasted put it . . .

> *Lake starts to make up packages of goods tied with newspaper and string.*

Estelle I'm listening to the men.

Lake What?

Estelle The men underneath.

Lake Rubbish. They're miles away those tunnels; not even close.

Estelle They're going to come right under.

Lake Since when?

Estelle I can hear the machines.

Lake Course you can't.

Estelle They're building a labyrinth, a huge labyrinth for the Krauts.

Lake Not under here, they're not. We're too near the sea; they'd flood. And look, it's past nine o'clock. Even if they were down there, they'd have gone home to the camp for their tea, wouldn't they?

Estelle They don't have any tea. They have a lump of bread – that big – a lump of mouldy bread.

Lake How do you know?

Estelle Everybody knows.

Lake You ever gone in that camp and watched them eat?

Estelle Course not.

Lake Well then. Come and help me with these orders.

Estelle I can't.

Lake Why not?

Estelle I'm in an enchantment.

Lake Well, that's marvellous. (*As she fills an order.*) Shultz . . . Spam, a sugar . . . It's dwarves you can hear down there, working in their gold mine.

Estelle Are you scared of them, Mrs Lake?

Lake Those men? Course not.

Estelle I am.

Lake Why?

Estelle They got faces like ghosts.

Lake Well don't think about them. I'm sure I never do.

Estelle I saw one in the lane when it was getting dark, all pale and bony. You never see them by themselves but this one was alone. He said something in foreign.

Lake Nonsense.

Estelle I had a sandwich in my pocket so I threw it at him and ran away. I looked over my shoulder and he was on his knees in front of it with his mouth open, horrible in the dark like a big O.

Lake They got no business talking to you. Tinkers and sodomites from all o' Europe.

Estelle D'you know what he was wearing under his jacket?

97

Lake What?

Estelle A coal sack. They work in blackness down there, I imagine it at nights – miles of broken rocks and water dripping on their heads. I can hear them shouting in my dreams all foreign through the earth and when they collapse or die, the Krauts just shove them in the concrete. They bury them in the walls – did you know that?

Lake Rubbish.

Estelle If you climb up the barn you can see their camp –

Lake (*firmly*) No you can't. Get off the floor.

Estelle I don't want to.

Lake Why not?

Estelle Well. (*Suddenly smiling.*) I made something.

Lake What?

Estelle A square of power.

Lake Where?

Estelle I'm lying in it aren't I?

Lake Don't make me laugh.

Estelle Whoever's in it shall be compelled to take their clothes off and dance, nude.

Lake (*amused*) You little devil. Come on then.

Estelle What?

Lake Strip off; let's see you dancing.

Estelle I don't have to; I made it, didn't I?

Lake (*laughing*) Square of power? You clown . . .

Estelle What?

Lake A square of power don't mean a thing!

Estelle It does.

Lake Come on, out the way then and see if I strip off.

Estelle Well you won't, will you? You know about it so you can defend yourself.

Lake A *circle* is power, not a square; a circle.

Estelle I don't want a circle.

Lake (*laughs*) Square o' power . . .

Estelle Stop laughing at me!

Lake All the power in that's just goin' to seep out the corners.

Estelle (*disappointed*) Is it?

Lake Course it is.

Estelle gets up and flops into a big leather chair, deeply upset. She curls up.

Schüle: one Spam, one coffee . . .

Estelle (*close to tears*) I hate this house.

Lake Oh sweetheart.

Estelle I want The Hermitage back. What would Myles say if he knew there were Krauts living there?

Lake Well now –

Estelle What if he knew you were selling them food? What if he knew that Mummy went out with that Captain?

Lake Myles isn't here. He doesn't know what it's like – and if he was here he'd be doing same as us: coping. Anyway, your mother doesn't go out with anyone – where did you hear that?

Estelle I'm not stupid.

Lake She was *friendly* with Captain Reicher but she never went out with him. And he's gone now, hasn't he? (*Pause.*) I know we've lost the big house but we're a lot better off than some: we got *officers* staying up there, not scum. Besides, this is a good little place; nothing wrong with it.

Estelle It hasn't even got a bloody toilet.

Lake Watch your mouth. Why don't you rub that mess out?

Estelle It's not a mess, it's a square of power.

Lake Fine.

The door opens. Lily enters, breathless, distressed. The chair hides Estelle from her.

Lily Lake – I need you.

Lake I'm busy.

Lily There's a man down by the beach. He's unconscious. I need you to help me bring him back. Come on.

Lake What are you talking about?

Lily Lake, he's dying and I need you to help me!

Lake Who is he?

Lily I don't know.

Lake Well, what's he wearing?

Lily Nothing. It looks as though he's been in the sea. I think he must've crawled up the beach.

Lake The beach is a minefield down there.

Lily I know. We can't let him die. Can you imagine, for him to survive the minefield and then die because he's cold? I put my coat round him but it's not enough. Come on.

Lake You expect me to go with you just like that?

Lily (*shocked*) Yes.

Lake He's one of them foreigners, isn't he, from the camp?

Lily He's dying.

Lake Well I'm sorry, but I think you should leave well alone.

Lily Lake!

Lake I know it sounds hard, but you can't go around helping those people; you know you can't. He'll be some Pole or something, all eaten up with disease.

Lily I don't believe it!

Lake I'm sorry for the man, truly I am, but he's probably dead by now anyway and he shouldn't be your trouble.

Lily I'm not leaving him.

Lake Then go up The Hermitage and get the Krauts to help.

Lily is speechless.

Estelle I'll come.

Lily (*noticing her for the first time*) You're supposed to be in bed.

Estelle I'll get my coat.

Lake You will not.

Estelle Wait.

Estelle runs out of the kitchen. Lily calls after her.

Lily Bring something to put round him!

Lake I know what you think of me.

Lily Do you?

Lake But anyone in their right mind would do the same. You know the penalty for helping those men; signs are up everywhere.

Lily I know.

Lake One word: Death. They don't even tell you how. Woman from Câstel just complained, *complained* about screaming she heard in the camp and they tortured her.

Lily No they didn't.

Lake And those people who had one hiding in their house; sent away to camps in Europe, the whole family! . . . And when you got this naked corpse, what are you going to do with it? 'Cause you can't bring it here.

Lily Course I can.

Lake It's not your house.

Lily It's not yours either! . . . I can't leave him, Lake. I'd have nightmares.

Estelle returns, warmly dressed, carrying a blanket and an old coat.

Estelle I'm ready, come on.

Lily Besides, there isn't a mark on him. He's not from the camp.

Lake A deserting Kraut then.

Lily He might be English.

Lake A suicide.

Estelle Let's go.

Lily What if he's English? That plane that came down over the bay this morning. What if it's him? Would you condemn him, Lake? A pilot like Myles?

Lily and Estelle leave. Lake is livid.

Lake How dare you? Taking the child out. I'm not a coward, you bloody cockney. Madness. You're the coward, girl; you're scared o' the bloody pigs, scared to pluck the fowl. After the war he'll come home and sling you out. You don't even know him, you –

Suddenly the overhead lights come on. Lake starts with shock and turns to the light switch, as if someone has switched it on. Her groundless fear makes her even more angry.

Now what? Just to torment us; power back on when everyone's off to bed . . .

A car pulls up outside. Lake panics. She quickly begins to clear away the kitchen table, shoving food indiscriminately into crates and boxes. She extinguishes the lamp.

Oh no. Don't bring him in. Don't bring him in. You can't bring him in.

There are quite a lot of groceries remaining on the table, when Von Pfunz enters, short and formal, holding the door open for Jeanne. Jeanne, elegant and aloof, sweeps past him.

Jeanne Hello, Margaret, this is Major Von Pfunz . . .

Von Pfunz Hello, good evening!

Jeanne stands in the chalk square as she speaks, and takes off her hat, coat and gloves. She holds them out for Lake.

Jeanne He's new to the Channel Islands, so we must do our very best to make him feel welcome. He's taken over from our dear Captain Reicher.

Von Pfunz Hallo, yes . . .

Jeanne And he doesn't speak any English. He's a buffoon.

Lake nods at Von Pfunz. Von Pfunz grins back.

You see how cosy we've made things, Major? You wouldn't think we'd only been here a week. House; nice?

Von Pfunz Very nice . . .

Von Pfunz is peering at one of Lake's boxes. Lake eyes him nervously.

Jeanne We've managed to squeeze in more comfortably than we thought – although the bathroom facilities are proving quite a rural adventure. Ein Cognac?

Von Pfunz Ja, ja, Cognac, very nice.

Jeanne approaches Lake on her way to get the drinks.

Jeanne (*quietly*) Why can't you be more careful? A fool could tell what you've been doing.

Lake I didn't know you were going to bring him back.

Jeanne He insisted, you bloody stupid woman.

Lake You have to get rid of him.

Jeanne I want to find out where they've sent Reicher.

Lake Not tonight. The cockney's gone running –

Jeanne Anyway half his men buy from us; what's he going to do?

Von Pfunz (*reading off a tin, smiling for approval*) Sardines in brine.

Jeanne Mrs Lake has been collecting tirelessly for the church bazaar.

Lake Get rid of him.

Jeanne No.

Lake I mean it.

Jeanne Put Estelle to bed would you, Margaret? (*Turning to Von Pfunz with a drink.*) I hope your officers are appreciating The Hermitage, Major. Thanks for letting us take our bric-a-brac before you kicked us out. Here, Cognac. It's Captain Reicher's but I'm sure he won't mind. He's gone for good, hasn't he?

Von Pfunz Thank you very much.

Jeanne Still here, Mrs Lake?

Lake leaves.

Are the ghosts at The Hermitage bothering you at all? I do hope so. We're one of the oldest families on the island, so there's plenty of them. Lascalles is my maiden name and we go right back to the tenth century. My ancestors invaded Britain with William the Conqueror.

Von Pfunz giggles. It has started to rain.

What about yours? Tyrolean goat herds, perhaps. Light me a ciggie, would you? Eine Zigarette bitte, Von Major.

Von Pfunz Ah! Ja, ja. Ciggie . . .

Von Pfunz lights cigarettes for himself and Jeanne, in a Hollywood kind of way.

Jeanne Thanks. So suave. Really, I'm powerless in your sway. Are you married? Do you cheat on your wife with prostitutes? Is she ugly too? My husband was ugly; there's no shame in it. He's been dead for five years now and I don't miss him at all. I married a pig. Well, of course I had to. I was pregnant with another man's child. My son's twenty-six now, so handsome it hurts you to look. He flies a plane for the RAF and he's going to die in the war, I know it. There's an ashtray over there. Ashtray. For flicken ashen. Can you fetch it?

Von Pfunz Ah . . . aschenbecher! Ash tray . . .

Von Pfunz eagerly fetches an ashtray.

Jeanne Goodness, what rain! My son's name is Myles. Shall I tell you a secret? I *love* him . . . (*Pause.*) He left me three years ago and came back just before the war, married. Exactly the kind of girl he knew I'd hate; a little cockney madam and a Jew, to boot.

Von Pfunz's smile looks stuck to his face.

Well, I must say it's been a very pleasant evening, Major. Very Nice Evening.

Von Pfunz Ja. Schön. Very nice!

Jeanne I enjoyed watching that piece of veal you had stuck to your lip. Mmm. Nice Food.

Von Pfunz Very nice food, ja.

Jeanne I'd do anything for a good meal, you know. I'm so sick of the taste of Spam I'd probably even . . . Well; these are hard times, aren't they? Of course, you're a powerfully attractive man; one rarely encounters such an erotic charge. I don't want to be personal, but is the rest of you as shiny as your face? How do you keep up that lustrous gloss? God, I wonder if I could bear it . . . No. I'd have to be drunk or insane. Do tell me about your wonderful name, Major; it sounds like flatulence. Where does it come from? Von Pfunz – your name?

Von Pfunz Ah! Twenty-nine October.

Jeanne Well, I can see we're going to be firm friends! Where did they send Captain Reicher? He's not coming back, is he?

Von Pfunz Cap-tain Reicher? (*He giggles.*) Ja!

Jeanne Yes, hilarious isn't it? Did they send him to Russia? . . . We were lovers but I'm sure you know that. I'm sure you think you've come to take his place. Fantastic. Lucky old me . . .

Von Pfunz Fan*ta*stic!

Jeanne Cheers.

They clink glasses.

Von Pfunz Roll me over in the clover.

Jeanne Oh dear.

Von Pfunz Down the hatch.

Von Pfunz drains his glass. Jeanne takes it from him and refills it as she speaks.

Jeanne Hitler's done a lot for your country, hasn't he? A lot of people here think so; you'd be surprised. That's a splendid uniform, much smarter than ours. There's a lot of people here who like the Krauts you know, especially women, women who'll be sorry if you leave. Guernseymen can be pigs you see, real *pigs*, and you're a very handsome race. Some of you anyway. And some of you look like goblins.

Von Pfunz (*taking the brandy*) Nice thank you.

Jeanne Most of us can differentiate between Germans and Nazis you see. Germans are fairly acceptable in a dull, teutonic kind of way, but you're a Nazi, I can tell. Reicher talked a lot about Nazis. In general, he said there are three kinds: The Fanatic, quite mad and therefore worthy of serious respect; The Sycophant, who would follow orders to shoot his own mother – and The Intellectual; bright enough to know what's going on and brutal enough not to care. Which kind are you?

Von Pfunz (*in perfect English*) Oh, I must be the fourth kind, Mrs Becquet.

Jeanne (*takes a sip of her drink*) I see. And what kind is that?

Von Pfunz He sits on a pale horse and his name is death. So to speak. (*He bursts into peals of giggles.*) I've been wonderfully entertained this evening. You're very charming.

Jeanne (*pause*) Thank you.

Von Pfunz Is it true you slept with Reicher? – I didn't know. I'm so sorry about my poor manners and my unfortunate name. Von Pfunz. It comes from a small town north of Munich.

Jeanne How nice.

Von Pfunz My father and mother ran a school for the children of the rich. Not much time for herding goats. They were very cultured and were kind enough not to dress me in leather clothes. I never had a wife. Just never met the right woman and if I did I would be loyal to her until death devoured me. There. I think I have answered all of your questions and now you can answer mine. When you said you'd do anything for a good meal, what did you mean?

Jeanne Well . . . nothing.

Von Pfunz What did you mean by my lustrous gloss?

Jeanne I didn't mean anything . . .

Von Pfunz You said you'd have to be drunk, or insane. To do what, exactly?

Jeanne I'm sorry, I don't remember saying that.

Von Pfunz unbuttons his jacket.

Von Pfunz Please be honest; I love the truth. I have erotic charge for you. You make a joke but this joke hides often what is true. You want to touch me; that is what you meant.

Jeanne I suppose it's too late for an apology?

Von Pfunz Don't demean yourself, Mrs Becquet. I'm not asking you to apologise.

Von Pfunz undoes his trousers. He takes Jeanne's drink from her. He sips it. He returns it. Jeanne puts out her hand to touch him. She withdraws it.

Jeanne I'm going to need my polish and a cloth.

Von Pfunz turns away, furious and embarrassed. He does his trousers up. He turns back to Jeanne and lifts his hand to straighten his hair. Jeanne flinches in fear, as if about to be hit. Von Pfunz is genuinely surprised.

Von Pfunz Did you expect me to hit you?

Jeanne No.

Von Pfunz I think you did. You must believe in your heart that you deserved it.

Jeanne No.

Von Pfunz Force of habit then. Your husband was a violent man.

Jeanne No.

Von Pfunz But he was a pig?

Jeanne Your English is very good, Major.

Von Pfunz No really; I don't speak a word.

Jeanne Why did you stop me talking? I would've told you everything eventually.

Von Pfunz Was there any more to tell?

Jeanne Perhaps you were trying to protect me from myself.

Von Pfunz I was becoming bored.

Jeanne That's always a danger when you don't understand the language.

Von Pfunz I'm not surprised that Reicher was so taken with you; you must have had him in the palm of your hand. Did you know what his job was?

Jeanne I had an idea.

Von Pfunz It is to be my job too. Did he ever talk about it?

Jeanne Of course not.

Von Pfunz Did you ever ask him?

Jeanne I wasn't interested.

Von Pfunz Everyone is interested, Mrs Becquet. People do a good job at pretending the camps don't exist, but in reality, they want to know all about them. Have you ever been in a labour camp?

Jeanne No.

Von Pfunz All of life is there . . . Humanity in all its extremes. I've gained a deep, almost religious understanding of humanity from what I have seen in our camps. My job is to liaise, you see, between the work organisation and the military. The camps here are small and dull but in many ways I was glad to get the posting. It's certainly warmer than Poland.

Jeanne Yes.

Von Pfunz And so lovely. As I sailed past all the little islands, I thought it tragic that Homer lived too far south to sing their praises. Really, this place is a haven. Pretty gardens, antique churches – all the poet needs for inspiration. Do you think I will fit in?

Jeanne I'm afraid not.

Von Pfunz Why?

Jeanne I don't expect you fit in anywhere, do you?

Von Pfunz (*giggling, but shocked*) Oh dear! You really are the most insulting woman I've ever met! To hear the truth, Mrs Becquet. It is a privilege. (*Pause.*) How many people know that you married because you were pregnant with another man's child?

Jeanne One.

Von Pfunz Your husband never knew?

Jeanne And never will.

Von Pfunz And your . . . *liaison* with your son?

Jeanne What?

Von Pfunz That was your secret, wasn't it?

Jeanne I said I loved him.

Von Pfunz But we both know what you meant.

Jeanne I hope I'm not being insulting again, Major, but you wouldn't know what I meant in a million years.

Von Pfunz What happened to his wife, the Jew?

Jeanne When the invasion looked imminent, she fled. Sailed off to England on a boat packed with cowards and I haven't seen her since. We were never close.

Von Pfunz How long have you been trading on the black market?

Jeanne Since the beginning of the war. Are you going to arrest me?

Von Pfunz No.

Jeanne Then perhaps we could drop the subject.

Von Pfunz You're not a patriot, are you?

Jeanne Of course I am. But I'm a pragmatist. My husband died heavily in debt. I've done only what was necessary to keep my house.

Von Pfunz Do you make a great deal of money?

Jeanne That's really none of your business.

Von Pfunz I could make it my business.

Jeanne Then arrest me.

Von Pfunz Not yet.

Jeanne Why not?

Von Pfunz I'm hoping we may become . . . well. I'd like to be – (*He sighs.*) I have seen terrible things in this war. I have been ill with it. Ill in my soul . . .

Jeanne (*coldly*) Oh dear.

Von Pfunz (*smiles*) You are so *rude*, so completely dismissive . . . It's a long time since I met someone so . . . forthright and true. I'm hoping, perhaps we could –

Jeanne Do I have any choice?

Von Pfunz There's always an element of choice in human affairs. When someone tells you they have no choice they're invariably lying. They've merely assessed their position and gone for the line of least resistance; the option which will cause them least trouble. It's a local virtue apparently, amongst the brave Britishers of Guernsey . . . (*Approaching Jeanne, who is now in the chalk square.*)

> I'd like to look at you
> As you are, naked in the light
> Jeanne Lascalles.

Jeanne Is that an order?

Von Pfunz It's a poem.

> You are the one
> Who sees me as I am, and laughs
> Jeanne Lascalles.

> *Jeanne turns her back on Von Pfunz.*

Do you dislike poetry?

Jeanne Bad poetry, yes.

Von Pfunz Of course; with such a fine poetic tradition, who could blame you? As a young man in Munich I spent many a happy evening curled up by the fireside with my *Treasury of English Verse*. So many fine men . . . so much delicate misery. I have always felt a kindred spirit. But you see,

> Blasted with sighs and surrounded with tears,
> Hither I come to seek the spring
> And at mine eyes and at mine ears
> Receive such balms as else cure everything.

Jeanne Major.

Von Pfunz (*touching Jeanne's shoulder*)

> But O, self traitor, I do bring
> The spider love, which transubstantiates all
> And can convert manna to gall
> And that this place may thoroughly be thought
> True Paradise, I have the serpent brought.

Von Pfunz undoes the zip on Jeanne's dress. He slowly touches her skin. She suddenly turns round and looks at him with contempt. She pulls her dress off and throws it to the floor. She throws her shoes off. She lifts her arms to undo her bra.

(*shocked, hurt*) Stop!

Jeanne stops.

I see you are a prostitute.

Pause. The door opens and Estelle rushes in, soaked to the skin. She looks at them, aghast. Jeanne, leaving the chalk square, fumbles into her dress.

Estelle.

Von Pfunz (*buffoon-like*) Hallo good evening!

Jeanne Estelle . . .

Estelle leaves, slamming the door.

Estelle!

Jeanne opens the door and shouts into the darkness.

Estelle! . . .

Jeanne closes the door. She does up her dress, consumed with shame and rage. Von Pfunz buttons his jacket.

Von Pfunz I hope we haven't shocked the little lady.

Jeanne Of course we have!

Von Pfunz I thought she might be used to seeing her mother in various stages of undress with German officers.

Jeanne GET OUT!!

Von Pfunz Well, I'd love to stay and question her as to why she's outside, two hours after curfew, but some other day. My bedroom at The Hermitage is the one with panelled walls and a fine view of the sea. Was that yours?

Jeanne It belonged to my late husband. I hope he haunts you.

Von Pfunz Does he haunt you?

There is a knock at the door and Lily enters, soaking wet from the rain. She glances nervously at Von Pfunz.

Lily We wanted to apologise for being out after curfew. There was a sick cow in the top field and I asked Estelle to come with me, to hold the torch. I'm sure we should have left it till the morning . . .

Jeanne Get Estelle and go to your room.

Von Pfunz (*buffoon-like*) Jeanne, please you introduce me?

Jeanne Lilian, this is Major Von Pfunz. Major Von Pfunz, Lilian Becquet.

Von Pfunz Hallo . . . Sister of Jeanne?

Jeanne Yes –

Lily No, I'm her daughter-in-law.

Von Pfunz (*removing his hand*) Ah! . . . son's wife, son Myles; flies a plane?

Lily That's right.

Von Pfunz Very nice . . . Is cow better?

Lily It's fine.

Von Pfunz I have a look? I know many sick cow facts.

Lily Thanks, but Estelle and I got awfully wet in the rain. We rather want to dry off and go to bed now.

Von Pfunz Well! Rather want very nice, dry off yes. Good evening. (*To Jeanne, kissing her hand.*) Enchanted. You are an oracle of truth.

    Von Pfunz leaves.

Jeanne There are no cows on this farm, Lilian.

Lily I meant to say pig, a sick pig.

Jeanne He'll find out.

Lily I meant to say pig and cow just popped out before I could –

Jeanne Where's Estelle?

Lily She's in the barn.

Jeanne What the hell is she doing outside at this time of night?

Lily Mrs Becquet, there's a sick man outside and I'm going to have to bring him in.

Jeanne What?

Lily I thought Lake would've told you.

Jeanne What are you talking about? What sick man?

Lily I found him on the beach. He's freezing to death and I need to bring him in.

Jeanne Who is he?

Lily I don't know; he hasn't spoken and he's got no clothes, nothing to identify him. Estelle's with him in the barn, covering him with straw to keep him warm, but he'll die soon, if we don't help him!

Jeanne You've left my daughter alone in the barn with a naked man?

Lily I put a coat round him!

Jeanne Good God!

Lily He could be British! Four drowned British have washed up on that beach this year. You heard that plane go down . . . It could be him.

Jeanne It went down at eight o'clock this morning into the dark, cold sea. Be serious. If he's found here, they'll shoot us, do you understand?

Lily Nobody saw us bringing him here.

Jeanne I can't believe you're putting yourself in such danger! You know your situation here . . .

Lily What do you mean?

Jeanne I mean, if they find out what you are!

Lily How can they? No one knows, except you.

Jeanne (*pause*) Why did you drag Estelle into this?

Lily Lake wouldn't come with me. I had to help him, Mrs Becquet.

Jeanne Why?

Lily He looks like Myles.

Jeanne (*pause*) Do what you like. If he dies, dump him back on the beach where you found him. Living or dead,

I want him out of here before it's bright. I'm going to bed. I don't want my daughter upset, and I don't want to see him.

Lily runs outside. Jeanne pours herself a drink. She drinks it.

May the ground open and swallow me.

She exits. The door opens and Lily and Estelle enter, dragging a man between them. He's naked except for an old coat. Bits of straw fall off him.

Lily Get him over to the fire.

Estelle He made a noise.

Lily When?

Estelle In the barn. Like a 'b' and air going through his mouth.

Lily That's good.

Estelle Then he puked up.

Lily Oh.

Estelle All salt water and yellow stuff.

Lily Oh.

Estelle And he moaned but I couldn't tell what language.

Lily Put him in the chair . . .

They lay him down in an armchair in front of the stove.

Estelle, run upstairs and find all the blankets you can. Bring him the pillows off my bed and the spare eiderdown. And find him something to wear. We have to get him warm.

Estelle What are you going to do?

Lily I'm going to make him drink something.

Lily goes to pour a glass of Cognac.

Stop gawping, Estelle. Get the blankets.

Estelle exits. Lily puts the Cognac to the man's lips.

Drink, come on, drink. You're somewhere warm. Out of the darkness. Don't die, bloke, live . . .

Lily moves to kiss him on the lips. As she does so, the lights go out, leaving the kitchen in total darkness, except for the firelight coming from the stove. Lily starts with the shock.

(*to the man*) Stay there. I'm going to find a light.

Lily fumbles towards the kitchen table. She searches for matches.

Estelle (*calling, off*) Lily! Turn the lights back on!

Lily I can't can I? The power's gone! . . .

Lily lights the lamp. Estelle comes in, staggering under an armful of blankets and linen.

Estelle I hate this house.

Lily Make him a bed there near the stove, and we'll lift him on to it.

Estelle I brought him this to wear. It's Daddy's old one.

Estelle throws an old-fashioned dressing gown at Lily.

Lily Blimey . . .

They both work rapidly.

Estelle.

Estelle What?

Lily When you came in and saw your mum and that Major, what did you . . . I mean, you looked like you'd seen a ghost.

Estelle So?

Lily What were they doing?

Estelle Nothing.

Lily So . . . did you just get a fright?

Estelle All this hate came up and blocked my throat.

Lily Have you seen him before?

Estelle No, I just hate him. (*Gazing at the man.*) He's got cuts on his legs.

Lily Oh . . . He must've hit them on the rocks.

Estelle There's barbed wire in the sea.

Lily Estelle, I don't like this. He's too still.

Estelle He's just sleeping, isn't he?

Lily He's hardly breathing.

Estelle Move him over here.

Lily Right. Yes.

Estelle It'll help him. It's on a square of power.

Lily (*to the man*) Come on, live.

Estelle Pick him up, Lily!

Lily Live!

> *They pick the man up and manage to get him on to the floor. Estelle immediately lies down next to him.*

She puts her arms and one leg around him.

Lily What are you doing?

Estelle I'm warming him with my body heat. I'm going to save his life. You put the blankets over us.

Lily You can't do that.

Estelle Why not?

Lily That's not what you do.

Estelle It's how you save people in the Alps.

Lily How d'you know?

Estelle I read it.

Lily We should be doing something!

Estelle Turn him to his side so if he pukes up in the night, he won't choke on it.

They turn him.

These girls were on a skiing trip from their Swiss finishing school and an avalanche blocked off their route so they hugged each other all night to stay warm. But there was one stuck-up girl who wouldn't touch anybody and she went off by herself. Soon, she found herself sinking into the snow and all she wanted to do was sleep and sleep. In the morning the others were rescued but the stuck-up girl was frozen in a block of ice.

Lily Right.

Estelle 'Cause that's what happens when you die of cold; you fall into a deeper and deeper sleep and if no one warms you up with their body heat like your friends or a St Bernard, you go further and further inside yourself into a land of dreams and eventually your spirit leaves your body and floats up to the firmament. It'll go all over me now.

Lily What?

Estelle If he pukes. I'm changing sides.

Lily puts the lamp on a nearby chair. Then she lies down beside him.

Estelle What are you doing?

Lily Same as you, what d'you think?

Lily curls up against the man. She puts her head to his chest.

Estelle He smells of the sea, doesn't he?

Lily Yes.

Estelle How long do you think he was in there?

Lily I don't know.

Estelle Can we call him something?

Lily If you like. We could call him George, after the King.

Estelle (*shyly*) Gabriel.

Lily Why d'you want to call him that?

Estelle It's my favourite name.

Lily Blimey.

Estelle Wake up, Gabriel.

Estelle kisses him. Pause.

Lily You'd better go to bed now.

Estelle No! . . .

Lily You should've been asleep hours ago, come on.

Estelle I want to stay!

Lily You can't, Estelle . . .

Estelle Why not? (*Pause.*) He won't die; I know he won't! Don't make me go to bed!

Lily I promised your mother.

Estelle Lily, please!

Lily You have to go.

Estelle It's NOT FAIR! Nobody ever lets me do *anything*!

She gets out of bed, fighting her tears.

Lily Come on, Estelle.

Estelle Everybody *hates* me! . . .

Estelle leaves. Lily looks at the man. Pause.

Lily Gabriel.

Scene Two

A sunny afternoon, two days later. An attic room with a small window. A large stock of black market goods has been laid to one side and a makeshift bed set up. Gabriel lies in it, unconscious. Jeanne is glancing through an old magazine. After a while, she puts it down. She looks deeply troubled. She stands and lights a cigarette. She looks at Gabriel.

Jeanne Oh I'm sorry, do you mind if I smoke?

Jeanne leans over Gabriel and blows smoke in his face. She shakes him, irritated. She moves away.

Mrs Lake seems to think I should talk to you. I think it's a waste of time, myself. It's uninspiring, talking to the dead. When the time comes, would you rather be buried or cremated? Because if it was up to me I'd throw you back in the sea, right now . . . and I'm not afraid of my cruelty, only my cowardice. I can't sleep with you in my house. I'm having nightmares. I want you gone. (*Pause. Jeanne touches his forehead.*) You poor boy . . .

Jeanne hears someone approaching. She immediately sits down and opens the magazine. Lake comes in with a tray of soup.

Lake I made him some soup.

Jeanne He won't eat it, will he?

Lake No.

Jeanne Then why bother?

124

Lake He might like the taste of it on his lips.

Jeanne It's a waste.

Lake My kitchen, my soup. (*To Gabriel*.) Hello, my angel! It's Mrs Lake! (*To Jeanne*.) Have you been talking to him?

Jeanne No.

Lake You should talk to him.

Jeanne I don't expect he understands.

Lake That's not the point. He needs friendly voices.

Jeanne Does he now?

Lake Friendly voices help.

Jeanne How do you know?

Lake I brought him out of that fever, didn't I? That fever would have killed him.

Jeanne Drugs brought him out of that fever; black market drugs that I paid for.

Lake (*to Gabriel*) Well then, my lamb, you're going to help Mrs Lake now, aren't you? You're going to eat up all this soup she made you!

Jeanne I've got a fear, Margaret. I've felt this . . . dread the last two days and I can't sleep. I can't sleep and when I do I have these ghastly nightmares, so vivid I think there's blood on my hands –

Lake Shut up. (*To Gabriel*.) There we are. Lovely mashed swede and a bit of chopped up Spam.

Jeanne Don't tell me to shut up. I pay your wages.

Lake Black market pays my wages. I don't want him hearing things like that. It'll trouble him.

Jeanne If he's troubled, Margaret, don't you think it's because you're trying to asphyxiate him with soup?

Lily (*entering*) Mrs Becquet! There's a bunch of Krauts in front of The Hermitage. They've got Estelle. That Major from the other night – he's holding on to her.

Jeanne (*going to the window*) What's happened? What's she done?

Lily I don't know. I just saw it out my bedroom window.

Jeanne (*to Lake.*) Margaret, get your coat.

Lake I'll stay here and watch him.

Lily I'll watch him.

Lake (*defensively*) He's having his soup.

Lily (*in horror, noticing*) What are you doing to him?

Lake Sustenance.

Lily He can't eat that.

Lake It's wholesome, nourishing food.

Jeanne Margaret, I want you with me, right now. Please don't leave my side.

Jeanne leaves.

Lake Feed him that soup.

Lily You must be joking.

Lake Then it's your fault if he dies.

Lily I saved his life!

Lake leaves. Lily takes a napkin from Lake's tray and wipes Gabriel's face.

Wicked old bag; what's she done to you? . . . There. This is what happens when I leave you. I'm sorry. I had to get

some sleep. (*Lily goes to the window.*) There they go.
Flying up the lane on their bloody broomsticks. (*Pause.*)
It's not even eight miles long, this island. I can cycle
round it in half a day. And I've grown to hate it, Gabriel.
I hate every rock. I want to smash every stupid little
garden and prissy little house. I've lived such a *useless* life
here, up to my ankles in chicken shit, growing veg for
them to flog to the Krauts. If only I was in London or
France or anywhere, I could be *doing something*!
(*Returning to the bed.*) I almost fell over you. You were
so pale I thought you were quartz. You scared me. I was
out celebrating my anniversary, you see. In the minefields.
Three years to the day since I came here as a bride.
'Guernsey's one of the island jewels of Europe,' he'd say.
'They'll love you there,' and he'd look at me and laugh.
I loved his laugh. When we got here . . . I shouldn't tell
you. (*Pause.*) 'Lily's my Jew-girl,' first thing he said, and
he gives me this great, long kiss right in front of her. It
was like he . . . Still. Three months I had with him, that's
all. I can hardly remember it now. (*Touches him.*)
They're softer than mine, your hands. Mine are ruined,
picking sprouts out o' the frost.

   Pause. She kisses Gabriel on the lips, with passion.

(*Whispers.*) Please don't be a madman. Please don't be a
Kraut. Please wake up and be my friend. (*No response.
To herself.*) Stupid cow.

   *She goes to the window again. During the following,
   Gabriel opens his eyes. For a while he's too
   bewildered to move, but he gradually begins to focus
   on Lily. He slowly sits up.*

What's it like, flying? I can't imagine how beautiful
everything must look from up there. The very thought of
being above the clouds, above the clouds in all that light;
it's beyond me . . . makes me want to cry, just thinking

about it. (*Pause.*) I get these attacks, Gabriel, where I start going mad inside 'cause I can't get away. Feels like I can't breathe. Sometimes, when I'm in the fields all alone and the sky's pressing down, or in the lane where the white weeds grow, it gets on top of me so much, all the green and the clouds and the smell, that I shut my eyes and with all the force of my person I say: Give me wings so I could rise up off my feet, so I could strive away and see this place fading in the distance. . . Give me wings so I could see the sea stretching out beneath me, all blue, all dazzling, and I think, that feeling, that feeling I want, of freedom, of floating, that feeling . . . that'd be worth dying for, wouldn't it? (*She is crying.*) Oh! . . . I was going to walk right into those mines and blow myself to kingdom come! . . . I would've done it too but I'm glad I didn't now, and I owe that to –

Lily turns around. Gabriel is staring at her, bewildered. She starts with shock. Pause.

You're awake.

Lily wipes her eyes. She goes to the bed.

I don't know what to say. You're awake. Can you speak? Do you understand me?

Gabriel I thought I was dead.

Lily (*taking his hand and gripping it tightly*) No . . . you're not dead. See? Your hands are warmer than mine. (*Smiling with joy.*) English . . . You're him, aren't you? The man in the plane.

Gabriel (*pause*) Who are you?

Lily I'm Lilian Becquet. Lily.

Gabriel Where am I?

Lily You're at the Lodge on the Hermitage estate. It's a farm near St Saviours. On Guernsey, the island of Guernsey. What's your name?

Gabriel I need some water.

Lily Here.

Lily gives Gabriel some water.

Gabriel Thank you. (*He drinks.*) I don't know.

Lily You don't know?

Gabriel No.

Lily Well, you've only just woken up. It's the shock I expect. What you've been through's made you forget.

Gabriel What happened to me?

Lily Your plane crashed into the sea.

Gabriel My plane.

Lily I was down by the beach three nights ago and I saw you lying on the sand. It looked like you'd dragged yourself out of the waves. At first I thought you were dead, then you moved your hand. Your fingers uncurled . . .

Gabriel You saved me?

Lily Yes. Me and the people who live here.

Gabriel Did I say anything?

Lily No, you weren't able. You've been ill for three days. Unconscious. We thought you were going to die, Gabriel. It's a miracle –

Gabriel What did you call me?

Lily Oh. Gabriel.

Gabriel You said you didn't know my name.

Lily We made it up. We had to call you something.

Gabriel Gabriel?

Lily My sister-in-law chose it; she's only ten.

Gabriel I can't remember anything. I don't know what I look like. I have no memory of myself at all.

Lily Wait, there's a mirror here . . .

She hands Gabriel a mirror. He looks at himself, concentrated, but unrecognising.

Gabriel I don't know who this is.

He puts the mirror down, troubled.

Lily You should rest. You're alive. You've survived. Give yourself time.

Gabriel Yes.

Lily Rest, and think. Anything, any image in your head, no matter how small . . . Hold on to it and the rest will follow, I know it will.

Gabriel (*pause*) Falling.

Lily What?

Gabriel Darkness. Falling . . .

Lily You remember falling?

Gabriel nods.

I expect you bailed out of your plane, got your parachute off in the sea . . .

Gabriel No. Falling.

Lily I don't know what you mean.

Gabriel No plane, no parachute. I was free. (*Pause.*) Why were you crying?

Lily I wasn't crying. (*Looking down.*) I'm not like that, Gabriel.

Gabriel Not like what?

Lily I never cry. (*Looking up.*) Would you like something to eat?

Gabriel Yes, yes, I'm hungry.

Lily Right. I'll get you some food.

Lily stands to move away. Gabriel takes hold of her hand.

Gabriel Tell me your name again.

Lily Lily.

Gabriel Lily. Thank you.

Scene Three

The kitchen, a short while later. During the course of the scene, evening falls. By the end, it's almost dark. Lily is at the table rapidly making sandwiches. She is humming as she works, in high spirits. Suddenly Estelle enters, breathless, afraid.

Estelle Hide me!!

Lily What's happened?

Estelle Mummy's going to murder me!

Lily Estelle, what've you done?

Estelle (*in terror*) Hide me, she's coming! . . .

Lily Go in the cupboard. I'll see if I can calm her down. Come on, quick.

Lily holds the cupboard door open. Estelle hands her a small book.

Estelle You have to take this.

Lily What is it?

Estelle It's his.

Lily The Major's?

Estelle I stole it.

Lily You did not.

Estelle I did. It's his diary. You can destroy a person when you know their secrets.

Lily (*flicking through it*) Estelle, it's in German.

Estelle (*disappointed*) Is it?

Lily Course it is; he's a Kraut, isn't he?

Estelle I didn't look . . .

Lily How could you be so stupid? He'll know you've taken it –

Estelle (*disappearing into the cupboard*) Shut me in!

Lily And he's going to come looking for it, isn't he?

Estelle Shut me in!!

Lily shuts Estelle in the cupboard. She looks frantically round the kitchen.

Lily Oh bloody hell! . . .

She shoves the book in the bread bin, just as Jeanne enters, furious, almost crying.

Jeanne Where is she?

Lily Who?

Jeanne Estelle!

Lily I don't know.

Jeanne I saw her come in here!

Lily You can't have. What's she done?

Jeanne (*close to tears*) She has *embarrassed* me!

Lily Oh dear.

Lake enters. She sits down by the door, exhausted.

Jeanne I'll *murder* her when I get my hands on her! Of all the *stupid* games to play!

Lake Get me a drink, quick.

Jeanne (*turning on Lake*) You're too fat; that's all that's wrong with you!

Lake Don't. I need a drink.

Jeanne (*going to fill a glass of Cognac*) I should never have bought you with me. You're a liability.

Lake You were damn glad I was there. You're scared of that man.

Jeanne Don't be ridiculous.

Lake Why be scared of him?

Jeanne I'm not.

Lily Is he coming here?

Jeanne (*handing Lake the drink*) No.

Lily Good.

Jeanne He was going to but I put him off. I had to *prostitute* myself.

Lily How?

Jeanne I offered to show him the neolithic tombs.

Lily Well . . . that's not so bad is it?

Jeanne You go with him then! You spend the day with that *reptile*.

Lily What happened, Mrs Becquet?

Jeanne Estelle's been breaking in there.

Lake She's been haunting them.

Lily Pardon?

Lake Creeping into The Hermitage and haunting them.

Lily Why?

Jeanne It's her plan, she says, to get the place back; so utterly ridiculous I'm ashamed.

Lily What's she been doing?

Jeanne You know the kind of thing; banging doors in empty rooms, moving things every time they put them down –

Lake She made a blood stain in the morning room.

Lily No.

Lake Every time they cleaned it up, she put it back.

Jeanne It's gone on for three days. And then they catch her and she behaves *ridiculously*. Shouting hysterical rubbish like Joan of bloody Arc.

Lily What did they do?

Jeanne They laughed.

Lily So they thought it was funny?

Jeanne I said they laughed; it's not the same thing.

Lily But they took it well? (*Giggles*.) They really thought they had a ghost?

Lake Oh you got to hand it to her, she was clever. She picked on that clockwork monkey Major – put dead mice all over his floor from every trap in the house.

Jeanne And the little savage scratched words into the panelling on his wall.

Lake Wrote 'You're in your coffin.'

Jeanne He won't forget this.

Lily You're in your coffin? . . .

Jeanne Or forgive it. (*Pause.*) I'm an idiot. She's with the madman in the attic, isn't she?

Lily No.

Jeanne I'm going up.

Lily No you can't! He's awake.

Lake Lord Jesus . . .

Lily Don't go up; he doesn't know who you are.

Jeanne So the Sleeping Beauty wakes. Is he German or English?

Lily He's English. I should take this food up now. I told him I'd only leave him for a minute.

Jeanne So who is he then? What's his story?

Lily Well, he hasn't got one as a matter of fact.

Jeanne Of course he's got one.

Lily He's lost his memory.

Jeanne Oh, how convenient.

Lily It's not his fault.

Lake He can't remember anything?

Lily Nothing, not even his name. I mean, after all he's been through, he's probably in shock, isn't he?

Jeanne But he strikes you as perfectly sane?

Lily Yes.

Jeanne (*sitting, relieved*) Well . . . thank God he's not going to die here. (*Pause.*) So, he's alive and awake and now, thank God, we can get rid of him. Margaret, go down to the village.

Lake You can't get rid of him just like that!

Jeanne I can and I will. He can walk away on his own two feet, and he's going, this afternoon.

Lake I want to see him first.

Lily You'll disturb him.

Lake Course I won't disturb him; he's my boy!

Jeanne No! Margaret, please. We've done our bit; we've saved his life. Go down to the village and talk to the crones –

Lake Why should I? No one'll help. You're not liked or trusted; who am I supposed to ask?

Jeanne I know you know people. You know everyone! Get someone in your coven to take him in.

Lake Oh!

Jeanne Margaret, help me. Please, I beg you. I want him out of my house!

Lake Shame on your soul.

Lake walks out, leaving the door wide open.

Lily Mrs Becquet, if you were to talk to him –

Jeanne Just get him ready to leave.

There's a crash inside the cupboard. Jeanne looks furiously at Lily and opens the door. She pulls Estelle out. Estelle runs for the stairs. Jeanne grabs her by the hair.

Estelle Ow!

Jeanne Did you think you'd get away with it?!

Estelle I want to see him!

Jeanne You little – !

Jeanne pulls Estelle towards her, viciously.

Estelle Gabriel!

Jeanne Did you think if you hid long enough I'd *forget?*

Estelle Aaahh!

Jeanne This is the end of your freedom. From now on, you WILL NOT LEAVE THIS YARD!

Estelle Mummy, no!

Jeanne (*slapping her*) You have *humiliated* me!

Estelle I didn't mean it!

Jeanne How could you be so *stupid?* Those men are not to be toyed with or played with! They are Nazi officers!

Von Pfunz appears in the doorway. He watches.

Estelle They took our house!

Jeanne slaps Estelle. Estelle howls.

Jeanne They're the occupying power! They can take any damn thing they like! I have fought for years to keep good relations with them and you have *ruined it*!

Lily Stop it, please!

Jeanne Do you think the Major's just going to forget it? Do you?

Estelle I don't know!

Jeanne NO HE'S NOT! He's going to MAKE US PAY! Because of *you*, I have to spend a whole day with that twisted *death's head*, showing him round the bloody (*Slap.*) ruins! (*Slap.*)

Estelle (*bawling*) I'm sorry! . . .

Jeanne Why did you (*Slap.*) do it? You *know* what's at stake!!

Estelle I wanted to do something *brave* . . .

Lily It's not her fault! I put her up to it!

Jeanne is just about to round on Lily when she notices Von Pfunz. Lily turns to see him. Jeanne releases Estelle. A horrified silence. Estelle smothers her sobs.

Von Pfunz Good afternoon.

Jeanne Major. How nice to see you again.

Von Pfunz Excuse me for disturbing your peace. I wish to talk to the little lady. (*Pause. To Lily.*) How is sick cow?

Lily Oh . . . much better thank you. It's gone back to its proper owner now. We were looking after it for another farmer, you see.

Von Pfunz Oh?

Lily He was . . . having a new roof put on his barn. So we took his cow for him. Anyway it's gone now.

Von Pfunz (*he giggles*) Fan*ta*stic.

Jeanne Won't you come in?

Von Pfunz enters the kitchen, neatly closing the door behind him.

Would you like a cup of tea?

Von Pfunz No thank you. I have come to speak with the little lady.

Jeanne (*pause*) You've picked a bad moment. You'll have to call back.

Von Pfunz Forgive me but I prefer to speak with her now. Alone, thank you.

Estelle I've already said sorry.

Von Pfunz It's not an apology I seek. Really, I find them tedious and I know in truth, you are not sorry at all.

Estelle I am.

Von Pfunz Only for being caught. In my more detached moments, I must admit I find what you did extremely 'spirited', if I may make such an obvious pun, and also rather funny. Don't you agree, Jeanne?

Jeanne No.

Von Pfunz It is always a joke to torment those who are sleeping.

Jeanne She has been punished, Major, as you can see.

Von Pfunz Punishment has never been an attractive ethic to me, ladies, for the simple reason that it doesn't work. When a person believes they've committed no offence, no amount of punishment will make them *feel* their crime. (*Glancing at Lily.*) And so many times, the mistake is made of punishing the innocent while the guilty go free. No. Punishment creates only martyrs.

Gabriel enters, breathless and weak on his feet, a white sheet wrapped around him. The women look at him, aghast.

Lily Gabriel. What are you doing out of bed?

Gabriel I heard crying.

Jeanne This is my nephew, Major – Gabriel Lascalles. He's . . . recovering from flu.

Gabriel (*to Estelle*) Are you all right?

Estelle nods, completely overawed.

Are you hurt?

Estelle shakes her head, slowly.

Jeanne Gabriel, this is Major Von Pfunz of the German army.

Gabriel How do you do?

Gabriel politely holds out his hand, completely unperturbed by Von Pfunz's uniform.

Von Pfunz (*shaking Gabriel's hand*) Very nice pleasure, yes.

Gabriel Deutsch. Eigentlich sind doch englisch und deutch sprachverwandt. Manche sind der Meinung, daß deutsch hart klingt, aber ich finde, es hat eine bestimmte Ausdruckskraft und Schönheit ganz für sich. Es ist die Sprache dunkler Wälder und kalter Winter; die Sprache eines schaffenden Volkes. Natürlich offenbart sich die deutsche Seele wahrhaftig erst in deutscher Musik . . . (*German. It's the sister language to English, isn't it? People say it's harsh but I think it has a strength and a beauty entirely of its own. It's the language of dark forests and cold winters; the language of a people who strive. Of course it's German music that really illuminates the German soul . . .*)

Von Pfunz Und die Seele der Briten durch die Dicht-kunst. (*And poetry that illuminates the British.*)

Gabriel Da haben Sie wohl recht. (*I suppose you're right.*)

Von Pfunz Sie sprechen ein ausgezeichnetes Deutsch, Herr Lascalles. (*You speak excellent German, Mr Lascalles.*)

Gabriel Tatsächlich? (*Do I?*)

Von Pfunz Als sei es ihre Muttersprache. Kein Akzent und nichts . . . (*Like a native. No trace of an accent at all* . . .)

Gabriel (*puzzled*) Oh . . .

Jeanne Gabriel is my brother's boy, from Torteval. He's recovering from a jolly bad fever. The air on this part of the island is so much better . . . His parents insisted he come.

Jeanne Lilian dear, why don't you take him upstairs?

Lily Come on, I made you this food.

Lily takes the tray and goes to the door. Gabriel stands.

Gabriel (*to Jeanne*) Am I really your brother's boy?

Jeanne Of course you are, dear.

Gabriel (*puzzled*) . . . Then you know who I am?

Jeanne Of course I do! . . . You've been very ill. Your poor parents have been so worried.

Gabriel Well . . . thank you. (*To Von Pfunz.*) Warum tragen Sie eigentlich diese Uniform? (*Why are you wearing that uniform?*)

Von Pfunz Sie sagt ihnen nichts? (*You don't recognise it?*)

Gabriel Ich fürchte nein. (*I'm afraid not.*)

Von Pfunz Dann haben Sie ein sehr beschütztes Leben gelebt. (*Then you've lived a very sheltered life.*)

Gabriel Schick ist sie ja. (*It's very smart.*)

Von Pfunz Danke schön. (*Thank you.*)

Lily Gabriel.

Gabriel Sorry. Excuse me.

Gabriel exits with Lily. The light is beginning to fade.

Jeanne He's been terribly ill, the poor boy. It was touch and go for a while . . .

Von Pfunz Do you know, he asked me what my uniform was.

Jeanne Really?

Von Pfunz He didn't recognise it.

Jeanne I think the fever must have temporarily affected his mind. I mean (*She laughs.*) he didn't recognise me, either . . .

Von Pfunz Extraordinary, isn't it? He was telling me how much he admires German music, how it illuminates the German soul. Tell me, what does he do for a living?

Jeanne He works on his father's farm.

Von Pfunz A man of his education? He speaks German like a native.

Jeanne Well, it's the war you see . . . it's rather clipped his wings. He was actually educated at Oxford, specialising in modern languages but when war broke out he was stranded here. Tragedy, really. He longed to be in the RAF, like Myles. He had a broken leg, you see, which he contracted when his horse threw him on a cliff path. He was in traction when they were evacuating men of military age. The occupation has prevented him from fulfilling his potential because he refuses to work for the enemy. He helps on his father's farm. Maurice Lascalles and Son of Torteval. Vegetables. (*Pause.*) They grew orchids and carnations before the war but of course, demand has dropped.

Von Pfunz May I see his papers?

Jeanne Certainly. His father has them in Torteval. I can send Mrs Lake over for them tomorrow, while we're sightseeing. Would that be convenient?

Von Pfunz It thrills me to hear you lie, Jeanne. Every word excites me. To hear you lie when I know you are capable of such truth . . .

Estelle That is the truth! He's my cousin Gabriel from Torteval and if you don't believe it you can jump off the earth.

Von Pfunz Well! The poltergeist . . .

Jeanne What do you want her for, Major?

Von Pfunz I discover that she has taken something from my room.

Estelle I didn't take anything.

Jeanne She says she didn't take anything.

Von Pfunz I'm afraid she's lying. Where can she have learnt such behaviour?

Jeanne I can't leave you with her, I'm sorry.

Estelle I'm not scared of him, Mummy.

Von Pfunz What do you think I will do? Hit her? I have never hit a child . . .

Jeanne (*to Estelle*) I'll be in my room. You only have to call.

Jeanne exits.

Von Pfunz You know what I want.

Estelle No.

Von Pfunz Come on, little phantom; you have a book of mine.

Estelle No I don't.

Von Pfunz I would like it back.

Estelle I haven't got it.

Von Pfunz Don't waste my time, please.

Estelle I don't know what you're talking about. Sorry.

Von Pfunz I ask you kindly to return it.

Estelle I can't, can I?

Von Pfunz That book is my only friend and I am a lonely man.

Estelle I haven't got it.

Von Pfunz I'm irritated by lies. I respect only the truth.

Estelle That is the truth.

Von Pfunz (*pause*) Estelle, I wish to make it clear that you are in *very deep trouble*. There is a road I could send you down, and this road, you have no idea where it ends.

Estelle You can't do anything to me. I'm a child. It's against the law.

Von Pfunz So. There is something essential about the war that you have failed to grasp: whoever is winning, and that is us, can do what they like. War is governed by force and chaos, not the law. This is a real war, Estelle, not some stupid game in your head. Over the water millions of people are dying. It is out of control. Force and chaos are terrible masters. I have killed people, yes I have, an ordinary man like me. If you had known me before the war you would have said, Von Pfunz? He is a nice fellow, a good old chap but now, imagine, I could kill you. There is no justice left, only force. If you were a little Polish girl or a Jew and you had taken my book, I would take you outside the door right now and shoot you in the back of the head (*He touches her; she flinches.*) and no one would say a word.

Estelle Maybe you just lost it.

Von Pfunz (*moves away, irritated*) Did you give it to your sister-in-law?

Estelle No.

Von Pfunz I think you did. Perhaps I should take her outside and shoot her instead?

Estelle She hasn't done anything.

Von Pfunz She is the cunning mind behind you. I heard her say so herself.

Estelle She was lying!

Von Pfunz So are you. People will laugh at you for taking my book. Do you know what is in there? There are no state secrets or Nazi plans. Do you know what it is that I write? I am a poet; does that surprise you? (*He giggles.*) I hardly think you're going to bring about the fall of the Third Reich with my poetry book . . .

Estelle I haven't got it.

Von Pfunz (*lighting candles*) What about your handsome cousin? Has he got it?

Estelle No.

Von Pfunz Why do you lie, Estelle?

Estelle I'm not lying.

Von Pfunz Has your Mummy got my book?

Estelle No.

Von Pfunz Perhaps you wouldn't trust her with it?
Perhaps you think she spends too much time with
Germans?

Estelle No.

Von Pfunz Do you like her spending time with us?

Estelle Don't care.

Von Pfunz Do you like her selling food to us while the
islanders are hungry? She's a parasite, don't you think? . . .
Would you like to see her going to jail?

Estelle She hasn't done anything!

Von Pfunz What had I done to you, when you stole my
book? What had I done to you when you leant over me
in the night and put those *things* on my face? When I
woke in that horrible way did you listen to my fear and
laugh? Did my anguish amuse you?

Estelle No.

Von Pfunz Why did you do that to me?

Estelle Don't know.

Von Pfunz Why not one of the other men? We are all the
same.

Estelle No you're not.

Von Pfunz We're all the enemy.

Estelle None of them talk to you! They all leave the
lounge when you go in. They don't like you!

Von Pfunz Then we have something in common.
(*Leaning over her.*) Forgive me, but no one likes you
either, do they? You have the haunted look of a child

147

who is lonely. A child who must imagine her friends out of thin air, communing with the ghosts. Perhaps they are your only real friends, the shades of night. It will always be that way. Do you understand me, Estelle? I know exactly the kind of woman you will become . . . unloved. (*He caresses her face.*) You are in your coffin.

Estelle attempts to turn her head. Von Pfunz grips her face, hard.

Give me my book.

Estelle I threw it in the sea!

Von Pfunz (*shaking her*) You're lying!

Estelle Mummy! MUMMY!

Von Pfunz Damn you!

Estelle screams. He releases her. Jeanne enters, flicking the lights on.

Estelle He said you were a parasite. He wants to shoot Lily and put you in jail!

Jeanne Of course he doesn't. He's making nasty, idle threats.

Von Pfunz is giggling.

Perhaps you'd go now.

Von Pfunz I don't yet have what I came for.

Jeanne And what's that?

Von Pfunz My book.

Jeanne Give the Major his book.

Estelle I haven't got it.

Jeanne Is that the truth?

148

Estelle Yes.

Jeanne Then go to your room.

Von Pfunz I must have this settled!

Jeanne If she's got it, you'll get it back. You can rely on me.

Estelle exits. Pause.

Major, did you just come here to terrorise my child, or is there something I can do for you, before you leave?

Von Pfunz Yes. You can help me with a problem I have.

Jeanne What's that?

Von Pfunz I am worried for you, Jeanne, worried that you have a Jew sharing your home, eating the same food, spending time with your child . . .

Jeanne Major –

Von Pfunz She is a bad influence, this we can see. Why don't you throw her out?

Jeanne She's my son's wife.

Von Pfunz Why didn't she go back to England before the invasion? She must have known the danger.

Jeanne She wanted to! I asked her to take Estelle to a cousin of mine in London. I knew I had to stay on the island; my house, you know, I wouldn't leave my house. Anyway, they got down to the harbour and everything was panic and mayhem. Estelle got frightened in the crowd and ran away. By the time Lilian found her, the last boat had sailed.

Von Pfunz So it's the child's fault that the Jew is stranded here? Amazing, the damage innocence can cause . . . My problem: I have looked up her records and

149

not only is she registered as a Christian, but her birthplace is given as Guernsey. I know this not to be true. Can you explain?

Jeanne Major, I have to beg you not to continue this line of questioning.

Von Pfunz I'm only looking for the truth.

Jeanne Please, just leave things be.

Von Pfunz Why must you protect her so? It's obvious you don't like her.

Jeanne What I feel about her is not the point! I know I've got my faults but that kind of treachery isn't one of them. I couldn't live with myself.

Von Pfunz Ah. A matter of conscience.

Jeanne Yes.

Von Pfunz The civilised person is capable of negotiating with conscience. One learns this in a war. Conscience will collaborate.

Jeanne I've gone down that path as far as I intend.

Von Pfunz But once you are on it, the path goes on forever. And you soon find you can live with anything. Jeanne, I have to report her.

Jeanne Why?

Von Pfunz All Jews must be registered.

Jeanne What for?

Von Pfunz Their own protection.

Pause. Jeanne shakily pours two drinks. She hands one to Von Pfunz.

Jeanne What's your name, Major? Your Christian name?

Von Pfunz I have two; neither is relevant.

Jeanne Well, Von Pfunz, I know you appreciate frank speech, so I'll speak frankly. I want to make a bargain with you.

Von Pfunz What bargain?

Jeanne I'll enter into any kind of relationship you might like, if you'll do one thing for me; leave my family alone.

Von Pfunz Well! (*He giggles.*) That's a very interesting offer, Jeanne.

Jeanne Yes.

Von Pfunz What can you mean by it?

Jeanne Exactly what I said.

Von Pfunz You'll do anything I like, if I leave your family in peace?

Jeanne Yes.

Von Pfunz I'm overcome! (*He giggles.*) It's like Christmas and my birthday all at once. Jeanne Lascalles will do anything I want . . . Unfortunately, I can't think of anything.

> *Jeanne is lighting cigarettes, Hollywood style. She hands one to Von Pfunz.*

Jeanne I'm being honest with you because I know you respect that. Don't lie to me. You can think of plenty.

Von Pfunz You're right, of course. But forgive me Jeanne; I'm not sure that I like your bargain.

Jeanne Why not?

Von Pfunz Well, (*Giggles.*) it rather takes the spontaneity out of our relationship, don't you think? If I know that every moment you are with me is merely an act of martyrdom for your family? The more outrageous I was in my demands, the better you would feel. (*Laughing.*) Impossible! . . . Is this how you seduced Reicher?

Jeanne Reicher was an attractive man. Are you? Do you think you'd stand the remotest chance with me, if I didn't have an ulterior motive?

Von Pfunz Ah.

Jeanne Of course not. You know I find you disgusting; what's the point in lying?

Von Pfunz None ever.

Jeanne This is a way of keeping relations between us absolutely honest. You want me; I want to live without threat of harassment. Every 'prostitute' has a price and mine is peace of mind.

Pause. Von Pfunz is genuinely hurt and depressed.

Von Pfunz It's a sad picture of yourself you paint. You fling my insults back at me most cleverly, but the picture you paint is very sad.

Jeanne Perhaps you'd like some time to think over what I've said.

Von Pfunz Jeanne . . . Look how you tread yourself in the mud. It makes me so sad that your life has brought you to this. No wonder you have become bitter and desperate. To see your brightness squandered on this tedious struggle – sardines and Cognac – and your family like chains around your neck. You should be in Berlin, or Rome, or anywhere where there is *life*. You deserve to be alive. You are priceless.

Jeanne So, my bargain is a bargain then.

Von Pfunz Unfortunately, there's only one thing I want from you, and it's beyond your power to give.

Jeanne What is it?

Von Pfunz You can't imagine.

Jeanne I can imagine quite a lot.

Von Pfunz Jeanne . . . Sometimes our desires are so deep that we are not even sure of them ourselves. How can we ever be sure of what we really want? In speaking even our deepest desire aloud, it may become suddenly foolish, absurd on our lips, and no longer our desire . . .

Jeanne Are you worried that I would despise you?

Von Pfunz looks down.

I despise you already. Ask for what you want.

Von Pfunz I can't.

Jeanne Why not?

Von Pfunz (*sighs*) So. Your bargain is tempting but I must turn it down.

Jeanne No.

Jeanne kisses Von Pfunz. She holds her body close to his. Von Pfunz doesn't move or respond. After a moment, he lifts her away from him.

Von Pfunz Don't demean yourself, Mrs Becquet.

Von Pfunz goes to the door.

Jeanne You impotent fool.

Von Pfunz takes a step back into the house.

Von Pfunz You're very like your child, Jeanne. You play with this war like a game in your head.

Jeanne What do you mean?

Von Pfunz You think you are *inviolate* . . . Well, I have some information for you; confidential.

Jeanne Then keep it to yourself.

Von Pfunz A launch of ours was lost at sea three nights ago. One of the passengers was a young man, from Berlin. When the wreck was found this morning, his body was not in it.

Jeanne How sad.

Von Pfunz He was on his way to Alderney, to visit a new camp there. It's run by the Schutzstaffel.

Jeanne The who?

Von Pfunz Hitler's brightest angels . . . the SS. This young man was an officer.

Jeanne Why are you telling me this?

Von Pfunz No reason. He was quite an aristocrat, apparently; educated at Oxford, like your nephew. He spoke English like a native.

Jeanne I'm sorry. I fail to see the relevance of this.

Von Pfunz Perhaps there is none. I just want you to be aware that penalties would be serious for hiding information about him . . . if you had any. I fear for your safety this evening, Mrs Becquet, so I am posting a guard around the house.

Jeanne Why on earth would you want to do that?

Von Pfunz I was going to blind my eyes to this, Jeanne! I was going to let it go! Anyone else I would have arrested already. Six armed men. I do this for you.

Von Pfunz goes. Jeanne locks and bolts the door. She sits. Her self-control crumbles.

Scene Four

The attic, later. Lily is sitting on the chair, mending a white shirt. Estelle is at the window, occasionally glancing out of it. Most of the time her attention is fixed on Gabriel, who is trying on a pair of cricket shoes.

Lily Do they fit?

Gabriel Yes. They're your husband's?

Lily Yes.

Gabriel I'm very grateful to him. (*He walks in them.*) Ja, schön . . .

Lily Why do you do that?

Gabriel Do what?

Lily Speak German. When you've forgotten everything else.

Gabriel Well. My mind's not empty, if that's what you mean. It's full. (*Taking off the shoes.*) Of things, you know: facts – fragments. German's so fluent I've been thinking in it. I know other languages too and music; I can hear phrases of it in my head. I haven't lost my knowledge – it's my whole experience that's gone. I don't remember a single thing that I've done or person that I've loved – nothing I can call mine. (*Pause.*) Except the falling.

Estelle Falling?

Lily He remembers falling.

Estelle Out of the sky?

Gabriel I don't know.

Lily Try and think about the plane.

Gabriel I don't remember a plane. (*Thinks.*) I can't explain. It's more than just an image or a memory; it's a *thing* . . . consumes me.

Estelle Is it frightening?

Gabriel No. It's frightening when I look in the mirror and don't recognise the face. I might as well have been born this afternoon.

Estelle Gabriel –

Gabriel Don't get me wrong; I'm glad to be alive.

Estelle smiles. A beam of a torch light suddenly shines into the room from the yard below. It moves around and disappears. Estelle peers round the edge of the window.

What's that?

Lily I expect Mrs Becquet's on her way to feed the hens. Here, try this on.

Lily joins Estelle at the window. For a moment Gabriel briefly clutches his head.

(*quietly to Estelle*) Are they still there?

Estelle It's hard to tell how many in the dark.

Lily What are they doing?

Estelle I don't know.

Lily Searching the place or what?

Estelle Just hanging around.

Lily Go downstairs and ask your mum what's going on.

Estelle We have to tell him. I know you said don't worry him with questions but he needs to know they're there, then he can think what to do.

Lily What can he possibly do?

Estelle Lily, he has to prepare.

Gabriel (*approaching*) Prepare for what?

Gabriel seems to be in some pain. He briefly holds his hand to his head.

Lily Are you all right?

Gabriel Who's out there?

Lily No one.

Gabriel Don't lie.

Estelle There's some soldiers.

Gabriel (*looking out of the window*) What soldiers?

Estelle Krauts.

Gabriel What do they want?

Estelle Come away from the window; they might see you.

Gabriel Why shouldn't they see me?

Estelle pulls Gabriel back into the room.

That man in your kitchen. They're the same, same uniform.

Lily Yes.

Gabriel Why are they here?

Lily They're guarding the house.

Gabriel What for?

Lily You mustn't trouble yourself with it.

Estelle He's got to trouble himself with it.

Gabriel Are you connected with Germany in some way?

Lily Pardon?

Gabriel I mean, why are they German?

Pause.

What have I said?

Lily You're in occupied Europe, Gabriel. Guernsey's occupied.

Gabriel I don't understand.

Estelle The Krauts have taken over the island. They bombed St Peter's Port and landed here in boats, thousands of them. They forced us out of our house and they're making us learn German in school. They march up and down all day and then at night they go to the pictures and watch films about Hitler. They've put barbed wire in the sea and planted mines on the beaches –

Gabriel (*appalled*) Why?

Lily Gabriel, do you not remember *anything*? (*Pause.*) We're at war.

Gabriel looks utterly lost. He puts his hand to his head in increasing pain.

What's the matter?

Gabriel But – wh – It's –

Lily Gabriel, what is it? Here –

Gabriel The Ger – we're the – the –

Lily What is it?!

Gabriel suddenly cries out. He flings himself on to the bed.

Gabriel!

Estelle What's wrong with him?

Gabriel cries out in agony.

Lily I don't know!

Estelle They'll hear him! They'll come inside! Put something over his mouth.

Lily You'll smother him! Leave him.

Lily has to physically keep Estelle away from Gabriel.

Estelle They'll take him away!

Lily Give him space and shut up!

Estelle Gabriel!

Gabriel passes out. Jeanne enters unnoticed, with a glass of Cognac. She is drunk.

Is he all right? . . .

Lily There must be something – He must've injured his head, when he fell. Estelle, I don't know . . . This happened to him once before, when I was watching him. The way he cried out. The pain, here. I thought it was the fever . . . some kind of pressure building up. Maybe that's all it is

Gabriel slowly comes round.

Gabriel Lily . . .

Lily How are you?

Gabriel I was falling.

Lily Like before?

Gabriel nods.

Nothing else?

Gabriel It takes hold of me.

Lily How?

Gabriel The speed . . . hurts.

Estelle You mustn't do it again.

Lily Rest.

Gabriel There's another image.

Lily What?

Gabriel Snow.

Lily Snow?

Gabriel I'm standing in snow. Everything white . . . And the dead sound things make when it's deep. Something behind me . . . like a fear. I'm wearing black.

Jeanne Estelle, get off there.

Estelle (*staring with shock*) I'm cold.

Jeanne Get off.

Lily Mrs Becquet. Fancy you hiding there.

Estelle reluctantly gets off Gabriel's bed.

Jeanne Wie geht es dir, meine kleine deutsche Junge? (*How are you, little German boy?*)

Gabriel Danke, gut; es geht mir gut. (*Fine thank you; I'm fine.*)

Jeanne Do you know who I am?

Gabriel Mrs Becquet.

Jeanne And who are you?

Gabriel I've been given the name Gabriel. I was born this afternoon.

Jeanne Well, Gabriel, I never wanted another child in my house.

Gabriel By that, I mean I don't know who I am. I'm sorry.

Jeanne Why be sorry? No one's blaming you for anything, are they?

Gabriel No.

Jeanne So. Have you had plenty to eat and drink?

Gabriel Yes, thank you.

Jeanne I see Lilian's giving you my son's favourite clothes.

Lily It's all he left behind. And he's got to wear something, hasn't he?

Jeanne She found you naked, did you know that?

Gabriel Yes.

Jeanne It's a shame really because if you'd been clothed, we'd've known who you were, straight away. We only had your features to judge you by and they can be so misleading, don't you think?

Gabriel I'm sure.

Jeanne So . . . you wear black in your dreams. (*To Lily.*) Does he know the danger he's put us in?

Lily It's not his fault.

Gabriel What have I done?

Lily Nothing.

Jeanne You'd be dead if it wasn't for me and my family. We put our lives at risk to help you. I've kept you in this house against my will for three days.

Lily You said he could stay!

Jeanne I didn't say he could betray us.

Lily He hasn't.

Gabriel What have I done?

Lily It's not his fault! He didn't know who the Major was. He can't remember the war.

Jeanne Don't be absurd!

Gabriel What war?

Jeanne Of course he can remember the bloody war!

Gabriel I need to know.

Jeanne What kind of a game are you playing?

Lily Leave him alone, Mrs Becquet; you'll make him ill again!

Jeanne This is *my house!* Don't you tell me what I can and can't do!

Lily retreats, defeated.

You don't know anything about the war?

Gabriel shakes his head.

Well. I have to say, I don't believe you. I have to say, I don't trust you an inch. So, without going into too much detail, the whole world has been at war for the last three years; that's everybody, everywhere. Ring any bells? Unless you've been living in a hermit's cave in the

Antarctic, you really can't have missed it . . . In Europe, the baddies are Nazis. They're German, they wear grey, and they want to rule the world. We're with the Allies, who wear green.

Gabriel So, the man I met –

Jeanne Is our enemy, yes. And tomorrow, because he's discovered we're hiding you, and because hiding you is a Very Serious Crime, he's going to come here like a cat tormenting mice. He'll spend the day playing with us and afterwards, he'll arrest my family and me. Then, when we've all been *raped* by him –

Lily Enough! –

Jeanne He'll have us shot.

Gabriel I didn't know . . .

Jeanne There was a German soldier in my kitchen, walking around with a gun on his belt. Did you think he was in fancy dress?

Estelle We fooled him, Gabriel. He thinks you're my cousin. We told him your name's Gabriel Lascalles and you come from Torteval. You work on Uncle Maurice's vegetable farm and you went to Oxford but the war's sadly clipped your wings . . .

The torch light shines into the room again. Jeanne goes to the window. She looks into the light. She raises her glass, then drinks. Pause. The light disappears.

Gabriel What do you want me to do, Mrs Becquet?

Jeanne Our punishment, Liebling, will depend on who you are. Some fugitives are more sacred than others, and perhaps you're only a stupid island drunkard who hit his head on a rock. Tell us the truth.

Gabriel I have.

Jeanne Are you a British pilot, Gabriel, like my son? Or are you German?

Gabriel I don't know.

Jeanne The fact is, the Major knows who you are.

Gabriel How?

Jeanne He says you're a shining SS officer who was washed off a boat on his way to Alderney.

Lily No.

Jeanne Do you know what they are, the SS?

Gabriel shakes his head.

They're the élite; Germany's hand-picked men. Lilian especially lives in terror of them.

Gabriel Why?

Lily (*to Jeanne*) Shut up!

Jeanne They're the most transcendent men on Earth, the first citizens of the new world. Sadly, their new world is only achievable by destroying the old. They regard most of us as sub-human and the Jews, whom they hate, as a plague.

Lily That's enough.

Jeanne I'm very sorry, Lilian. Believe me, I am. But this is one of Hitler's brightest angels; one of his chosen few.

Estelle You've made a mistake . . .

Jeanne There's a concentration camp on Alderney that you were on your way to visit. Alderney's a secret place these days. Half the troops don't know what goes on . . .

But we hear things. Is it true that you can't remember anything about yourself or the war?

Gabriel Yes it's true.

Jeanne Then what made you blank it out? What have you done that you can't live with? You could be this man, couldn't you? It's possible.

Gabriel Ja, möglich ist es. Alles ist möglich. (*Yes, it's possible. Anything is possible . . .*)

Jeanne I've had nightmares since you came here. Every night, since they dragged you in . . . (*Voice cracking.*) You look like my son.

Lily He does not!

Jeanne Do you hear me?

Gabriel Yes.

Jeanne You look like Myles, my son.

Gabriel I can't help that.

Jeanne He's dead, isn't he? My son is dead.

Estelle No! . . .

Jeanne That's the truth. I can feel it!

Jeanne sobs. She drops her empty glass. The torch light shines into the room again. It moves around and disappears. Only Lily and Gabriel notice. They look at one another.

Estelle Mummy . . . don't cry. It's not true . . .

Estelle touches Jeanne, who flinches, stands and stumbles towards the door.

Jeanne Ohh . . . God . . .

Lily What now?

Jeanne Going to be sick.

Lily grips Jeanne by the arm.

Lily Downstairs. Now. I'll get you a bucket.

Lily leads Jeanne out roughly. Estelle gets on the bed beside Gabriel.

Estelle Myles isn't dead. I'd feel it too, if he was. He isn't dead, I know it. Mummy's wrong. She's wrong about everything. I know you're not that man.

Gabriel kisses the crown of Estelle's head.

You came for me didn't you?

Gabriel What do you mean?

Estelle The night you came, I made a square of power. Everything that's happened has come out of it. At first I thought it wasn't going to work but Lily must've found you at the exact moment, the exact moment when I made my wish.

Gabriel What wish?

Estelle I went with her down to the beach to help bring you back. And when I saw you lying there in the sand, I knew that when I'd said, let my brother come like a bright angel, what I'd really meant was, let a bright angel come like my brother.

Gabriel Estelle.

Estelle It was my square of power again, that saved your life. I made sure we laid you right on top of it and you survived. You took the power and it went right through you. And I still didn't know it was you, but I was hoping, hoping all the time. And all you can remember is

falling . . . You remember falling and everything is new
to you –

Gabriel Estelle, this is –

Estelle (*hugging him*) I love you, Gabriel, I love you and
I want you to know that I've already started to help. I
decided the night you came and I've been braver than
ever in my life. I smashed his Hitler and wee'd in his
boot, and I stole his book to read his secrets and destroy
his plans. He's spreading lies about you because he can
see that you're pure and good. He told me what Force
was, Gabriel, and I knew he meant evil; all the while I
was looking at him thinking evil, evil, evil.

Gabriel Estelle, what is it you think I can do?

Estelle (*simply*) You've come to crush and destroy them.
You've got to kill Major Von Pfunz.

Lily comes in, with Von Pfunz's diary, hidden.

Lily Come on. Time for bed.

Estelle Where's Mummy?

Lily In the chair by the fire.

Estelle Was she sick?

Lily She'd eaten some biscuits that had gone off.

Estelle Can I go and see if she's better?

Lily She's asleep. Go to bed.

Estelle (*whispers*) I love you.

*Estelle kisses Gabriel and gets out of his bed. She
kisses Lily and exits. Lily puts Von Pfunz's book on
the bed.*

Gabriel What is it?

Lily Estelle stole it off the Major. I thought if you could speak German you could probably read it too and you might find something that will help you.

Gabriel Help me do what?

Lily Remember.

Gabriel I see. Is that wise?

Lily Gabriel . . .

Gabriel I'm only sure of one thing, Lily. Gabriel is not my name. What do you think?

Lily About what?

Gabriel About me. Who do you believe I am?

Lily I believe the same as you.

Gabriel And what's that?

Lily That you don't know.

> *Gabriel looks despairing. Lily goes to him – a gesture of comfort. Gabriel pulls her into an embrace. They kiss. It's becoming very passionate when Lily breaks away.*

No! I can't . . .

Gabriel I'm sorry. (*Pause.*) You love your husband –

Lily No, it's not to do with Myles. I don't love him. When we got married I thought I did, but it was false. It was false and I got stuck here. I want to tell you something else.

Gabriel What?

Lily (*looking straight at him*) I'm a Jew.

Gabriel What should that mean to me?

Lily You tell me. What does it mean?

Gabriel Do you . . . is it that you have a religious objection to – to us being –

Lily (*half laugh, half sob*).

Gabriel No.

Lily The Jews on this island have gone. No one knows where. I knew two women. Police came, handed them to the Krauts, never seen again. The only reason I'm still here is 'cause Mrs Becquet protects me. We hear rumours about things in Europe. God help me . . . (*They embrace.*)

Gabriel Why have you told me?

Lily I thought, if you were one of them I'd be able to tell.

Gabriel Can you?

Lily shakes her head.

Don't turn against me.

Lily I'm not. I just need to know you won't turn against me.

Gabriel How could I? You're all I have.

They kiss passionately. Lily breaks off, staring at him.

Lily Who are you?

The torch light shines in. Gabriel kisses her.

Gabriel This.

He kisses her again.

I'm this . . .

Scene Five

The kitchen. Moonlight. Jeanne is asleep in the chair by the fire, a blanket over her knees. She looks awful.

Estelle enters, wearing her night dress. She is holding a candle. She looks at her mother. She goes to a drawer in the dresser and takes out something wrapped in a red cloth. She puts the candle and the cloth bundle on the floor. She draws a chalk square. She kneels in it and makes her secret signs, as previously. She unwraps the bundle. Inside it is an old First World War dagger. She examines it. She holds it up by the tip and slowly lays it in the square. She stands back, her eyes fixed on the dagger.

Pause.

Estelle looks at Jeanne once more and exits with the candle.

The attic. Lily and Gabriel have made love. Lily is asleep, Gabriel awake.

He goes to the window and peers out. He sees Von Pfunz's book lying on the floor. He picks it up. He flicks through it. He sits on the bed and starts reading.

Scene Six

Dawn. The kitchen. Jeanne is awake, but unmoving.
Someone knocks loudly on the back door. Jeanne starts.
She stands and leans dizzily against the table. She
attempts to neaten her appearance, panicked and ill.

Jeanne (*calls*) Just a minute! (*More knocking. She*
fumbles across the room.) Would you wait a moment
please?

Lake (*off*) It's me.

Jeanne Margaret . . .

Lake (*knocking*) Come on, let me in.

Jeanne Wait.

> *Jeanne unlocks the door. Lake enters.*

Lake Bloody little bleeders wouldn't let me by. What's
been going on up here?

Jeanne I thought you were him.

Lake Who?

Jeanne Him.

> *Jeanne flops back into her chair and closes her eyes.*

Lake What's going on, Jeanne? Why are those lads out
there?

Jeanne Margaret, I desperately need a cup of tea . . .

Lake Marvellous.

Lake puts fuel in the stove and puts the kettle on the hob. Jeanne raises her head.

Jeanne Where have you been?

Lake Where you sent me. I walked up here last night, found it covered in Krauts. One of them's a lad I know so I says to him: 'Come on, I live here, you have to let me through,' but he wouldn't – didn't even tell me what was going on.

Jeanne Where did you go?

Lake Pub. Slept in the lounge. Mrs Garrett gave me a blanket. What have you done to yourself, Jeanne?

Jeanne I just had a couple of drinks.

Lake Then you don't need tea.

Lake cracks a raw egg into a cup. She pours in some milk and whisks it with a fork.

Jeanne Not one of those . . .

Lake Why are the lads out there?

Jeanne The Major saw the boy.

Lake He saw the boy?

Jeanne It was love at first sight. The boy started chatting in fluent German and now Von Pfunz is convinced he's some missing Nazi.

Lake He speaks German?

Jeanne nods.

Does he still not remember himself?

Jeanne shakes her head.

What's the Major going to do?

Jeanne I don't know . . .

Lake (*handing her the drink*) Drink.

Jeanne May the ground open and swallow me.

She drinks.

Lake It was a mistake to take that boy in, Jeanne.

Jeanne I knew that!

Lake It would have been kinder to let him die.

Jeanne Why? What have you found out?

Lake The truth.

Lily enters.

Jeanne Lilian.

Lily How are you, Mrs Becquet?

Jeanne I never felt better, thank you. How are you?

Lily I think you should see this.

Lily puts Von Pfunz's diary in front of Jeanne. Jeanne picks it up.

Jeanne What is it?

Lily The Major's book.

Jeanne The Major's book . . . Where did you find it?

Lily Estelle gave it to me.

Jeanne I might have known. (*Flicking through it.*) Damn, it's in German.

Lily Gabriel read it during the night.

Jeanne What's in it?

Lily Stuff about Poland. Things he's seen there.

Jeanne What things?

Lily (*sits*) They're killing Jews. On a scale you can't imagine. In these huge places like factories. Shipping trainloads of people into Poland and gassing them.

Jeanne What?

Lily I never read anything that made me sick before. Gabriel woke me in the night. He said I ought to hear. It's the truth. I never thanked you much for sticking your neck out over me, Mrs Becquet. But I'm truly grateful.

Lily suppresses tears.

Jeanne Lily . . . (*She hesitates.*) This is simply not true. Von Pfunz is a very sick man and he's making it up. We're talking about civilised Europe! Now please, calm yourself and tell me if there's anything in that book that we can hold over him, anything that damns him, in any way.

Lily The whole thing damns him.

Gabriel enters, dressed in cricketing gear.

Gabriel Good morning.

Jeanne Gabriel, I want to know about this book. I want to know what Von Pfunz says about himself. There must be something in here we can use.

Lily She doesn't believe me.

Gabriel Oh.

Lily Would you read her something please?

Gabriel I'll translate it for you. (*Reads title in German then translates.*) 'Abgegeben . . . ', 'Discarded . . . ':

> Like a field of corn or the sea
> hair heaped to the rafters
> high as hay.

The secret in this place
is loud in the sunlight
dark in the silence
like a brown curl it clings.
I tear it from me.

Jeanne What does it mean?

Gabriel What it says. He's seen a room filled with hair.
He's written almost everything in poetic form so it takes
a while for the darkness of it to reach your heart.

Lily Read another.

Gabriel (*reads the title in German, then translates*) 'Die
Unerwählten.' 'The Unselected.'

The Selector loves the dark, the mask
And cloak it throws around his task.
These shadowed wraiths,
Pouring out of wagon gates
A shambles of limbs unsteady,
Are creatures half born
To the spirit world already.
Survive or be damned.
They pass
Where the Selector stands
And it is done.
A firmament of human eyes
Stare into the shadows that are his
Yet he is calm at source.
For the Selector does not choose;
His hand moves left and right
An independent thing, a tool
Not of his but of the rule
That thralls us – Force.
The Unselected learn their fate
Too late to curse him to his face,

Nor does he care to feel
Their soon annihilated hate.
The Selector cloaked
In darkness stands
As judges must
When judgement is at hand.

Pause.

Lily (*to Gabriel*) Read the one about the child's shoe.

Jeanne I've heard enough.

Jeanne takes the book from Gabriel.

He mustn't know that you've read it.

Lily I have to go somewhere. I'm going to be sick.

Jeanne Take it up to Estelle. She has to give it back.

Lily exits upstairs with the book.

Gabriel To have seen such a place and turn it into poetry. Before I read that I didn't know anything. And now I don't want to know any more.

Lake I must tell you something, boy.

Gabriel What?

Lake There's no easy way to say it so I'll just say it. I heard this story last night from Mrs Garrett, a landlady who's got ears everywhere. She got it from a woman in St Peter's Port; one of your wife's people.

Jeanne You know who he is.

Lake Your name ain't Gabriel, it's John Gilbert. You work in a bank, translating for the Krauts.

Gabriel I what?

GABRIEL

Lake You been missing a couple of weeks and your family all feared you was dead.

Gabriel What family?

Lake This winter, you start getting this bad vision and pains in your eyes and they turn into these like fits, and no one knows what's wrong with you so they take you to the Kraut doctors and the Kraut doctors do all manner of tests and that, and then one of them takes you aside and says there's a thing growing in your head that ain't right, something growing in there and they're sorry but there's nothing they can do.

Jeanne My God . . .

Lake You go to pieces after that and run off. Then, the same day as Lilian finds you, three men see you over where they're building the tunnels, no shoes on, all besmirched and cut up on your legs. They reckon you been hiding down there. Last they see, you was running off to the beach, stumbling like you're blind, blinded in the light.

Jeanne This is unbelievable.

Lake I'm sorry, my boy, but I thought you ought to know.

Jeanne Margaret, do you know what this means? We can't be prosecuted for hiding him. If he's only an island man, what crime have we committed by having him here?

Lake None.

Jeanne That's right, none. (*To Gabriel.*) I'm so sorry. This is awful news for you; truly tragic, but at the risk of sounding callous, I have to say that it's very good news for us.

Gabriel Yes.

Jeanne It's one thing less, one thing less . . . Margaret, come and help me with my hair.

Jeanne exits to her room.

Lake I'm sorry.

Gabriel Nothing you've said makes the slightest connection with me. It's just as foreign and just as possible as anything else I've heard. John Gilbert. Blinded in the light.

Lake Well. Like I say, I'm sorry.

Gabriel There is one thing.

Lake What?

Gabriel I can see perfectly.

Lake exits to Jeanne's room. Gabriel has a spasm of pain. He overcomes it.

I am no one.

Gabriel's eyes suddenly alight on the dagger in the chalk square. He looks at it, puzzled. He picks it up. He stands in the square and examines it. He realises where he is standing. He kneels. Pause. He suddenly puts his ear to the ground, as if he has heard something below. Estelle enters from the stairs, neatly dressed, her hair loose. She approaches Gabriel.

Estelle Can you hear them?

Gabriel (*starting with shock*) Who?

Estelle The men underneath. They're coming right under the house.

Gabriel You've got men underneath?

Estelle Yes.

Gabriel What are they doing?

Estelle Making a labyrinth for the Krauts. Will you make them stop?

Gabriel (*pause*) What's this, Estelle?

He holds up the knife. Estelle takes it.

Estelle A knife. It's been gathering power.

Gabriel I see.

Estelle I wanted to get you a gun but the Krauts keep them all locked up. Daddy had one, but he buried it after the Great War and no one knows where. He had this in the trenches. Mummy says he used it for killing rats but I think it was Krauts. (*She hands it back to Gabriel.*) Will it do?

Gabriel For what?

Estelle For him. You just have to find your chance. I'll help all I can.

Gabriel (*goes to the armchair*) Estelle, I don't need this.

Estelle Why not?

Gabriel (*smiles, ironically*) I'm going to smite him with a thunderbolt.

Estelle giggles. The door bursts open and Von Pfunz enters, carrying a jackboot. Gabriel is hidden from his view by the chair. He puts the dagger in his belt behind him.

Von Pfunz Where is your mother? I want her now!

Estelle Why?

Von Pfunz You know why! (*Holding up the jackboot.*) Explain!

179

Estelle looks afraid and ashamed.

Next time you come near my house I will tell my men to shoot! That a little girl could do this! It sickens me. You are like an *animal*, a filthy dirty –

Gabriel (*stands*) Guten Morgen, Herr Major. (*Good morning, Major.*)

Von Pfunz Herr Lascalles. Versteckt hat sie sich, in meinem Haus . . . (*Mr Lascalles. She's been hiding in my house . . .*)

Gabriel (*smiling*) Ich weiß; und schikaniert hat sie Sie auch noch, die Kleine. (*So I gather; terrorising you single-handedly.*)

Von Pfunz Ein Verbrechen hat sie begangen. (*She has perpetrated a crime.*)

Gabriel What's she done?

Von Pfunz It is almost too shameful to say. She has urinated in my boot.

Lily enters, dressed. She stares at Von Pfunz. Estelle runs to her.

Mrs Myles. Good morning.

Lily I have to brush her hair.

Lily exits with Estelle.

Von Pfunz This is my finest boots. The best in Munich. I was to wear them for my day with Mrs Becquet. You can imagine my disgust. (*He puts his boot down. Pause.*) Your flu is better?

Gabriel Yes, thank you.

Von Pfunz You have good rest last night?

Gabriel Not really. I couldn't sleep.

Von Pfunz I sent my men to watch over you.

Gabriel It wasn't your men that kept me awake. I was reading.

Von Pfunz Good book?

Gabriel Poetry.

Von Pfunz Ah, you are a lover of poetry?

Gabriel It fascinates me.

Von Pfunz The treasure of England.

Gabriel Yes.

Von Pfunz I grew up with Keats and Donne. (*Giggles.*) I dabble a little myself.

Gabriel You write poetry?

Von Pfunz Yes. I am hoping one day to be published.

Gabriel Oh?

Von Pfunz You find it unusual for a soldier to write?

Gabriel A little, yes.

Von Pfunz But poetry is a voice of truth, and truth is revealed most clearly in extremities. Soldiers live in extremities; they are in the mouth of death.

Gabriel But surely not all soldiers see the truth, even when they're staring right at it.

Von Pfunz I quite agree. It is the soul of a poet that sees the truth, but sometimes such a soul is trapped in a soldier's life. It is the soul of a poet that can unravel the chaos he is in and make it something pure. You see, the poet believes that only when we struggle to understand on a greater scale, do we know that we're alive, that we're more than a machine . . . The poet sees the greater truth. (*Pause.*) I think you are fooling me. You know all this; you were at Oxford!

Gabriel What do you mean by the greater truth?

Von Pfunz (*giggles*) You ask me this before breakfast? (*Thinks.*) I mean an honesty so pure it hurts us. A superior state, of light, where all is clear. Such a thing is possible only as a dream – but the search is poetry. To choose the face of truth hardest to look into. That is where one finds something pure.

Gabriel I see.

Von Pfunz I think for most of us it's a moment that comes only with death.

Gabriel You see death as a greater truth?

Von Pfunz As a kind of purity, yes. It's rather a cliché, I know.

Gabriel So purity can be absolute darkness as well as absolute light?

Von Pfunz Yes . . .

Gabriel How would you define evil?

Von Pfunz (*giggles, delighted*) You are playing in a cricket match today?

Gabriel No. These are my clothes.

Jeanne enters, smartly dressed. Lake follows her.

Jeanne Major, I thought I could hear your voice. Forgive me for keeping you. I was just putting the finishing touches to my hair. (*Noticing the boot.*) What's that?

Von Pfunz That is my boot.

Jeanne What's it doing in my kitchen?

Von Pfunz It is the victim of an outrage.

Jeanne I'm sorry?

Von Pfunz Your daughter has emptied her bladder here.

Jeanne She's done nothing of the kind!

Von Pfunz You can see for yourself.

Von Pfunz takes the boot to the sink. He empties it.

That is the evidence. These are waterproof and I put my foot right in. I was revolted.

Jeanne How dare you suggest that Estelle did this?

Von Pfunz I demand that it is cleaned.

Jeanne One of your pig soldiers did it. Make them clean it!

Von Pfunz Madam, this has gone far enough. Your child will clean this while I watch!

Jeanne Over my dead body.

Von Pfunz I am lenient with her because she is your child but I have had the limit! She will clean this boot or I am telling my men to shoot all trespassers – and we shall see then if she can haunt us!

Jeanne (*appalled*) Are you threatening her life?

Von Pfunz I am saying I have had enough!

Jeanne (*livid*) You should remember where you are. You may be in the habit of shooting children – but this island is a civilised place. I take full responsibility for Estelle, so why don't you shoot me? Why don't you arrest all of us right now and take us out to be shot?

Von Pfunz Jeanne, this is not –

Jeanne Take whoever you're going to take, and get out! You're dis*gus*ting.

Von Pfunz (*shocked*) It was a figure of speech, you know, words I use all the time: I say all the time, 'Do this or that or I will have you shot'; these are not words I mean! I would not harm your child! . . . You must forgive my mistakes, my – It is language problems. Mrs Becquet, we must go to the ruins. I have ordered a picnic . . .

Jeanne Am I under arrest?

Von Pfunz No.

Jeanne Is anyone else here under arrest?

Von Pfunz This is mistaken –

Jeanne Then *get out!*

   Pause. Von Pfunz exits.

Jeanne What have I done? I meant to appease him. Oh God, I've buggered it up!

Lake (*looking out of the window*) He's doing something.

Jeanne He's lining up a bloody firing squad. God!

Lake No, he's talking to them. I don't know what he's doing.

Jeanne What have I done?

Gabriel Mrs Becquet, I was talking to him about the greater truth.

Jeanne I beg your pardon?

Gabriel The greater truth. I think he's a soul sunk into darkness.

Jeanne Thank you, I'll remember that useful fact.

Lake They're going! Look, he's told them to go!

Jeanne Why?

Lake I don't know, do I?

Gabriel In his book, there's a poem about you.

Jeanne What poem?

Gabriel He says you see him for what he is. He says you're –

Lake He's coming back. I'll lock him out!

Jeanne No! (*To Gabriel.*) What?

Gabriel Großartig.

Jeanne (*irritated*) Well, that's marvellous.

Von Pfunz knocks on the door.

Gabriel It means magnificent.

Jeanne (*to Lake*) Open it.

Lake opens the door.

Von Pfunz May I speak with Mrs Becquet please?

Jeanne (*to Lake*) Ask him the purpose of his call.

Von Pfunz Yes, Mrs Becquet, I have sent my men away. I wish to – They are not needed here now but you must let me in.

Jeanne Would you ask the Major to come in?

Lake stands back. Von Pfunz enters.

Von Pfunz I know why the child hates me. It is your house I live in, your island I occupy. I am the enemy. Of course she hates me for all these things. I forget, you see, what it is like for her. Things have different meanings to a child. They do not see the same. And really, I like her. She is brave and – I feel bad about so many things! Jeanne, I have sent my men away. I am not – I am not . . . disgusting.

185

Jeanne Major.

Von Pfunz I am a slave of force. This must be. If I were my own master I would never be hated by children. It *pains* me. I long to be her friend!

Jeanne (*pause*) Would you like a cup of tea?

Von Pfunz Thank you.

Jeanne Margaret, perhaps you'd make a pot. Please, sit down.

Von Pfunz Thank you.

Von Pfunz sits. Lake starts making tea.

Jeanne Well, this is more civilised isn't it?
Unpleasantness before breakfast can spoil the whole day.

Von Pfunz After discovering my boot, I lost interest in my eggs.

Jeanne A tragedy . . . Please, let me feed you. Margaret?

Lake starts making toast.

Jeanne Gabriel dear, would you put that thing outside? It's so unsightly.

Gabriel puts the boot outside.

Von Pfunz (*confidentially*) Jeanne, I must tell you. I reconsider your bargain. This night I was thinking. I wish no more nightmares. I wish –

Jeanne Say nothing more.

Von Pfunz is moved.

Von Pfunz I wish for truth between us. And so, this is hard but I must make you see it. Your daughter-in-law.

Jeanne What about her?

Von Pfunz You would like to see her live somewhere else, you know you would.

Jeanne No!

Von Pfunz These things are hard to admit, even to yourself. She must register her real identity and then I can move her for you.

Jeanne No!

Estelle and Lily enter. Estelle carries Von Pfunz's book.

Von Pfunz Here she comes. Look how she clings to the child. This is the bad influence.

Lily Major. Estelle wants to say something to you.

Von Pfunz Well.

Estelle I'm sorry for taking your book.

Estelle puts the book on the table. Lily sits.

Von Pfunz Thank you. (*He picks up the book, as if reunited with something precious.*) It would have been terrible to lose it. (*He pockets it.*)

Jeanne (*to Estelle*) You lied to me and you lied to the Major. What have you got to say for yourself?

Estelle Nothing.

Von Pfunz Why did you steal it?

Estelle I wanted to give it to someone.

Von Pfunz Who?

Estelle The Resistance.

Von Pfunz The Resistance! And how did you propose to get it to them?

Estelle Don't know.

Jeanne She reads too many adventure books.

Von Pfunz Estelle, I'm sad to tell you, that alone of all the occupations I have partaken in, Guernsey has no Resistance. Nothing organised, that we can find. It's what makes it so pleasant to stay here. There is no troupe of brave young men hiding in the hills, because there are no hills – and no brave young men! (*He giggles.*) Now. What am I to do with you? (*Giggling.*) I think perhaps, if I were to lock you in the tunnels, you would know what it was to feel haunted.

Lake (*slams a plate of bread and jam down in front of Von Pfunz*) Breakfast.

Von Pfunz Estelle, shake my hand. I am determined we shall be friends.

Estelle shakes Von Pfunz's hand.

Now, give me a kiss.

Estelle hesitates.

Jeanne Kiss him.

Estelle reluctantly kisses Von Pfunz. He pulls her onto his knee.

Von Pfunz There! How is that?

Estelle Mummy –

Jeanne Make friends!

Von Pfunz (*to Gabriel*) I hope our trip today will take us as far as Torteval, Mr Lascalles.

Gabriel Why?

Von Pfunz I'm longing to meet your family.

Gabriel Me too. I can't imagine what they're like.

Von Pfunz (*taken aback*) What do you mean?

Jeanne Sebastian . . . I have a confession to make.

Gabriel Mrs Becquet hat mir Schutz geboten. (*Mrs Becquet has been protecting me.*)

Von Pfunz Wie bitte? (*What are you saying?*)

Gabriel Ich bin nicht ihr Neffe. (*I'm not her nephew.*)

Von Pfunz Wer sind Sie dann? (*Then who are you?*)

Jeanne We discovered this morning that this poor boy –

Gabriel Vor vier Nächten bin ich an den Strand gespült worden. Lily hat mich gefunden und hierher gebracht. Diese Familie hat mein Leben gerettet. Ich war bewußtlos bis gestern, und als ich aufwachte, hatte ich alle Erinnerung über mich selbst verloren. (*I was washed up on the beach four nights ago. Lily found me. She brought me back here and this family saved my life. I was unconscious until yesterday and I woke remembering absolutely nothing about myself.*)

Von Pfunz Nicht möglich . . . (*No . . .*)

Jeanne I do think you might speak in English.

Gabriel Meine gesamte Erinnerung ist mir völlig entschwunden. Selbst mein eigenes Spiegelbild hat mir angst gemacht. Die Nebel haben sich zwar ein wenig gelüftet; aber trotzdem konnte ich mich gestern nur an ein oder zwei seltsame Bilder erinnern – allerdings nichts über den Krieg. (*I'm suffering from a complete loss of memory. My own image in the mirror made me afraid.*

The mist has cleared a little; yesterday, I remembered only one or two strange images, and quite remarkably, nothing about the war.)

Von Pfunz Was, Sie wußten nicht, daß Krieg ist? (*You didn't know there was a war?*)

Jeanne What are you telling him, Gabriel, dear?

Gabriel Stellen Sie sich nur vor! Als ich herunter kam und Sie traf, hatte ich keine Ahnung wer Sie waren! (*Can you imagine? I came down and met you, and I didn't have a clue who you were!*)

Von Pfunz Das ist wahr, meine Uniform! (*That's right, my uniform!*)

Jeanne Gentlemen please, I insist you talk in English!

Gabriel Today, things are much better. I know all about the war, and I know exactly who you are.

Von Pfunz Incredible . . .

Jeanne What has he said?

Von Pfunz He is a lost man.

Gabriel I was found naked, carrying no identification, nothing. They just took me in.

Von Pfunz Who are you, my friend?

Gabriel My past is one day old. I've got no idea if I'm the same man I was, or if this has shaped me into someone else, completely. There's no reply to your question. I don't know who I am.

Von Pfunz This is unbelievable . . .

Jeanne It would be, only we found out who he is this morning.

Von Pfunz Oh?

Gabriel (*giggling*) Die denken, daß ich ein überge-
schnappter Bankangestellter bin, der auf die Barrikaden
gegangen ist. (*They think I'm a bank clerk, who's gone
on some kind of a rampage.*)

Jeanne Speak in English, please!

Von Pfunz *What* did you say?

Gabriel They think I'm a bank clerk who's gone on
some kind of rampage.

Von Pfunz Ha! A bank clerk? Ha!

Lily (*to Lake*) Did you tell him this?

Lake It's the truth. His name's John Gilbert.

Jeanne He went missing from St Peter's Port a few days
ago.

Von Pfunz And does he speak fluent German?

Lake He works translating for your lot.

Gabriel Apparently I'm a dying man, Major. I've been
given a death sentence.

Jeanne Allow me to explain –

Gabriel They tell me I have a *thing* on my brain, a
tumour I suppose – the reason I remember nothing. I'm
dying.

Von Pfunz But this is absurd!

Lily (*to Lake*) How could you? How could you tell him
that? He's no more a bank clerk than I am.

Jeanne Keep quiet, Lilian.

Lily I've spent more time with him than anyone, and
I know!

Pause.

Von Pfunz Who do you think he is?

Lily I think he's one of you.

Von Pfunz Ja?

Lily Mrs Becquet told us one of your officers was lost at sea. I think it's him.

Gabriel Lily, why are you telling him this?

Jeanne She's just trying to protect him.

Von Pfunz She's telling me what she thinks I want to hear. But the last thing I want to hear is her lies.

Lily I'm not lying. You just asked me what I thought!

It becomes clear during the following that Gabriel is fighting pain. He tries to hide it.

Jeanne It'll be easy to have him identified. He's got a wife in St Peter's Port. You can take him there right now.

Von Pfunz Forgive me, but I was speaking of the canker in your house, of this malignance under your roof. Everything this woman has ever said to me has been a lie.

Lily stands.

Lily He knows . . .

Von Pfunz What do I know, Fraülein?

Lily (*agonised, to Gabriel*) You told him.

Gabriel No.

Von Pfunz Mrs Becquet told me.

Jeanne Lily . . . he deceived me.

Von Pfunz You were calling for help.

Jeanne He tricked it out of me, I swear!

Von Pfunz Your spirit was speaking with mine.

Jeanne You have to believe me, I'd never do this! He's been holding it over me for days!

Lily Mrs Becquet, he'll kill me.

Von Pfunz Nonsense.

Jeanne If you try and take her from here I've got ways of stopping you. I know the entire civilian Controlling Committee and I'm a personal friend of the Bailiff. This won't be allowed!

Estelle gets off Von Pfunz's knee. During the following she goes to Gabriel and looks at him.

Von Pfunz Jeanne, I understand your compassion but it is *malign*. You must tear it from your heart. Even the child turns from the Jew, you see? It is the natural thing. (*To Lily.*) I want you to come with me to St Peter's Port this afternoon. There, we shall go to your own police and you must tell them, nice British bobbies, all the correct information. We just want the truth.

Lily He'll kill me!

Estelle (*whispers*) Now, Gabriel . . .

Von Pfunz You should be proud of your race. You should state what you are.

Lily I'll end up in that place, Mrs Becquet, my hair in that room full of hair. My dress in a a pile with a million others and the rest of me discarded. That's the truth, isn't it? 'Die Unerwählten'.

Von Pfunz (*bewildered*) She has read my book.

Estelle (*whispers*) Now.

Gabriel (*through controlled pain*) I read it to her. Last night.

Von Pfunz *Why?*

Gabriel I thought she ought to hear.

Von Pfunz That is my private book . . .

Gabriel This morning, we read a couple of pages to Mrs Becquet and Mrs Lake. I think it would be fair to say that they found it obscene.

Von Pfunz It is *sacrilege* you have done.

Estelle Smite him.

Von Pfunz My poems, you don't understand –

Gabriel Yes I do.

Estelle Do it now!

Gabriel I asked you to define evil and you couldn't.

Von Pfunz Because it does not exist! There is only force. You must see this – only force and chaos – my words make this clear. There is no evil!

Gabriel is fighting considerable pain.

Gabriel You're too steeped in it to see it.

Gabriel stumbles into the chalk square.

Von Pfunz What happens with him? . . .

Estelle (*trying to support him*) No, no, don't fall, don't fall! Gabriel!

Gabriel I will not let you.

Gabriel goes into a spasm of pain.

Lily Give him space, Estelle. Let him breathe.

Gabriel passes out and lies still, face downwards.

Estelle Gabriel!

Von Pfunz What is wrong? Why does he do this?

Jeanne We tried to tell you and you wouldn't listen. He's brainsick and dying.

Von Pfunz Jeanne, send to The Hermitage for my men. They will get the doctor here.

Von Pfunz tries to turn Gabriel over.

Estelle Leave him where he is.

Von Pfunz Little girl, don't order me around. I have first-aid facts.

Von Pfunz turns to Jeanne. Estelle pulls the dagger out of Gabriel's belt.

Von Pfunz Jeanne, you do nothing. Send for my men!

Lily (*becoming hysterical*) They'll take me away. They'll take me away! You'll have to drag me screaming, SCREAMING –

Jeanne ESTELLE! . . .

Estelle plunges the knife into Von Pfunz's belly. Von Pfunz stands and staggers.

Von Pfunz Das Kind . . . ich bin verwundet . . . (*The child . . . I'm hurt . . .*)

Lake Lord Jesus.

Jeanne (*to Estelle*) What have you done?

Estelle is in deep shock. She is ashen, silent, the knife still in her hand. Von Pfunz collapses against Jeanne.

Von Pfunz Jeanne . . .

Jeanne Margaret, help me!

Lake Put him in that chair.

Lake and Jeanne help Von Pfunz to a chair.

Lily Estelle, it's all right. It's all right.

Lily hugs and comforts her.

Jeanne (*trying to open Von Pfunz's jacket*) I can't get this damn thing open, Margaret.

Lake Here.

Lake shoves some cloths at Jeanne.

Jeanne Get him a drink.

Lake fills a glass of cognac.

Lily Give me the knife, Estelle. It's all right.

Estelle lets go of the knife.

Jeanne Lily, go to the Hermitage and get his men. He needs a doctor.

Lily No.

Jeanne For God's sake – (*Aside, to Lily.*) What if he bleeds to death? You'd see Estelle take the blame?

Lily I won't help him.

Lake I'll go.

Jeanne Margaret.

Lake heads for the door.

Lake You sure that's what you want?

Jeanne Don't tell them who did it. Just say there's been an accident.

Lake Keep him talking if you want him to live. And keep that cloth pressed on the blood. Jeanne, I'm not running.

Lake exits.

Lily I'll look after things now. You go to your room. Now, Estelle. I mean it.

Estelle understands. She flies up the stairs.

Jeanne I told you to leave my family alone and you wouldn't listen. If you'd damn well listened this would never have happened!

Lily has the knife. Von Pfunz perceives her intention.

Von Pfunz My God. (*He giggles weakly.*) You come to finish me off . . .

Jeanne Lily, don't. This is my house –

Lily Then you do it!

Lily holds the knife to Von Pfunz's throat.

Von Pfunz It is easy to kill. You will see . . . And then you will be just like me.

For a second, Lily hesitates. Von Pfunz grabs her hand and takes the knife from her.

Von Pfunz (*with contempt*) You see? We are not all as brave as a ten-year-old child.

Lily knocks Von Pfunz off his chair. He cries out in pain. She pushes past Jeanne and runs upstairs, distraught. Jeanne helps Von Pfunz into a sitting position.

Von Pfunz This has killed me.

Jeanne (*taking the knife from him*) Pull yourself together.

Von Pfunz Not the knife. This dance of scorpions with you. I have found myself able to live with anything . . . but not this pain. It has torn me apart from the minute that I saw you. I cannot fathom this wretched pain.

Jeanne I don't know what you're talking about.

Von Pfunz I must say everything to you.

Jeanne Don't.

Von Pfunz It is my deepest desire –

Jeanne I won't listen.

Von Pfunz My deepest desire to be loved by you. I know that is not possible. (*Pause.*) I shall say the Jew stabbed me.

Jeanne What?

Von Pfunz I shall protect your little girl. The Jew shall take the guilt.

Jeanne No. (*pointing to Gabriel*) Say he did it!

Von Pfunz I can't do that.

Jeanne Why not?

Von Pfunz It would be a lie.

Jeanne Please, if you love me –

Von Pfunz No. I save the little girl because I love you. In Poland, it is true. I saw things that would – I saw the ground move in the thaw, so many bodies buried underneath. I thought it was hot springs . . . The dead are all the same, Jeanne, all the same. Me, you, all the same. There is no salvation. They make fertiliser from the bones. This room of women's hair, a vault, vast, they turn it into cloth, sell it for sixteen pfennigs a yard. And I see this. I see it with my soul . . . So I write my book, and I think, what is the greater truth? I do this so the children of the future will thank me. This creates a pure Europe. I blight myself, I tread my soul in this mire for them. The cruelty becomes clear. It is like a dream in my mind. A pure Europe, like light . . .

Jeanne (*pointing to Gabriel*) He stabbed you.

Von Pfunz You don't listen.

Jeanne He stabbed you!

Von Pfunz No!

Jeanne stabs Von Pfunz.

Jeanne Then I have to.

Von Pfunz Jeanne . . .

Jeanne I do listen. And this is what I think.

Von Pfunz dies. Jeanne pulls the knife out of him. Her hands are covered in blood. She shudders. She looks at Von Pfunz.

Disgusting.

Jeanne goes to Gabriel. She puts the knife in his hand. She smears blood onto his hands and his cricket whites. She goes to the sink and washes her hands. Gabriel comes round.

Gabriel Falling . . .

Jeanne approaches him. She looks at him and gently touches his hair.

Mrs Becquet.

Jeanne You poor boy. I'm so sorry . . .

Gabriel I could see a river. Like a flash in my mind. A great river. Sun on it, the noise, everything. It seemed familiar.

Jeanne There aren't any rivers on Guernsey.

Pause. Gabriel lifts a hand to touch her. He sees the blood. He becomes aware of the knife. He sits up. He sees Von Pfunz.

You went into a frenzy and stabbed him.

Gabriel No . . .

Jeanne I saw you do it.

Gabriel (*pause*) Estelle.

Jeanne She's been in her room all morning. The Major tried to arrest you. Surely you remember? . . . You resisted. You stole my knife and plunged it into him. Twice. I tried to save his life.

Gabriel Is that the truth?

Jeanne Yes.

Gabriel I don't remember.

Jeanne You don't need to.

Gabriel (*looks at the corpse*) Dead. So. I killed him.

Jeanne nods her head.

Then that is the sum of my life.

Jeanne You look like my son.

Gabriel Your daughter believes in angels.

Jeanne kisses Gabriel. She immediately stands and looks away.

Jeanne Do you want them to find you here?

Gabriel No.

Jeanne Then run.

Gabriel Where's Lily?

Jeanne With Estelle.

Gabriel Will you tell her –

Jeanne Of course. Of course I will.

Gabriel I can't find words.

   Gabriel stands.

Which way is the sea?

Jeanne Down the hill. Run.

   He goes to the door.

Gabriel I don't know who I am.

Jeanne You're Gabriel Lascalles.

Gabriel (*slowly nods*) Auf Wiedersehen.

   Gabriel leaves.

Jeanne Forgive me.

   Jeanne suddenly cries. Lily appears at the door. She looks at Von Pfunz.

Lily Who killed him?

Jeanne Gabriel.

Lily I knew he would. Where is he?

Jeanne Gone. To the beach.

Lily Who are your tears for, Jeanne?

Jeanne I'm not crying.

Pause. Lily goes to Von Pfunz. She pulls the book out of his pocket. She holds it.

Lily I couldn't do it.

Jeanne That is because you are good.

Lily (*pause*) I can't stay here, Jeanne.

Jeanne Where will you go?

Lily I don't know.

Jeanne Then stay.

Lily looks at Jeanne. Neither gives much away. Estelle enters, smiling through her tears.

Estelle I saw Gabriel, running to the beach. So fast . . . his feet weren't touching the ground. I could tell.

Jeanne reaches for Estelle's hand.

SILENCE

For Susan Buffini, my mother

Silence was first performed at The Door, Birmingham Repertory Theatre, on 14 October 1999. The cast was as follows:

Silence Zita Sattar
Ymma Rachel Sanders
Agnés Patricia Gannon
Roger Nick Fletcher
Eadric Alex De Marcus
Ethelred Martin Freeman

Director Anthony Clark
Designer Rachel Blues
Lighting Tim Mitchell
Dialect Coach William Conacher
Fight Director Terry King

Characters

Ymma
a lady

Agnés
a servant

Eadric
the king's man

Silence
a youth

Roger
a priest

Ethelred
the king

Setting

Dark Age England

ACT ONE
Canterbury

ACT TWO
The Open Road

ACT THREE
Cumbria

Act One
Canterbury

ONE

A field in Kent.
  Ymma, a young noblewoman, is bent double in mid-vomit. Agnés, her servant, holds her hair. Eadric, a warrior, watches from a distance.

Agnés There we go. Get it all out. That's it.

Ymma Don't let them look at me.

Agnés (*to Eadric*) Show her some respect. She's the daughter of a saint!

  Eadric turns and walks away.

Ymma Pigs . . . (*Retches.*)

Agnés (*speaking out*) This is the fourth time since we left Normandy. The first was on the ship. We were approaching the English cliffs, gazing at the white land of our future. I was feeling almost hopeful, but Ymma went very quiet and said:

Ymma This is the beginning of the end, Agnés. This is the Kingdom of – (*Retches.*)

Agnés When we landed, the king's men met us on the harbour and loaded our belongings on a cart; bag after bag full of clothes. All she said to them was:

Ymma Don't come near me.

Agnés And she threw up again, spattering someone's boots. It was mortifying. An hour or so later, she made us stop outside a church. I thought she meant to say an urgent prayer to her sainted mother, but when I followed her in, I found she'd done a vomit in the font. I thought it blasphemous and I told her so.

Ymma Empty. Everything's out. There's only bile left . . .

Agnés You've got it in your hair.

Ymma I don't care.

Agnés You can't meet the king with vomit in your hair. Here. (*Agnés wipes her up.*) This is awful. You'll just have to tell him you're not used to English food.

Ymma Leave me.

Agnés Ymma, we have to get to Canterbury before nightfall. The men have been telling me about the raids they get after dark; Vikings, coming up the rivers like angels of death . . . We're late – it took me ages to clean up that font – and I'm scared.

Ymma I'm staying here.

Agnés You can't!

Ymma Why not? It makes no difference where I die.

Agnés Ymma, this is a new start in a new land –

Ymma It's a punishment, the whole damn thing. I'm here to be buried alive!

Agnés Your brother could have shut you away, locked you in an abbey for the mad! – But he's given you this wonderful chance. The English king's deciding your fate –

Ymma It's a trap!

Agnés It's whatever you make it! It all depends on how you behave. And look at you . . . Ymma, what about *me*? If you mess this up, what happens to me? It's so unfair!

Ymma (*stands*) I'm going to walk.

Agnés To Canterbury? You can't.

Ymma If this is my fate, Agnés, I'm going to meet it on foot, with my eyes wide open.

Agnés What about those men?

Ymma Make them follow me, fifty yards behind. They've been undressing me in their pigshit minds since we landed at Dover, and I don't want them close enough to hear my thoughts. If they question my behaviour, you can tell them I'm having a vision.

Agnés *What?*

Ymma I'm the daughter of a saint. Tell them I'm in an ecstasy of the spirit and that the Holy Virgin is at my side, leading me to my fate.

Agnés That's blasphemous!

Ymma It's not blasphemous, it's a beautiful lie. If you make it enchanting enough, they'll believe it.

Agnés Right. I'll tell them she's barefoot, immaculate, veiled in blue – whatever you like – and don't blame me if we get struck down!

Agnés exits. Ymma slowly surveys the landscape

Ymma Kent. What a dump.

TWO

A chapel.
Water dripping. Silence, an adolescent lord, is before the altar, kneeling in a strange, un-Christian way. Roger enters, a youthful priest. He watches puzzled, disturbed.

Roger Lord Silence? I am a priest. My name is Roger. The bishops have sent me to find you. I've been selected from all God's servants in this holy place – on account of my youth and my mild and humble nature – to tell you of your fate, which the king himself has decided. I congratulate you, my lord. You're to be married to a French princess, Ymma of Normandy. It's my task to prepare you for that Blessed Sacrament.

Silence Pardon?

Roger The king, in his wisdom, is giving you a wife.

Silence Why?

Roger He has seen fit to decide your fate.

Silence What right has the king to decide my fate?

Roger He has divine right. He is a king.

Silence I'm puzzled, Sir. I have been puzzled since the moment I arrived and now I'm utterly confused. Does the king think me a fool?

Roger My lord –

Silence He sent envoys up to Cumbria, requesting my assistance. When I arrived, after an arduous journey, I was taken to his bedchamber and he said:

Ethelred (*from his bed, his face averted*) You have to help. My coasts are plagued with Viking raids and my people torment me with demands for protection. I hear you are of Viking blood. You know Viking language, Viking culture; you have an insight into the Viking mind. I want you to work with my men, to guide them, that they may better understand this demon race and purge it from our shores.

Silence I said, Sire, I am honoured. The Vikings of course are not a demon race but I agree they must be

stopped. They're even raiding up in Cumbria, where
their own people have lived for generations. Majesty, our
feelings are the same.

*Ethelred has sat up, his crown askew: a naked,
scrawny youth. He is gazing at Silence.*

Ethelred (*aghast*) What are you?

Silence I am Silence, Lord of Cumbria.

Ethelred This is impossible . . . The Lord of Cumbria is
a warrior!

Silence So I am.

Ethelred You're a LITTLE BOY!

Silence (*with dignity*) I'm fourteen.

Ethelred Are you telling me it was you who raised the
siege of York?

Silence That was my father. He is dead.

Ethelred I have been made a fool of! Madness and
chaos . . . Who brought this infant here? I'll have them
blinded!

Silence And his men pulled me out. No wonder the
Vikings are raiding this land. If I ruled Cumbria that
way –

Roger My lord, you cannot question the quality of
a king.

Silence My priest says that one should question
everything.

Roger To question a king is treason.

Silence She says that ignorance is our greatest enemy
and that only by questioning can we defeat it.

Roger She?

Silence A king who keeps his subjects in ignorance can only be a tyrant!

Roger Your priest is a woman?

Silence Yes. Her name is Surr.

Roger My lord, I –

Silence (*going to the altar.*) I'm going to light a candle. It's for my father. In times of trouble, I ask his advice.

Roger He is with Christ, my son.

Silence I'm glad. It's good to hear that Christ is in Valhalla.

Roger Uhh!

Silence It's a place of perpetual light.

Roger (*appalled*) Jesus Christ is *not* in Valhalla!

Silence (*lighting a candle*) You said he was with my father.

Roger But –

Silence My father is in Valhalla; if Christ is with him, he must be in Valhalla too.

Roger No, Valhalla / is a heathen myth –

Silence And now I'll make sacrifice.

Roger What?

Silence Where do you keep your lambs?

Roger Are you intending . . . to slaughter a lamb on this altar?

Silence Of course. My priest says that when the way before you is shrouded in mist, the future is written in entrails. Priest . . . have I said something wrong?

Roger faints.

THREE

The king's chamber.
    Ethelred is under his blankets. Eadric kneels by his bed.

Eadric And as we watched . . . Sire, there appeared a light beside her, and within it, slowly taking shape, was a lady veiled in blue. She was barefoot, immaculate, with her hands in an aspect of blessing. I wanted to drop to my knees but I didn't. I held back.

Ethelred (*appearing from out of the blankets*) What?

Eadric I held back.

Ethelred You saw *what*?

Eadric A lady. She hovered, Sire, with shining raiment underneath . . . I'm not a religious man, you know this. I'm a soldier. The only time I've ever seen things like this is after eating woodland fungi – the kind that gives a feeling of euphoria in battle – and I haven't touched any, I swear it.

Ethelred Are you telling me you saw the Blessed Virgin walking with Ymma of Normandy?

Eadric I wouldn't like to say. But whoever it was, she didn't have no mud, even on the soles of her feet. Incandescent is a word I'd like to use. Radiant. Possibly diaphanous . . .

Ethelred Eadric, it was a trick of the setting sun.

Eadric I saw it.

Ethelred It was her shadow or something.

Eadric It communicated with my mind. Sent me thoughts so beautiful I wept. I feel changed.

Ethelred Eadric, you are my strength of arm, my executioner, chief architect of all my violent acts. Please believe me when I say this is rubbish.

Eadric Sire, lies do not come from the mouth of Eadric Longshaft. I saw a shining vision!

Ethelred Very well, you saw a vision. It spoke to your mind. Who am I to argue? Only the king. (*Pause.*) I've decreed the lady's fate. She's marrying Silence of Cumbria.

Eadric I beg you, Sire; meet her before you decide.

Ethelred Her brother sent her here for punishment, and puishment she'll get. Cumbria is a wasteland on the edge of the civilised world and its lord is a juvenile fool.

Eadric But what if she is holy? I saw her walk in Godlight!

Ethelred Too late. The proclamation's already been read.

Eadric She is so other-worldly, Sire, that she cannot keep down her food!

Ethelred Well, what can I do? I won't go back on it. I can't change my mind, can I?

Eadric No, Sire.

Ethelred You know what they whisper behind my back! Feeble, vacillating, vague . . . Do you think I like it? It *pains* me. Oh God, all this trouble! If you're so taken

with her, Eadric, make her your responsibility, not mine.
When she's wed, you can escort her up to the icy North
and play with visions all the way. Oh, I am exhausted
in my labours for this land, worn out with my exertions
and no one, no one cares. Eadric, have pity. If you're
human, have pity on your king . . .

Eadric looks at the king, without pity.

FOUR

The chapel.
*Water dripping. Roger approaches Silence, zealously
excited.*

Roger Lord Silence, since we spoke, I've been seeking
the help of God. I threw myself down in my cell and
said, 'God, what am I to do? Lord Silence is a heathen,
a worshipper of fiends –'

Silence Pardon?

Roger '– but when I look at him, I see no evil in his
face; he is but a youth who's been led astray.'

Silence I don't worship fiends!

Roger 'How may I, Roger, who has crept out his youth
in sandals, meek in the shadow of crypts and cloisters,
how may I save him from damnation?' At that moment,
I saw a great flurry of leaves swirl away in the wind
towards the North and I knew that God was sending me
a sign. He was saying, 'Roger, take this boy. Fill him
with my Word. Go with him to Cumbria and educate
him in my ways.'

Silence I have a God: Odin. I see no need to learn about
yours.

Roger Lord Silence, your heathen faith endangers you most terribly. Please hear me. If they find it out, they will slaughter you. You must discover God.

Silence So you wish to teach me – to keep me safe?

Roger Yes! Safe in his hand forever more. I prayed that my days would not end in the library, crumbling in parchments, and now my prayers have come true. Please, let me take you by the hand and lead your spirit into grace.

Silence (*moved*) Are you saying . . . that you wish to be my friend?

Roger Your friend, yes. Your guide, your brother.

Silence I have no friends here. I am alone.

Roger Alone, no longer. You have me. (*Embraces Silence.*) And the Lord!

Eadric enters, with Ymma and Agnés.

Eadric (*indicating Silence*) The Lord of Cumbria.

Roger Women! My God, it must be her. Quick, kneel, pray – do something!

Ymma There must be some mistake.

Roger Lady of Normandy and . . . other gracious lady, please accept a welcome from God's humblest servant in this place. I am a priest. My name is Roger. I offer up a prayer of thanks at your safe arrival –

Ymma Am I to marry you? Or the little boy?

Silence Lady, I am Silence, Lord of Cumbria. My borders stretch from Lancaster to the land of Strathclyde. I come at the king's own request from Ragnarok, my castle in the North. It's his will we should be wed and there's nothing we can do. So hello.

Ymma I'm to marry your father, surely.

Silence My father's dead.

Agnés (*to Ymma*) He'll grow, my lady.

Ymma Agnés, I had imagined cruelty. What I've got is ridicule. It's worse . . . I'm to be married to a child.

Silence I've been ruling Cumbria since I was born. No one there would dare to call me child.

Roger Gracious lady, noble lord, this marriage is wished by our royal king –

Ymma Then curse him. Curse him! (*She exits.*)

Agnés My lady's unwell. The rigours of the journey; English food –

Ymma (*re-enters*) Tell me, Priest, how are we to consummate it? He's a baby! (*Re-exits.*)

Agnés I'm sorry; please don't judge her, or me. We're not like this. (*She exits.*)

Roger She spoke of consummation; I feel faint. Why did she scorn you? People marry children all the time.

Silence I'm fourteen! I'm not a child!

Roger No, no, no, of course not! . . . But my lord, her objections shouldn't be taken to heart. I've done much reading on the subject of women and I know their characters well, though my experience of them is scant. They are weak, capricious creatures –

Silence She doesn't want to marry me –

Roger Nonsense –

Silence And I don't want to marry her!

Roger My lord, have pity!

Silence Pity?

Roger She cannot help herself. Women are foolish. It tells us so in our Holy Books. The soul of a woman is an inferior thing, a dark shadow, compared to the brilliant soul of a man. It's made of tarnished metal, a weak and rusting substance that must be constantly polished by a strong male hand. Women are naturally inclined to evil. They are created inferior, responsible for our fall and all our agonies on Earth. Now, Ymma of Normandy is a woman alone. She has no male hand to guide her, no one to save her from herself. Think of the peril she is in. If you don't wed her, who will bring her meagre soul closer to God?

Eadric looks heavenwards, closing his eyes.

FIVE

The king's chamber.
    Ymma enters in a rage. She is trying to get her dress off, clawing at the back. Ethelred appears from his blankets and watches her, amazed.

Ymma Damn you bastards! Damn my damn brother! Damn this nation of Saxon pigs and their bastard, BASTARD KING! They will not break me. I'll not break! Hate. Hate this dress, hate it!

Ethelred Good evening.

Ymma (*turning, shocked*) What are you doing? This is my chamber!

Ethelred No, it's –

Ymma Get OUT! Agnés, AGNÉS! . . .

Ethelred This is *my* chamber. I am Ethelred, your bastard, bastard king.

Ymma laughs incredulously. Ethelred puts on his crown. Pause. Ymma kneels.

Ymma Your Majesty. I'm lost –

Ethelred I don't recall ordering a whore this evening.

Ymma I am Ymma of Normandy, Sire.

Ethelred You come into my bedchamber with a mouthful of curses and you start to take off your clothes. What am I to think?

Ymma I thought this was my chamber.

Ethelred You can only be a whore.

Ymma I thought I was alone. In private!

Ethelred So in private you think the king's a bastard and you curse his name? Continue. You were undressing.

Ymma I . . .

Ethelred Please carry on. Don't let me interrupt you. Do you require payment first? I never pay first. To speak truthfully, I never pay at all. That is my prerogative as king; and if a whore displeases me, I have her killed. Undress.

Ymma When I saw the white cliffs of this land, I should have thrown myself from the boat rather than set one foot on it. I could have been at peace by now, under the weight of the great sea.

Ethelred May I remind you that to disobey a king is treason, punished by death.

Ymma (*turning on him*) I would rather be dead than standing here. So, bastard, why don't you kill me? Kill me!

Ethelred is speechless.

Is this how you live? I hear you never leave your bed.
It stinks in here, like a fetid prison. Are you a prisoner,
Your Majesty?

Ethelred What do you mean?

Ymma You look as if you've never had a moment's
freedom in your life.

Ethelred Like all true monarchs I am slave to my
subjects. And I serve them best by being here, in my bed.

Ymma So you lie there scratching while the Vikings
ravage your land?

Ethelred I am engaged in a battle – a grave battle!

Ymma With fleas and bedbugs?

Ethelred With God!

Ymma Oh, with God . . .

Ethelred I am trying to save my England from
destruction. I can only do this by discovering God's will.
He is angry and I, his instrument on earth, must appease
him. There is no greater work I could do.

Ymma You're afraid, aren't you?

Ethelred To be afraid of God is a virtue.

Ymma But you're afraid of everything. The most
powerful man in England and you're shaking with fear.

Ethelred Your brother said in his letter that you were
dangerous. He said you had all the malice and cunning
of the viciously insane.

Ymma Then why don't you kill me?

Ethelred What did you do for him to cast you out?
He's put the mark of Cain on you. What crime did you
commit?

Ymma My brother is a snake but he's a powerful snake.
You're just a snake. Look at you.

Ethelred Eadric! EADRIC!

Eadric enters.

This is a whore. It has offended me.

Eadric Sire –

Ethelred Take her away. Watch until she is wed. See she
doesn't harm herself.

Ymma You coward.

Ethelred You've been sent to me for punishment and
you'll live to savour every moment of your fate!

*Eadric escorts Ymma out. Ethelred rocks in his
blankets.*

I am *not* afraid . . .

SIX

The chapel.
 Water dripping. Silence and Roger.

Roger . . . So that is the story of our Lord, Jesus Christ.
I'll fill in the details later but all you need to know is
that he died to take away our sins. Which brings me to
confession. Tomorrow you must stand pure before God
and in order to be pure, you must be confessed. It is
time, my son, to clean your soul. I'll discuss the dark
cornucopia of human sins and vices in due course but

223

as we're so pressed for time we must begin with sins of the flesh.

Silence Sins of the flesh?

Roger The most insidious sins of all. What else can reduce a man to the behaviour of a beast? Silence, you must know that even if you have not sinned with your body, you may have sinned in your thoughts. All thoughts which linger on the flesh are sinful. Even our dreams can sin.

Silence I'd like to confess my puzzlement. I'm extremely puzzled, Sir.

Roger You must call me Father.

Silence On the journey from Cumbria, Father, the king's envoys were telling me of fucking.

Roger That is a sinful word! The word you need is . . . consummation: the Sacred Act.

Silence Sacred Act . . . They told me how the Thing between my legs will grow out of nothing.

Roger Ah, Thing, yes –

Silence That it will make me into a man, from a boy, into a man and never go back – And I'm worried. Really frankly extremely puzzled and worried.

Roger Silence. This is not exactly a confession –

Silence Yes, but I'm not worried about sin, I'm worried that it won't happen with me.

Roger That what won't happen?

Silence The Thing won't grow.

Roger Ah . . . Has the Thing never grown of its own accord? . . . Perhaps as the result of a dream, a devilish planting of desire in the mind during sleep? Or perhaps as the result of accidentally brushing against the flesh of another?

Silence My priest told me that some men had Things and some men didn't.

Roger My son, all men have Things! Your heathen priest is an ignorant woman. Disregard all she says! You have a Thing and the Thing will grow. It's a natural phenomenon. You'll become familiar with it in time and really, the feeling is quite . . . innocuous.

Silence Has it ever happened to you?

Roger Occasionally . . . I am able to subdue it with the power of prayer. Silence, you must have had some experience of your Thing?

Silence I once had a dream where – (*Pause.*)

Roger Where what? I am your confessor, Silence, and you must tell me all. It may have been an evil dream and we need to find out so that you can repent and I can absolve you. That is how confession works.

Silence I was in the forest. It was winter light, coming horizontal through the trees, and there was snow lying heavy on the ground. I was naked.

Roger Ah.

Silence But the strange thing is that I felt no cold, just a kind of . . .

Roger An excitement of the flesh?

Silence Yes. My nerves were all on end. I felt completely alive. I was hunting. Only, it wasn't an animal I was hunting. It was a man.

Roger A man?

Silence With dark hair and arms like Odin himself.

Roger Oh.

Silence He hid in the trees ahead – and he came at me out of nowhere! I leapt on him and fought – and he drew me close to him. I thought he was going to kill me but –

Roger But what?

Silence He kissed me.

Roger Ah.

Silence And everything went peculiar. I was pulling his hair and kicking, but he held me closer and closer and I could feel my legs go limp so I grappled and yelled, 'I'll fight you to the end you –'

Roger Barbarian, yes!

Silence And he threw me to the ground and my lips went on his and we . . . There came a feeling, here . . . Like flying! My senses soared – all six of them at once! – and I awoke.

Roger And upon waking . . . was your Thing not large?

Silence No, Sir.

Roger There had been no expulsion of liquid?

Silence Um. There was some moisture, yes.

Roger Ah. This moisture. Did you know what it was?

Silence No, Sir.

Roger It was the seed of life. A man puts this seed into the woman, with his Thing, during The Act. You shall put it into your wife and create an heir for Cumbria. Do you understand? (*Silence nods.*) You must not think of

the barbarian in the forest. It was an evil dream, doubly
evil because . . . he was a man. Now, do you repent of it?

Silence Yes, Sir.

Roger You must call me Father. I absolve you, in the
name of the Father, the Son and the Holy Spirit, Amen.
You can pray, if you like, for your Thing. You must ask
God to make it large only when it is fitting; that is with
your wife, in the marriage bed, preferably not more than
twice a week and never on a Holy Day. (*Adjusts his
crotch in embarrassed discomfort.*) You must go now.

Silence Why?

Roger Our lesson on sin is over. I am overcome with
a desire to pray privately. Please go.

Silence Is it something I've said?

Roger No. I'm just asking you to leave!

Silence (*watching him*) . . . It's your Thing, isn't it?

Roger Silence, do not shame me!

Silence . . . The Thing is shameful then?

Roger Yes! Yes!!

Silence leaves, puzzled and upset.

Power of prayer: God calm me . . . Bishops. I must think
of bishops, dead fish and bishops, bishops, bishops . . .

SEVEN

A large chamber.
*Ymma is wearing a wedding gown. Agnés is pinning
on her veil. Eadric watches.*

Agnés The king's had a dozen nuns working through the night to finish this on time. I heard they almost went blind, huddling round candles. You look wonderful. Good luck, Ymma. My heart is with you, on this, your wedding day. (*Pause.*) Well, thank you, Agnés. You've made me look lovely; what skill you have. Oh, that's all right; it's the pinnacle of a lady's lady's career, dressing her lady for her nuptial feast.

Ymma Are we to have this *thing* here all day?

Eadric I'm under orders. I must watch.

Ymma And what about my wedding night? Will you stay and watch that too, dog?

Agnés Forgive my lady; she's overwrought – girlishly excited. (*to Ymma*) Please! This is our last chance. I beg you, just accept it.

Ymma Agnés, shut up, or I will scream like a maniac until they lock me away.

Agnés Pinnacle of my career and this is it. (*Picks up two posies. Hands one to Ymma*) Here. Try not to wilt them.

The wedding: music. Silence stands beside Ymma, who is staring straight ahead. Eadric watches; Ethelred observes. Roger, conducting the service, is extremely nervous.

Roger And the Lord God caused a deep sleep to fall on Adam and He took one of his ribs and closed up the flesh thereof: And the rib, which the Lord God had taken from man, made He into a woman (*joining their hands*) and brought her unto the man. And Adam said:

Silence (*as a vow*) This is now bone of my bones, and flesh of my flesh.

Ymma (*in reply*) She shall be called woman.

Roger Because she was taken out of man. Therefore shall a man leave his father and mother and cleave unto his wife: and they shall be one flesh.

Silence tries to kiss Ymma. Can't reach. Roger blesses them.

And they were both naked, the man and his wife, and were not ashamed.

Ethelred Amen!

Ethelred leaves. Roger and Agnés bring forward a bed. They leave. Eadric backs out, his eyes still on Ymma. Silence and Ymma are alone. The moment grows agonising.

Silence I like your dress. (*Gently touches it.*)

Ymma (*flinching*) What are you doing?

Silence I wanted to touch it.

Ymma Well. I'm your wife. I suppose you can touch anything.

Ymma holds out her arm. Silence touches the fabric.

Why are you called Silence?

Silence My mother chose it. I was born just after my father died. They say she was depressed.

Ymma removes her arm.

Your mother was a saint, wasn't she?

Ymma So they say.

Silence Did she have a halo?

Ymma A what?

Silence A crown of celestial light. The pictures in the church have them. The priest told me what they were. I thought they were hats.

Ymma No. My mother didn't have a halo.

Silence Then how did people know she was a saint?

Ymma They made her a saint after she was dead.

Silence So . . . during her life, she was just ordinary?

Ymma Yes.

Silence I thought saints had powers, like gods.

Ymma Only after they're dead. Their remains have power.

Silence What like?

Ymma I don't know – healing, casting out spirits, whatever.

Silence Can your mother do that?

Ymma If you don't mind, I'd rather not talk about her.

Silence Why not?

Ymma Because your questions are childish.

Silence You shouldn't speak to me like that.

Ymma How should I speak to you?

Silence With respect.

Ymma (*she turns her back*) Undo this, would you? It's so tight it's making me sick.

Silence I'll call your maid.

Ymma No, I don't want her in here. You do it. (*Pause.*)
My lord.

*Silence gets under the veil and starts to clumsily undo
the gown.*

Silence I don't think you should judge me on account
of my age. It's an accident of birth, not something I can
help. I'm willing to try and if you were too, we'd . . .
(*Laughs, playing with the veil.*) This is so clean; like
being lost in mist. It's like snow! . . .

Ymma Tell me about Cumbria. If I'm to live there,
I should know the worst. I've heard that people share
their beds with pigs and drag their knuckles on the
ground.

Silence (*hurt. Pulls roughly at the back of the dress*)
I can't do this. Do it yourself.

*Silence moves away, caught up in the veil. Fights with
it. Manages to get it off. Ymma tries to undo the back
of her gown. She can't. It's like a straitjacket. She
reaches the point of tears.*

I'm sorry, let –

Ymma Agnés, AGNÉS!

Agnés (*enters.*) What?

Ymma Get me out of this. Those nuns have sewn their
misery into every seam.

Agnés Right. (*to Silence*) Oh dear. Nervous fingers . . .

Ymma My husband was about to tell me of Cumbria,
that vast bogland in the freezing North, where fate has
flung us.

Silence From the minute I met you, you've been rude to
me. You know nothing about me, or my home!

Ymma And I'm wedded to it for the rest of my life!

Silence turns away.

Agnés (*to Ymma*) Look at him. He's trying not to cry.

Ymma So what?

Agnés He's a little boy . . . You could have had some brute who'd have raped you twice by now and beaten you for crying. If I were you I'd count my blessings.

Ymma Well, you're not me, are you?

Silence Cumbria is beautiful. It's a land of green mountains and still waters, of forests and cold rivers and I only have to think of it to know that I am strong. My priest says Ragnarok, my home, was there before the Romans came. For a thousand years people have lived within its walls – and now it's ours. We're a new people, a bold people – Viking and British – and we love our land. But the land is wild. I am lord only of the people, not of the land. The land is free. That is Cumbria, lady. More beautiful than you deserve.

Ymma (*pause*) Thank you, Agnés. You may leave.

Agnés I'll just turn the bed down.

Ymma I said go.

Agnés goes.

I'm spiteful and cruel. I carry rage around in my heart. I've never earned anyone's love. I'm vicious and vengeful and even my servants despise me. I'll make you a terrible wife.

Silence You remind me of my priest.

Ymma What?

Silence She's holding the reins of my government while I'm away. She's powerful like you, but she isn't angry.

Ymma Your priest is a woman?

Silence Yes. Why are you so angry?

Ymma It's my nature . . . (*She sighs.*) I should have been a man. My anger would have been a virtue then. But I'm not a man. I'm this.

> *Ymma takes off her dress and stands in her shift. She throws the dress to Silence. Pause. Silence carries it to a chair, and lays it down as if it were a dying person.*

Silence So. Consummation . . .

Ymma Yes.

Silence The Sacred Act.

Ymma Sacred? Is that what they told you? (*a slight, contemptuous laugh*) Well, come on then. (*She sits on the bed.*) Forgive me, but the sooner we . . . achieve it, the sooner we can go to sleep. It's been a long day.

Silence Some other time, I think.

Ymma Pardon?

Silence Out of consideration for your unpolished soul, I've decided to defer it.

Ymma Lord Silence, they'll check the sheets in the morning.

Silence What for?

Ymma To make sure we've sealed our fate. If the marriage isn't consummated, it's worthless. Didn't they tell you that? It's a bond of blood.

Silence Blood? . . .

Ymma (*pause*) Won't you look at me? (*Sighs.*) Oh you poor little boy –

Silence Get into bed and shut your mouth! I am not poor! I am not little! I am not a boy! I'm a MAN!

Ymma (*getting into bed*) Right. Please yourself. (*She pulls the covers over her head.*)

Silence I'm saying my prayers . . . And then you'd better watch out! (*Prays.*) Dear Lord, bring happiness to my union. Now. (*Checks to see if anything is growing.*) Now! I need it NOW, GOD! (*Fumbles. Panics. Kneels in an un-Christian way.*) Odin, help. With your power, make me a man. Please. PLEASE! . . .

> *Silence approaches the bed. Jumps on Ymma and clumsily kisses her, groping her breasts. Ymma can't breathe. Eventually she shoves Silence off.*

Ymma God Almighty.

Silence (*distraught*) It won't / happen!

Ymma You could have warned me.

Silence I can't do it! It won't grow.

Ymma What are you talking about?

Silence My Thing!

Ymma Of course it'll grow. You're nervous, that's all.

Silence No! I saw the envoys pee and I can't do it like that.

Ymma Don't be stupid.

Silence (*sobs*) I don't know where it is!

Ymma Oh for Heaven's sake! . . . Here.

Silence Don't touch me!

Ymma Silence, I can grow it for you.

Silence No!

Ymma Pull yourself together – (*struggling*) – this is difficult enough as it is.

Silence Get off!

Ymma Come here! (*Tears open Silence's trousers.*) I'll sort your Thing out!

Silence Leave me, witch! I said GET OFF!

Ymma Don't be such a baby! (*hand in trousers*) What's . . .? Oh my God, you haven't got one!

Silence wails.

You're a girl . . .

Silence WHAT?

Ymma You're a girl!

Silence UHH!

Ymma Mother of God . . . I married a girl.

Silence I'm a BOY! I'm my mother's son, Lord of Cumbria!

Ymma Silence – (*feeling under her clothes*) you've got breasts.

Silence No –

Ymma And look – boys have bollocks – where are yours?

Silence NO! –

Ymma You're a girl!

Silence God HELP ME!

Ymma . . . Don't tell me you didn't know.

Silence I'm Lord Silence of Cumbria! Lord Silence! A man!

Ymma Look at us . . . We're both the same.

Silence looks. She buries her head in the bedclothes and whimpers.

This is incredible. How have you lived your whole life not knowing what you are?

Silence I'm a boy, a boy. They said I was a boy.

Ymma Why would they do that? They've turned you against your own nature!

Silence Jesus protect me. Odin protect me.

Ymma What if my mother had done it to me? Oh my God, I'd be Duke of Normandy! . . .

Silence Don't let me be female. Women have shrunken souls . . .

Ymma Do you see what your mother's done? She's given you power, freedom and power! You're a lord. As a woman you'd have lost everything; as a man, you have it all!

Silence (*helplessly*) What will I do? . . .

Ymma A little girl. (*She laughs.*)

Silence Don't laugh.

Ymma The king of England has married me to a little girl.

Silence Don't you dare! (*She pins Ymma down.*) I will kill you if you laugh! I mean it.

Ymma Do you know what our marriage is, Lady Silence? It's a sacrilege. Solemnly, in front of God, that priest has joined two women in wedlock. Do you know what the Bible says about that?

Silence No.

Ymma Abomination. You've deceived the king. Do you know what he'll do to you when he finds out?

Silence Send me home?

Ymma Silence, he'll put your head on a pole. Nothing will be punishment enough.

Silence Why didn't Surr tell me? And my mother . . . How *could* they? Abomination; what will I do?

Ymma I don't know. It's a shame you're not pretty. Pretty women can be so moving when they plead . . .

Silence When will you tell them? Will you wait until morning or do you want to do it now?

Ymma Agnés, AGNÉS!

Silence Yes, yes, get it over. Do it now. Let me die.

Agnés enters in her night attire, carrying a candle.

Agnés What?

Silence Forgive me!

Agnés That's all right, my lord. I'm used to being called out of bed at the most horrendous hours to indulge Ymma's whims.

Ymma My husband, Lord Silence of Cumbria is . . . thirsty. He'd like some wine.

Silence looks at her in amazement.

Agnés Right. Wine.

Ymma Can you imagine? He tells me he's never tasted French wine.

Agnés Oh, my lord hasn't lived.

Ymma No. But he's going to start living now. I've been telling him, Agnés, French wine is like poetry. It's known as the drink of love, and of freedom and truth. We should toast our union with it. We've made a vow to be flesh and bone together. We should love and protect each other, don't you think?

Silence Yes . . . Bring us wine, thank you.

Agnés Well, I'm delighted. Oh, I could cry. I thought she'd break your arms, my lord.

Ymma Out!

Agnés Congratulations, you're truly a man now. (*She leaves.*)

Silence (*embraces Ymma.*) Thank you. Thank you.

Ymma You strange creature. Strange, strange creature. Silence . . .

Silence (*they part*) A woman's wisdom lies in her silence.

Ymma What?

Silence My mother used to say it, when I was a b – a child. I never understood it before. Your face is so perfect it frightens me. Your clothes amaze me. I can't be the same as you; you're beautiful.

Ymma Silence, are you aware of what I've just done?

Silence You've saved my life. My bride is beautiful and she's saved my life.

Ymma If they find out what you are, they'll have my head. It would be difficult trying to function without it.

Silence Yes.

Ymma So we must learn to lie.

Silence No, why should we lie? We need only stay silent. You can hide anything in a silence. (*Pause.*) What'll we do about the sheets? We have to seal our fate.

Ymma Blood and spit. Give me your knife and I'll cut myself.

Silence No. Let me.

Ymma To tell you the truth, I was going to have to do something about them anyway.

Silence Why?

Ymma Oh . . . I'm not a virgin.

Silence (*speaking out*) Later that night, as the dawn in the window gave us every shade of brilliant blue, my wife and I enjoyed a jug of ruby wine and watched the room slowly saturate with colour. Why had she called herself spiteful and cruel? She was warmth and laughter unfolding before my eyes. We promised over our bond of blood, that neither of us would ever reveal my true identity. She said the truth was a jewel to be hidden. As the first beams of sunlight began to fill the room with gold, we began to plan our lives in Cumbria. She said we should allow each other freedom in all things and our freedom would cleave us together. It seemed impossible that we were a sacrilege and impossible that I was the same creature as my strange and beautiful spouse. I thanked the gods, abomination though I was, for bringing me to her, and making her my wife.

EIGHT

A courtyard.
   Ethelred is huddled in blankets, rocking in distress.
He wears his crown but little else.

Ethelred (*looking skywards*) Is it God I wrestle with, or the devil? Why do you play with me? What does it MEAN?

   Roger enters, dressed for travelling. He is shocked by
   Ethelred's appearance.

Roger Your Majesty? . . . I am a priest. My name is Roger.

Ethelred Priest –

Roger Forgive me, but you seem . . . Perhaps you have some clothing or some footwear I could bring?

Ethelred I'm troubled by a dream. I wish to know if it has power.

Roger Um, dreams are not my area of expertise, Majesty. I'm more of a parchment man –

Ethelred I dreamt last night of the end of the world.

Roger The end of the world?

Ethelred The apocalypse. It's made a wreck of me! Priest, I must have the meaning.

Roger Sire, permit me to find you a bishop, or a more senior –

Ethelred No, you, now! I awoke – in my dream – to find that the ground was shaking. Like this – all shaking! I came out here, where we are now, and there was a rumbling and people wailing in distress, women, old men, pathetic people of all kinds. I thought 'bastards' and I raised my hand to bless them. Then it came. There was a roar. Masonry shattered and the land cracked open.

Roger Goodness.

Ethelred Flames went as high as the moon.

Roger What did you do?

Ethelred Screamed. I screamed and screamed.

Roger Ah.

Ethelred In horrible silence, as one does in dreams. It was the apocalypse, Priest.

Eadric enters, laden with weapons. He listens.

Roger I've – I've had similar dreams myself . . . Perhaps they are the inevitable fear of our times, living as we do on the edge of destruction.

Ethelred You believe we're on the edge of destruction?

Roger Oh yes. There are signs and portents all around us – the Vikings, for example. My theological brothers believe that they are the last enemies of the righteous, and that the end is very close.

Ethelred Priest, do you think my dream could be a portent of the end?

Roger Well . . .

Ethelred Because there's more.

Roger Oh.

Ethelred There I was, screaming in the fire, but in the midst of God's carnage, in the very eye of the last catastrophe, I was untouched. Others were consumed

all around but I was unburning, unbloody! And then,
I saw her . . .

Roger Who?

Ethelred Ymma of Normandy.

Roger Ah.

Ethelred There, at the crux of the dream. She was
crawling towards me, her clothes all torn, covered in dirt
and grime, her thighs grazed, breasts heaving –

Roger Heavens above.

Ethelred And in her face, was . . .

Roger Was what?

Ethelred (*moved*) Love.

Roger She is the daughter of a saint.

Ethelred She grasped me. I gave a small cry, a kind of
'aahhh . . . ' and fell into her arms. She was brimful of
deep depths. She clutched me.

Roger Ah.

Ethelred And then we kissed. It was like music in my
mouth.

Roger Oh.

Ethelred We fornicated. In the flames.

Roger Uh.

Ethelred I think it was love, Priest. It was profound.
And when we finished, all was quiet. We had survived.
(*Pause.*) What do you make of it? Will it help me pray
for salvation? To know that I've fucked my way through
the apocalypse?

Roger Majesty, I can give you a penance for this dream.

Ethelred I'm not looking for a penance! I'm looking for the meaning.

Roger (*adjusting his crotch*) Perhaps it means you should pray. There is much to be said for the power of prayer.

Ethelred She walked through these gates with a Holy vision. She found her way to my room. God put her in my sight. She opened her heart to me, touched me with the truth, and I've married her to – (*suddenly realising*) I should have married her myself! Oh GOD! (*Flings himself down.*) Why didn't you *tell* me? Oh, you BASTARD! . . .

> *Eadric drops his weapons. He lifts Ethelred into his arms and roughly calms his tantrum, as if this is a duty he's done many times before, but doesn't relish. He looks accusingly at Roger.*

Roger I am a priest. My name is Roger. I – I was just passing, humbly on my way to meet the newly-weds. I'm to accompany them into the North.

Eadric Why?

Roger They will need guidance.

Eadric I'm the guide.

Roger Spiritual guidance, my friend. God's protection.

Eadric I'm the protector.

Roger Well, splendid . . . You and how many others? What kind of a retinue are we to have?

Eadric None.

Roger We have only one protector?

Eadric The fewer people who travel, the less chance of attack. I've disguised the cart as best I can to resemble a peasant vehicle. We go unobtrusively. It's our best chance.

Roger It is perilous then?

Eadric The roads have never been worse. But it's my belief that the cart is blessed and will come to no harm.

Roger What makes you say that?

Eadric We travel with the daughter of a saint.

Silence (*enters*) Father, guess what? The sacred act was indeed sacred –

Roger My son, you're before the king.

Silence (*kneels*) I'd like to thank you, Sire, for giving me my wonderful bride. May Odin reward you with a place in Valhalla! –

Ethelred *What?*

Silence In heaven! May Jesus Lord Christ God bless you and reward you, Amen.

Ethelred (*appalled*) Priest, he is a heathen!

Roger No longer, Sire! He received baptism just before he was wed. I intend him to become God's own vessel, a shining light of Jesus in the North!

Ethelred So, I have married the daughter of a saint to a godless Viking devil.

Ymma (*enters, with Agnés.*) Good morning, Sire.

Ethelred Leave us, all of you, NOW! LEAVE US!

All exit except Ymma.

Don't look at me, I'm a mess. Avert your eyes. (*Ymma looks away.*) You can see the husband I've given you. He's a fool, a heathen savage! I've made you ridiculous.

Ymma Not at all.

Ethelred I wish to apologise. I had your fate in my hands and look what I did!

Ymma I'm happy with your choice.

Ethelred No! I wish to rectify the situation. It may not be too late.

Ymma Sire –

Ethelred Speak freely: did you consummate? If not, I can have it annulled. I can annul it and you can stay here, in court. You can forget the whole idea of going to Cumbria. I can send him packing and have you, Ymma, here, with me.

Ymma As your whore?

Ethelred No, NO! As my wife. As Queen, consecrated Queen of England.

Ymma You would annul my marriage to Lord Silence and marry me yourself?

Ethelred Yes. With my unreserved apology.

Ymma Why?

Ethelred Ask not for a reason. Let it grow. Like a bloom . . . Ymma, you asked me for freedom. This is it: freedom and power.

Ymma I have knowledge of my husband.

Ethelred (*devastated*) Is that the truth?

Ymma My husband has knowledge of me.

Ethelred But think what I'm offering; consecrated queen!

Ymma I'm sorry. It would offend God.

Ethelred No, no, God wishes it! Oh, I could kill myself for calling you a whore. What was I *thinking* of?

Ymma I belong to Silence of Cumbria with vows I cannot break!

Ethelred He's a pagan; the marriage is void! (*Grabs her.*) Ymma, I know where your feelings lie.

Ymma Get / – (*struggling*) NO!

Ethelred I've seen the love on your face. I've felt the passion of your kiss. / In my dreams –

Ymma Don't touch me! Get – DON'T TOUCH ME!

> *Ymma punches Ethelred in the face. He reels backwards and passes out. Pause.*

What have I done? What have I done? (*Sinks to her knees.*) Every time a good thing comes, every time I think my life might shine, just for a moment –

> *She sees Eadric. She looks at him aghast. Silence enters.*

Silence What happened?

Ymma I hit him. It's over. He'll come round and this dog will carry me away!

> *Eadric picks up Ethelred. He takes him to a corner. He drops him in a heap. He hurls the crown away. Ymma and Silence watch, flabbergasted.*

Eadric Let's go.

Roger (*entering*) Where's his Majesty? I was going to ask him to bless our cart.

Eadric He's gone.

Ymma We're leaving. Now! We go by no main roads, we pass through no towns. We ask help from no one and we don't stop until we reach the North. We go like *fugitives*!

> *Eadric bows. Ymma sweeps past him. Eadric exits, after her.*

Silence Father, my wife is amazing.

Act Two
The Open Road

NINE

The cart.
Ymma, Roger and Agnés in the back, Eadric and
Silence in the front.

Silence It was our second day in the cart.

Ymma For hours I looked over my shoulder, expecting
the king and all his men to descend upon us. But nothing
happened. No furies came.

Silence I was looking at our saviour, Eadric Longshaft,
trying to think who he reminded me of, when he said
something strange.

Eadric Dog.

Ymma begins to sing. She has a high, eerie voice.

Silence Every time I look at you, Eadric, I think I've seen
you somewhere before. Did you know that?

Eadric No.

Silence My wife . . . I didn't know she could sing. I learn
something about her every day; like finding new jewels
in a box full of treasure. Are you married?

Eadric Was.

Silence What happened?

Eadric (*resents being asked*) She's dead.

Silence Oh . . . How did she –?

Eadric Vikings took her. I found her spoiled.

Silence Spoiled?

Eadric So I killed her. Anything else?

Silence He didn't speak again for the rest of the day.

Roger (*speaking out*) The open land; we are exposed, dazed and wriggling, like beetles under a lifted stone. I cannot raise my eyes. When I try, my stomach lurches and my head spins. It makes me want to weep in shame. Why am I afraid? How is it possible for a man to be afraid of fields?

Agnés Father, are you cold?

Roger No, good lady.

Agnés You're shaking. I thought you might be –

Roger No no no. Not cold . . .

Agnés I was wondering if you'd hear my confession sometime.

Roger I . . . I've never been confessor to a woman.

Agnés Please. It seems this kingdom's at the mercy of the Vikings; wild, savage killers sweeping over hills, raping, burning . . . We're crawling along in an open cart, prey to every danger. It would comfort me to know I could confess, if I was going to die.

Roger I – Silence, would you sit with me?

Silence What's the matter?

Roger (*attempting to stand*) I'm a little dizzy. It'll pass.

Agnés He's going to faint!

Roger Good lady, it's – (*He faints.*)

TEN

A dungeon.

Ethelred (*filthy and alone*) Guard! Guard! Let me out,
you peasant, I'm your king! They found me dazed and
crownless, lying in a drain. They locked me here with the
rubbish of creation, thinking me a madman or a knave!
It is a portent . . . God's destruction is coming and order
is flung upside down. Pagans marry saints and kings rub
their faces in the mire. We are truly on the brink of the
end! How may I prevent it? What must I do? Ymma,
you came like salvation into my dream. You had to *hit*
me to make me see! I must not be afraid. I must take my
power. I must earn, with action, the taste of your love.
I will break my chains and hurl them away!! (*to the
guard*) I am Ethelred Rex! Free me, you slave, or I will
murder you! . . .

ELEVEN

The cart.
    *Eadric and Ymma in the front. Roger has a cowl over
his head, protecting his eyes from the view. He resembles
the figure of Death.*

Eadric On the third day, she sat with me. We passed
through the outskirts of London at dawn. The walls still
had skulls of the Viking dead on view, from their failed
siege of '94. They will never take this marvellous city,
those cunts.

Ymma It stank like a witch's latrine. London . . . What a
dump.

Roger (*to Silence*) What is the Eucharist?

Agnés Our priest had decided to test the young lord on his catechism and a marvellous comfort came over me, listening to them speak.

Roger The Eucharist, Silence. We did it yesterday.

Agnés Although it was amazing how little the young lord knew.

Eadric She is silent. Her back straight in some kind of a royal way they must teach them from the cradle.

Silence The Eucharist is when God . . .

Ymma Where is the king? Every day I think today he will find us and he'll be revenged.

Eadric He'll never find us.

Ymma Why do you think that?

Eadric This cart is blessed and safe from harm.

Silence Turns himself into bread!

Roger (*sighs*) Silence . . . you must find the right words. It is the language of respect.

Eadric Every time I try to speak to her I –

Ymma What manner of man is the king?

Eadric He is a king. They cannot be judged like others. Sometimes, when I'm on duty at his door, I hear his thoughts. They come to me in purple.

Ymma Right.

Silence The Eucharist is the sacrament in which the Lord Jesus God is . . . baked?

Roger No, come on, Silence!

Silence In which . . .

Agnés . . . the soul and divinity of Our Lord is contained in the appearance of bread and wine! Sorry, Father, I couldn't help it. I love the catechism. I used to win prizes.

Eadric Every time I try to speak to her I –

Ymma (*pointing*) What's that?

Eadric It's the monastery of St Alban, where we may rest tonight. It's full of monks. They're famed for their devout lifestyle and their bee keeping. I find myself talking shit. It makes me hate myself.

Silence As I watched Eadric Longshaft, I suddenly realised who he reminded me of. He was the Barbarian, the Barbarian in the forest . . .

TWELVE

Canterbury.
  Ethelred is dressed in state, sitting on his throne, caressing it.

Ethelred I lay in my own dungeons for three days and three nights. I came within an inch of severing the thin cord of sanity which keeps our souls intact. When the bishops finally freed me, I put a knife to my gaoler's throat and ask him who was king. 'You!' he squealed – and in that word, I finally perceived the meaning of power. He who can inspire fear, is powerful. Like God. I cut his throat and felt myself grow stronger every second of his dying. The world is a different place to me now. I, Ethelred Rex, have realised the nature of God. And with this realisation comes the course of action I must take. God is as cruel as the jaws of the wolf. God is force. His word is chaos. And his will? His will be done.

THIRTEEN

The cart.
Three days later. Rain. Ymma next to Eadric, Roger
under his cowl, Agnés eating.

Roger Lesson twenty-two: Hell.

Agnés It had rained without break for three days. In
places, the road was like a river bed.

Ymma We crawled across the belly of England.

Roger Hell is eternal, a place of perpetual dark.

Silence I'd had enough of learning the priest's faith.
I wanted to sit in the front with Eadric.

Roger It is the hopeless destination of the damned.

Silence I had an urge to – (*She giggles.*) I wanted to see
what he'd do. Perhaps he'd –

> *Silence's imagination: music. The sun comes out. She*
> *caresses the back of Eadric's neck. He turns and pulls*
> *her into the front of the cart. She lies in his arms,*
> *delighted, as Roger continues.*

Roger In order to imagine Hell, one must think of the
worst pain our soft flesh can suffer, the worst
degradation our human spirits can bear and magnify it
to eternity. One must think of an exhausting pitch of
agony strung out like a screech until Doomsday.

Silence Eadric, I can't. My wife . . .

Eadric Don't ask me to control myself. I love you too
much.

> *Eadric kisses Silence. Silence swoons as Roger*
> *continues:*

253

Roger Hell is a burning lake, vaster than all the seas, where God sends those who offend him; heathens, sinners, abominations of every kind!

Silence looks up. The sun goes in. She returns to the back of the cart and listens.

God is terrible in his judgement! Once damned to Hell, there is no prayer and no penitence that will move him.

Silence Father, supposing that one was a heathen or an abomination – or both – and yet not a bad person. What would God do?

Roger He would damn you.

Silence But you said he loved all men.

Roger Yes, he may love them, but he won't save them. He's loving but cruel, omnipotent but heartlesss, benign but a force of terror! – I'm sorry!

Silence What is it?

Roger (*crumbling into distress*) We have to stop! I've upset myself . . .

Agnés (*to Roger, concerned*) May I offer you some cheese?

Roger No no no . . .

Agnés Or some dates? They come from the Holy Land. I like to think our Lord was comforted with dates, when he was in the desert.

Roger You're very kind.

Eadric How proud she is in the rain, as if she drinks it with her skin.

Ymma The king could have caught us ten times over, don't you think?

Eadric I have told you what I think. You do not listen.

Ymma Perhaps he awoke from that punch and remembered nothing . . . I hardly dare to hope.

Eadric (*putting his jacket over Ymma's knees*) An offering of comfort, lady.

Ymma (*flinching*) What?

Eadric It's deerskin – waterproof.

Ymma No thank you. (*She pushes the jacket away.*)

Eadric But you're wet. Your garments, wet and clinging –

Ymma I said no.

Eadric Is it not good enough? Even for your knees?

Ymma Listen. I am grateful for your help. I appreciate everything you've done, but as far as I'm concerned, you are here to drive this cart. When we get to Cumbria, my husband will pay you for your service, and then you can trot back to your boyfriend, the king.

Eadric yanks the reins in a sudden fury. The cart goes out of control. It careers into a ditch. Roger is flung into the arms of Agnés. Eadric falls on top of Ymma.

Silence (*excited*) A cart crash! We'd gone off the road!

Roger (*to Agnés*) Dear lady – forgive me.

Agnés (*hurt*) It's nothing.

Roger Your food!

Ymma Get off me. Get off!

Eadric (*holding her down*) You speak me wrong. Listen!

Eadric doesn't move. He stares at Ymma with such intensity that she is afraid. She struggles.

Ymma DOG!

*Eadric abruptly climbs off the cart. Ymma is
extremely shaken.*

Silence What's the matter? No wonder he's angry. You
treat him like an animal. If you don't like him you
should let me sit with him.

Ymma Stay away from him, Silence.

Silence Why should I?

Ymma Because I say so! (*She walks away.*)

Silence Don't order me around. You're my wife, not my
mother!

Eadric I need help.

Silence (*jumping off the cart*) What can I do?

Eadric Wheel's fucked.

Agnés We were at the edge of a great moor. The wind
was bitter and the rain poured.

Eadric (*to Roger*) Get out.

Roger I'll remain under here, good Sir. I suffer with
weak lungs and I fear –

Eadric Out!

Roger (*climbing out, eyes shut*) There was nothing for
it but to close my eyes and pretend that I was blind.
I resolved not to open them again until we were safely
installed in –

Ymma There's a cave here – we can shelter in it.

Roger Thank God!

Silence That's not a cave. It's a barrow.

Ymma What's a barrow?

Silence A tomb, where the ancient people buried their dead. Surr found one in Cumbria, full of skulls and weapons and the folded bones of a great eagle.

Agnés There'll be ghosts! Horrible shadowy things that suck men's souls!

Roger (*approaching*) Let me go in, dear ladies. I can hold up the cross of our Lord and bless the ground. Shadows will not harm you then. (*Barges past them into the cave. Loudly*) I am a priest. My name is Roger. Flee, things of night, in the name of God! (*Kneels.*) Let these rock walls close around me and keep me from that overwhelming sky. Oh please, please, you pagan devils, keep me safe inside. I'll drink blood in your service if you keep me here, just for a night, just for an hour. Blind me, have my soul, make me your creature but keep me from the nightmare of that moor . . .

FOURTEEN

The barrow.

Silence It took Eadric and I two hours to mend the wheel. The whole time he never spoke a word, except to say –

Eadric Give me that thing.

Silence He smelt of horses and rain and firewood and I kept thinking of my dream . . . See me, Eadric, see me for what I am.

Agnés We curled up in the barrow that night, all five of us. It was a terrible squeeze. I found myself next to the priest. (*She settles.*)

Roger Our small candle cast shadows dancing across paintings of the ancient people – a leaping deer and a man with huge eyes, naked, holding a simple spear. He looked like our first father Adam, before the Fall. A feeling of peace came over me as I looked at him. (*Whispers.*) Pagan, pagan, I consign my soul to your care. (*He settles to sleep.*)

Agnés (*asleep*) Mm, yes . . .

Eadric (*watching Ymma.*) Words have always caught me in their snares. They betray me even as they spill from my mouth. Words are the instruments of lies. One day, all humanity will communicate with thought, for the mind speaks the truth, always. It's for this reason that I practise the art of mindspeech. (*He concentrates.*)

Agnés . . . Yes, harder, there . . .

Eadric I find a dark space inside and imagine my message, like a beam of light travelling through the void. It leaves the sphere of my skull and like a lighted arrow, finds a route to the mind of the receiver . . . There are some who can speak over distances of miles, but I, who am a novice at the art, must be close. I am close now. My thoughts wind around her like a shroud. (*He whispers.*) Beloved, hear me . . .

> *Eadric closes his eyes. Pause. Ymma stirs. Pause. He touches her ankle. She wakes. She recoils.*

Ymma (*pause*) Stay away from me, or I will kill you. I mean it.

Eadric Your words mean nothing. Only your thoughts.

Ymma If you touch me, I will kill you. Stay away!

> *Silence moans and puts her arm around Ymma. Ymma turns and kisses her.*

Silence, I love you, my God-given gift . . . Nothing must come between us.

Silence You strange creature. Strange, strange creature . . .

> *Their kisses become more passionate. Eadric, furious, leaves the cave. He goes to the cart, opens a bag of Ymma's clothes and starts to tear one of her dresses. He stops. He holds the dress to his face. He falls to his knees. He is going to make love to the dress.*

FIFTEEN

A ship.

Ethelred I am full of the fire of revelation tonight. Perhaps it's the motion of this ship, or perhaps my clarity is God-given. As we cleave the waves, the whole journey of my life is rippling around me. I was sat on a blood-stained throne when I was ten years old; they padded the crown to make it fit. And the Vikings, seeing the land in the hands of a child, began their raids. They have blighted my life from the start. God's will is simple. I will drive that Viking blight from my shores. I will root out His pagan foes and do His apocalypse for Him. The boy Silence, as fresh-faced as I was when they made me king, is the crux of my revenge; he lies at the end of my path. The prize for his murder is Ymma. If the wind keeps with us, we'll be in Yarmouth at dawn. Then Hull, then Tynemouth. At this rate, I'll be in Cumbria before them.

SIXTEEN

Dawn. Outside the barrow.
Birds tweeting. Roger is kneeling in Silence's un-Christian way.

Roger Help me, help me, help me, help me –

Agnés (*enters*) Father, I've just had a wonderful dream.

Roger I cannot interpret dreams or hear confessions – or do anything right now, I'm sorry!

Agnés I don't want you to interpret it; I just thought you might like to hear it. I was lying in a boat in the middle of the ocean and all I could see were tumbling waves and the great vault of the sky. I had a sense of being the tiniest thing in all creation.

Roger Oh –

Agnés There I was, no more than a dot in God's immense design –

Roger Ng!

Agnés – and suddenly, I could hear angelic singing . . .

Roger Angelic singing?

Agnés When I was at the convent, our Abbess once said to me that angelic singing could only be heard by humankind in its dreams. She said that all of man's earthly music was merely an attempt to remember its fleeting beauty . . . It's strange how dreams can affect us. I've been so troubled on this journey but I think that hearing such music in a pagan tomb can only be an omen for something good.

Roger I pray it is. (*Lifts his cowl to see her.*) Forgive me – did you say you used to be a nun?

Agnés I was a foundling. The nuns cared for me. I lived with them until I was ten, then my lady's sainted mother purchased me and gave me to her daughter as a maid.

Roger My parents gave me to the bishops at the same age. Sold me into a worthy life.

Agnés It's the same for all the children of the poor. We have no freedom, do we?

Roger Lady, may I ask, if the question is not too intrusive: when you left your convent, did you by any chance, after such a long period of incarceration in a safe and familiar place, find yourself – oh this sounds so foolish! – did you find yourself unnerved, frightened, perhaps shaking in an unfathomable way at the sight of – fields?

Agnés (*understanding*) Oh . . .

Roger Did you find yourself yearning to be anywhere that would take your eyes from the swoon of the horizon, from the sheer, shuddering size of it? And when approaching an open moor, such as the one that looms ahead, did you ever find yourself praying that a mist might surround you, an eclipse, a cloud, anything, that you might not feel so horribly exposed to the endless land and the unspeakable vault of the sky?

Agnés Well, it's a long time ago but –

Roger And did you feel, when you were flung from the safety of all you held dear, that the nature of God had changed, that he was not the God you'd always believed in, not the friend you could rely on, but a wild stranger – or worse – did you begin to doubt his very existence, to feel the universe was so cruel and so chaotic that some other force must preside over it, some heartless, savage deity worshipped by the heathens who made this tomb –

or worse – nothing at all, a heaven empty of divinity, a chaos of life with no guiding hand? Did you ever feel that the sky could be godless?

Agnés (*moved*) Yes, I did! Not because of the land, but because of where fate had thrown me. It made me despair.

Roger My dear sister, tell me, did these terrible feelings leave you?

Agnés Yes. But they change you. I fought hard to reconcile myself with God. There's nothing else to believe in, is there? (*Roger sobs.*) Father, you're crying. (*She puts out a hand.*)

Roger (*he clings to it*) Help me.

SEVENTEEN

The cart.
  Eadric is asleep under Ymma's clothes. Silence enters.

Silence Eadric. Longshaft, wake up. What are you doing? These are my wife's clothes.

Eadric (*wakes with a jolt.*) I was cold . . .

Silence Oh, (*picking up a dress*) she was wearing this the first time I saw her, when she called me a boy and sneered. Look at that colour . . . (*Holds the dress against herself.*) Do you like it?

Eadric What?

Silence This shade – is it good? (*She giggles coyly.*)

Ymma (*entering*) What are you doing?

Silence (*showing Ymma the dress*) Look.

Ymma Silence –

Silence Eadric slept out here. He didn't have a blanket so he used your clothes.

Ymma (*to Eadric*) Is that true? (*Pause*) Did you touch my clothes? Answer me!

Eadric picks up a petticoat. He presses it to his cheek. Ymma is horrified.

Agnés, AGNÉS!

Agnés is elsewhere with Roger. He is holding on to her arm.

Agnés And this is mugwort; a humble plant but marvellous in the treatment of warts.

Ymma (*to Eadric*) Get away from my things!

Silence Ymma, what's he done?

Ymma Can't you see?

Agnés The detail of the moor will help you cross it. If you focus your eyes on all the tiny living things, the size of it won't trouble you.

Roger Look, a frog!

Ymma AGNÉS! (*to Eadric*) I feel sick when I look at you. Do you understand? DOG! How dare you violate my things!

Eadric gets off the cart. He exits. Agnés and Roger approach.

Agnés (*to Ymma*) What?

Ymma Get on the cart. Pick up my clothes. Take them over there.

Agnés What for?

Ymma Burn them.

Agnés *What?*

Ymma Burn them!

Silence Ymma, why?

Ymma Because they're *filthy*!

Agnés I'm not burning your clothes!

Roger These garments are objects of splendour. It would be a tragedy even to singe them!

Ymma Did I ask your opinion?

Roger No –

Ymma Then shut up! BURN THEM!

Silence No one's going to burn your clothes. I won't allow it!

Ymma Damn you, Silence, you stupid, naive fool!

Silence That's enough! You're my wife, Ymma, and you'll do what I say!

Ymma (*shocked*) Don't ever speak to me like that. You've NO RIGHT!

She exits. Pause. Silence bursts into tears.

Roger Silence, my friend, do not cry . . .

Agnés (*drawing Roger away*) Sooner or later I knew this would happen.

Roger What?

Agnés One of her rages. They take her to the very brink of madness. In her last one, she tried to kill her brother – fell on him with a knife, tore him. It's why he sent her here. Father, I want to confess: I hate her for dragging me with her. I'm full of resentment, full of envious thoughts. If I were her, I'd find it so easy to be happy. She's blessed with wealth and a beautiful face, yet she hates her life. I should pity her, but I can't. She holds my chains. (*to Silence, kindly*) Now, my lord. Dry your tears. What do you wish me to do?

EIGHTEEN

The moor.
    Ymma is vomiting. She finishes. She wipes her mouth. Eadric approaches.

Eadric It's hard being near you, lady.

Ymma Then keep away.

Eadric You make me forget myself.

Ymma How many women have you raped, Eadric? I know men like you. How many?

Eadric None.

Ymma Liar.

Eadric I say the truth.

Ymma Do you know what it means, rape?

Eadric Yes.

Ymma What?

Eadric I'll say it silently.

Ymma Rape means living through your own murder. No one will ever do it to me again. They're burning my clothes. Everything you touched will burn. Do you understand?

Eadric Listen.

He falls to his knees and closes his eyes. Ymma impatiently leaves.

(*mindspeaking*) I was a boy. The Vikings came with a hundred ships. They burned the town and caused terror. We fought them in the mud by the sea. They slew us. I ran. Three of them found me. They held me down. Like a pig. That is rape, lady. You may trample me. You may walk on my back with your rage. Please.

Silence enters. Eadric opens his eyes. Ymma has gone. Silence is watching him.

Silence Are you praying?

Eadric No.

Silence Where's Ymma?

Eadric Gone.

Silence She asked me to burn her clothes. I couldn't. The priest said why not leave them as a sacrifice to the gods of the tomb, so that's what we've done. I don't understand her, Eadric. I don't understand women at all. I understand you better. You're a man.

Silence gently touches Eadric's shoulder. He looks at her. She half smiles. She leaves. Eadric tries to wipe Silence's touch from his body. He spits.

NINETEEN

The cart.
Silence and Eadric in the front. Ymma sits alone, facing backwards.

Roger As we left the moor, I saw a small, brown bird pulling worms from the ground. It looked at me with eyes full of eloquence and seemed to say, 'Lo Roger, the wilderness is alive with purple flowers and the dew-strung webs of spiders.' The next day we crossed a stream of clear waters which I wanted to leap from the cart and touch. Rabbits. The evening thronged with rabbits. They reminded me of myself.

Silence My wife was silent. She seemed to be in a different place and not with us in the cart at all. It was like being with a stranger.

Eadric Dog.

Roger And then we entered a forest.

Silence The light came horizontal through the trees.

Roger For days, we gazed at a rich canopy of flaming colours. An ochre leaf dropped from a branch and landed in my lap. It was soft and lined, like the palm of my hand.

Agnés It's lucky.

Roger Lucky?

Agnés Very lucky. To catch an autumn leaf.

Roger Ah. (*He gives it to Agnés.*) May the luck belong to you.

   Agnés is moved.

Silence (*joining Ymma*) Ymma, I hate this. Why are you using your silence against me?

Ymma Because I fear that if I try to speak . . . it won't be a word that comes out of my mouth but a madwoman's shriek. I know these times of old. It's as if the world turns to ash and a chasm yawns between living things and me.

Silence Ymma, you can't talk like this! What do you mean?

Ymma I mean I'm nothing. I'm a thing that sits to be looked at, a thing that mustn't think. I mean my brother held me down, hand over mouth, and showed me the purpose for which I was born. (*She can't speak.*)

Silence Ymma. (*She takes Ymma in her arms.*)

Ymma I'm a pool, a dark glass into which men can peer and see themselves as strong. Let dark waters wash over me. Let me be ash. Let me be dust and disappear.

TWENTY

Tynemouth.

Ethelred Round up all those Viking-born and slay them! I don't care how many generations they've lived here; if they've been tilling the land since Alfred's time it's not long enough. They are not your brothers! They will never be sons of England and their loyalty will never be to this nation or this crown. They have taken our land and raped it, and until they are gone, we will never be free. Beloved people, I commend you to God, for his judgement is cruel. Pray he might not send it before we purge these savages from our shores. Men of England, march with me on the road to righteous murder! March with me to Cumbria! (*Pause.*) That was Tynemouth. I was brilliant. Filthy people kissed my hand and cheered. No one could believe it was me.

TWENTY-ONE

York.

Roger At the other end of the forest was the city of York –

Ymma (*jumping off the cart*) A dump.

Agnés A marvellous town, full of Roman buildings; quite the busiest place I ever saw. It seemed that one could buy anything here.

Silence Ymma, where are you going?

Ymma Wait for me. (*Exits.*)

Silence I began to feel our journey was in its final stage. At last, we were in the North!

Eadric Look at it. Viking shit. I wish all Vikings dead, dead and buried in a great stinking pit of my making.

Silence I'm a Viking.

Eadric I know. (*He spits.*)

Silence (*hurt*) He told me to –

Eadric Sit in the cart and guard it!

Silence So I did.

Eadric exits.

Agnés The priest and I took the opportunity to walk along the city walls. We looked at the view below us, a forested vale, as far as the eye could see.

Roger Naked winter trees. Such dignity in their bareness. You've reconciled me with the horizon. I don't know how to thank you.

Agnés Oh, it was nothing . . .

Roger Dear lady –

Agnés For both of us, it was a moment of –

A note of angelic music. They exit. Silence alone.

Silence What am I? I cannot be a husband to my wife. I cannot be a woman to a man. I am nothing. No wonder he spits at me. If only I could tell him that underneath I – Eadric . . . I'm sick of hiding. I want to be free. Help me.

Ymma enters, dressed as a man.

Ymma Silence? Do you like it? I was inspired by you. It's deerskin; waterproof. And look, lined with wool. Soft, pliable, strong; perfect. And look at the footwear. You could stamp on a snake with them.

Silence What did you do with your dress?

Ymma I traded it.

Silence Your last dress?

Ymma Yes. It's gone, every nun-made stitch of it.

Silence Ymma, I wish you'd traded anything else! Your last dress . . .

Ymma What about it?

Silence I wanted it.

Ymma What for?

Silence To see myself! . . . To see what I look like.

Ymma Oh, Silence . . .

Silence How can I know myself until I've seen myself? I don't know who or what I am!

Ymma You are Silence of Cumbria! Silence . . . We'll soon be home, my love. You have the whole future to know yourself.

Eadric enters, laden with supplies. He sees two men embracing.

Eadric Sodomites. (*He draws his sword, disgusted.*)

Ymma Are you going to murder us, cabbage?

Agnés (*entering with Roger*) Ymma, what are you doing dressed like that?

Ymma Look. (*She kicks the air in front of Eadric's face.*) Freedom. You might think about doing the same. We're going into wild lands and I want to protect myself.

Roger Ah. (*to Agnés*) Should I dress as a man, do you think?

Ymma Sit with me in the front, Silence. Teach me to drive the cart.

TWENTY-TWO

Ragnarok.

Ethelred Our march through Cumbria was triumphant. We slaughtered the heathen and pride was in our step. We came to the runt's castle with our banners unfurled and I, dressed in my finest furs, was carried aloft – my travel throne placed on a bier. The place was abandoned. The heathens must have heard of our approach and fled. I entered alone – as befits a warrior king – and in the hall, by a great fire, sat a solitary woman. She said she was a priest – but by the robes she wore and the mistletoe twined in her hair, I could see she was a witch.

I felt power surging through me, fabulous power, power of life and death. My hands were itching for a murder. I expected her to shriek, or spit, or beat herself with a sacred fish – but she did nothing. She stood silently, eyeing me. It was . . . audacious. It was then I had another revelation about power. Sometimes, to kill is not enough. One has to torture first.

TWENTY-THREE

A barn.
Eadric is serving stew around a fire.

Silence We were less than a day from my home, high in the mountains of Cumbria: my home.

Roger We stopped by the shores of a darkening lake, and as the heavens stretched out in a glorious canopy of winter stars, we made our camp in a disused barn.

Eadric Stew.

Roger Delicious. It's inspiring to watch a man cook. Makes me think men can do anything!

Ymma spits a bone out. She wipes her nose on her sleeve.

Silence Somehow, with her dressed like that, there seemed to be no difference between us.

Ymma One day, maybe not for a hundred years, maybe not for two, all women will be driving loaded carts up hills. That's my dream, Silence.

Silence I thought her more beautiful than ever. There was a light in her eyes that I had never seen before. And if she was beautiful dressed as a man, then maybe I was too.

Eadric I can hear her. In the high air, her thoughts have come, curling round me like a mist. 'Lord Silence is a sodomite,' she says. 'He's driving me to make myself ugly. For him, I have rubbed my female nature in the mud. Help me, Eadric. Return me to my natural state.'

Ymma burps loudly. Eadric looks at her, with understanding.

Tonight I will lift her high once more. Tonight, we will have truth and truth and truth. I've put three hundred mystic mushrooms in the stew.

Roger The season of Yule is upon us and the more I look at our humble surroundings, the more I'm reminded of our Lord's nativity.

Agnés Oh yes, born in a barn.

Roger When our meal is over I should like to say Mass – to celebrate the end of our journey and to thank God for keeping us safe.

Ymma Our journey isn't over yet. You've seen the villages we've passed: blackened shells, corpses rotting in the fields. There's Vikings everywhere. Why thank God about that? You should keep your prayers 'til you're safe in Ragnarok.

Eadric It's not Vikings.

Ymma What?

Eadric Those villages. Vikings kill different.

Silence He's right. Vikings cut runes into dying flesh as offerings to the gods.

Eadric The corpses I looked at are normal. Like we make. In Kent.

Ymma The king . . .

Silence There's always people raiding round here. It could be the Strathclyde Welsh, or the Celts or the crazy people from the Isle of Man. We'll be safe in Ragnarok. The walls are as high as trees.

Agnés Why don't you say the Mass? It would be such a comfort to us all, Roger . . .

Roger Dear lady, of course.

Eadric The mushrooms began to take effect during the sermon.

Roger Brothers and sisters, dear brothers and dear sisters, my friends, here we are, five humble souls protected only by a barn in a land where violence rages and chaos seems to rule.

Eadric begins to undress himself.

There are those who say this chaos is a sign. They say God is sending his destruction, preparing his vials of wrath to pour upon the Earth. The skies will darken, fires will roar and there'll be nowhere, nowhere to hide . . . So that, my dear friends, is my question for this evening. Is God going to destroy us? And if he is, is he wrong?

When Eadric is naked from the waist up, he begins to oil his torso.

Because . . . because I think he is. How could he even think of destroying us? It's an outrage. If he wanted us perfect, why did he create us flawed? And if he created us flawed, why does he blame us for it? God is *wrong*! We live lives of such misery, punishing ourselves in his name. Is his thanks to send destruction? Frankly, if it was the other way round, if we had the power to obliterate him, I wouldn't hesitate. Rid the world of God, I say, rid it of fate and shame; let all deities be gone! My friends, we may be only days away from the end. How should we behave? Should we gouge our cheeks and rub ashes into our hair? Should we wail out our sins like starving wolves in the snow? I say no! I say if destruction is coming then taste the life you never had. Pluck it like a late apple and lets its tartness fill your mouth. Gorge yourselves on the scent of blown roses, lick frost from spider's webs, smash the ice on drinking troughs and hurl it in splinters at the sun. I say glory in the world, exult in nature, immerse yourself in womankind!

Agnés Amen!

Roger Dear lady . . .

Agnés I love you!

They embrace.

Come outside. I want to show you something.

Agnés and Roger exit. The sound of drums begins, gradually coming nearer.

Silence After Mass, my wife developed a golden halo. And –

Eadric draws his broadsword. He swishes it around.

Eadric did that. The ground's becoming the sea . . . I'm fine really. (*She collapses.*)

Eadric I was reckless that night. The barn was filled with the shadow of goats. (*He points his sword at Ymma.*) I will see you dishonoured no longer.

Ymma You put drugs in that stew, didn't you?

Eadric The mushrooms of truth. I know what you want of me.

Ymma I want nothing!

Eadric Your freedom. (*He advances.*) Say with your mouth what I know from your mind and I'll plaster the roof with his guts, now, while he sleeps: let me, now!

Ymma No! NO!

Silence (*standing, with her sword drawn.*) Ha! Unhand my wife . . . big man.

Ymma Silence, he's drugged you.

Silence I will fight you, Frost Giant.

Ymma He means you harm!

Silence I am a thing of the forest, fleet of foot and sharp of eye.

Ymma Put down the sword and get out.

Silence See me for what I am. See my nature, Eadric!

Ymma Silence!

Silence Away with you, wife! This is man's affair.

Ymma (*she shouts*) Agnés! Bring the priest! PRIEST!

Silence I'll meet you in Valhalla, barbarian.

Ymma (*attempts to stop her*) What are you doing?

Eadric Let him fight. And when I've killed him, I'll get those fucking goats over there!

Silence lunges at Eadric. He soon disarms her. He picks her up, in a tight hold.

Silence Eadric . . .

Ymma Silence, what are you *doing?*

Silence kisses Eadric. He drops her, disgusted, and with instinctive violence, he pulls out his dagger. Ymma throws herself between them.

No, no. He's drugged; it's not his fault! He thought he was kissing me. Me, Eadric!

Eadric (*about to plunge in the dagger*) It said my name!

> *Ymma stops Eadric's mouth with a kiss. Eadric is paralysed by the force of it. Silence backs away as the kiss continues. And continues. At last Ymma breaks off. Eadric gazes at her, stupefied.*

Ymma Silence, get out. Run!

> *Silence exits, distressed.*

You love me, don't you?

> *Eadric nods. Without breaking the gaze, Ymma takes his dagger. She stands.*

I've never thanked you properly for the way you saved me in Canterbury, for the way you led us here, so bravely. You hide a lot in your silence, don't you? (*Eadric embraces Ymma's legs.*) There . . . (*She strokes him.*) What a shining soul you must have. You're strong, you're noble and you never lie, do you? Maybe my feelings could grow . . . (*She raises the dagger.*)

Roger (*entering*) There's drums!

Agnés (*following*) Coming up the valley!

> *Eadric flings himself in front of Ymma and picks up his sword.*

Roger A band of men with flaming torches!

Eadric (*turning on Roger*) Draw, Priest!

Roger Merciful God.

Eadric Keep your goats at bay.

Agnés Listen, drums!

The drums are close, and getting louder.

Eadric Move, now.

Agnés They're Vikings!

Eadric Worse. They're men of Kent.

Ymma (*at the door*) Silence! SILENCE!

Eadric Where's my fucking shirt?

Agnés Run! Hide!

Ymma SILENCE! . . .

Roger and Eadric pull her away.

TWENTY-FOUR

In the snow.

Silence (*alone, running*) Abomination! Stupid and naive!
I am so WRONG! He would have *killed* me . . . She is
the only one, the only one who doesn't judge me, the
only one who wants me to be free. My bride, my bride
who saves me with her kiss. YMMA! . . . I don't know
how long I ran. Towards morning, it began to snow.
I ran and ran, through the darkness, long into the
spinning light of day. I was flying. My mind soared,
snowlight swirled around me and dazzling iceflakes
melted on my tongue. (*slowing down*) At last I came to a
forest, white and silent in a shroud of snow. The air was
hushed and branches closed round me like a veil. And
then I realised . . . These were trees I knew, summer and
winter, familiar as the veins on my hands! This was my
forest! And there, looming out of the shade, its dark
shape outlined in frost, was Ragnarok, my home. Ymma,
wife of my heart. We're here!

Act Three
Cumbria

TWENTY-FIVE

Ragnarok.

Ethelred After thirty hours, the witch was nearly dead.
I had slept and watched, dreamt and listened in a daze
of fascination, as my men expertly broke her. To keep
myself amused, I began to tell her what she might expect
on the Day of Judgement. But she said: 'This, now, is
judgement. This is the winter and every winter is the
winter without end.' I questioned her as to what she
meant. It appears that in her theology, the end begins
when our mother, the sun, is torn out of the sky by a
ravenous wolf. The world freezes and we perish in
endless dark and cold. Every winter they fear it: an
apocalypse of ice. They only know they have escaped
it with the first warmth of spring. This wolf, this giant
evil, is the very spirit of chaos. I've been meditating on
his image; it is indeed powerful. So, as the wolf howls
with victory in the darkness, Odin and the hordes of
Valhalla meet him for the final battle on the frozen seas.
No one wins. All is destroyed, matter, spirit, evil, good,
everything, utterly lost. As the witch died, she told me
that the last act of Odin, with the jaws of the wolf
around his neck, is to fling fire over the world. 'It'll end
in flames,' she said. 'Everything will end in flames.' 'And
afterwards?' I asked, but she was dead. An eternity of
nothing, I suppose. The concept of salvation is too
refined for these barbarians.

*A light comes up on Silence. She is kneeling, her
hands tied behind her.*

What do you make of it, Lord Silence? There's not a lot of dignity in torture – but your witch impressed us all. I've hung her naked body from your walls, as a sign of our respect. Shall I do the same with you?

Silence It doesn't matter what you do. Surr isn't there on the walls and neither will I be if you kill me.

Ethelred You'll be burning in the fires of Hell.

Silence I don't believe in Hell.

Ethelred I must abandon you to an eternity of nothing, then.

Silence Odin's fire will melt the ice. And out of the water a new world will rise. The final flames become a new sun, who begins her journey across the sky. The end is the beginning. It continues world after world, life after life. The final destruction doesn't exist because life will defeat it in the end. That's what Surr was saying as she died. You are the wolf incarnate – but life will defeat you.

Ethelred The wolf incarnate. I like that.

Silence Life will tread upon your neck and the future will forget your name. I don't care what you do with me. This is my home. I know who I am here and I'm stronger than you. My curse on you, king. May the future laugh in your face.

Ethelred Let me show you the future, Lord Silence. Here it is, in my hand.

> *Ethelred brings down his fist on Silence's face. She collapses. Pause. He notices Eadric, who is kneeling before him. Ymma, Agnés and Roger have entered behind him. They stand in the shadows, staring at Silence.*

Eadric, what perfection! (*Hugs him.*) I knew you were close when I found this boy, skulking like a burglar at the gates. Here I am, like an eagle in my nest awaiting prey, and he delivers me himself!

Eadric We found villages; your work.

Ethelred Yes! I'm doing my own killing for the first time.

Eadric Our journey; you at the beginning and at the end.

Ethelred There's a symmetry in that. A kind of omnipotence, an alpha and omega.

Roger Sire, forgive me; I –

Ethelred Who's this?

Roger I am a – My name is Roger, Sire.

Ethelred Priest! You listened to my dream.

Roger Yes –

Ethelred It changed my life, that dream, put me on the path of truth.

Roger I am glad of it, but, Sire –

Ethelred God was speaking and you helped me hear him! I won't forget that, Priest.

Roger Let me ask you on my knees – Lord Silence – is he dead?

Ethelred Not yet.

Roger Sire, he's just a boy. / I plead for mercy, clemency and grace!

Ethelred Grace does not apply to heathens. He's a pagan, he's a traitor, he's venomous, he cursed me; I'd say he was kin to the Antichrist himself!

Ymma (*aside, to Agnés*) / What'll we do?

Agnés I don't know.

Ymma We have to get him out.

Agnés I can't do anything, can I?

Ymma Help me, Agnés, please, I beg you!

Agnés There's fifty men of Kent out there. How far d'you think you'll get?

Roger Please, your Majesty, if you murder this boy you will jeopardise your soul!

Ethelred Priest, it's not murder. When murder is justified it becomes something else.

Ymma (*drawing a sword*) Get away from him.

Ethelred (*noticing her*) YMMA!

Ymma Get back.

Ethelred What's *happened* to you?

Ymma Lord Silence is innocent of any wrong against you.

Ethelred You look AWFUL!

Ymma Let him go!

Ethelred Eadric, why is she dressed like this?

Eadric Not my fault.

Ethelred Priest, did you say nothing to her? You're supposed to be her spiritual guide!

Roger Well, it wasn't / my business. I –

Ethelred This is appalling! You look like a MAN! Something has to be done . . . (*to Agnés*) You, woman, where are her things?

Agnés We lost them on the journey, Sire.

Ethelred Well, that's no good!

Ymma Let him go!

Ethelred (*to Ymma*) I can't look at you dressed like that. I've come all the way up here pursuing your image and look what you've done!

Ymma I said release my husband!

Ethelred Get undressed!

Ymma What?

Ethelred (*to Agnés*) You, help her. Get that nightmare off! Eadric, take that thing from her, it's ridiculous! (*to Agnés*) You! MOVE! I'll avert my eyes until you resemble yourself.

Ymma Eadric, help me!

Eadric I am.

> *Eadric takes the sword. Agnés begins to undress Ymma.*

Agnés I'm sorry, my lady.

Ethelred (*to Eadric*) Eadric, take that boy away and kill him. I don't care how; just do it. Hang him, stab him, throw him from the tower, whatever. When the deed is done, come and tell me. I want you for my guard of honour, my best of men.

Roger Sire, the boy has never spoken treason or disloyalty –

Ethelred The boy is the past! You must look to the future, Priest. Your future may be very bright. I like you. You're insightful, compassionate; more truly a man of God than every bishop in this place.

Roger Sire, I have changed –

Ethelred I want you to marry me.

Roger Pardon?

Ethelred A union between us is God's will. I feel it in my heart and I know it with my soul. Our marriage will be sacred. I'm giving you the honour of conducting the service.

Roger Ah.

Ethelred Prepare for it, here, now! From now on, you are a bishop. (*to Eadric*) I gave you an order, Eadric; move!

Eadric picks up Silence. Ymma is in her shift.

Ymma (*desperate*) Silence is a girl!

Eadric stops.

Silence of Cumbria is a girl, a young girl of fourteen.

Ethelred *What?*

Ymma She is sinless. Until our wedding night she was ignorant of her sex, ignorant of everything. Please, you must let her go.

Agnés is aghast. She looks at Silence anew.

Roger I am more shocked than I can say. This is a grievous, fatal lie. And it is cruel!

Ymma Oh, Priest, think. It's the truth!

Ethelred Why are you trying to save him? I'm doing you a favour!

Roger That is Silence, Lord of Cumbria, my student, my friend, my brother. Do not rob him of his dignity at the moment of his dying!

Ethelred Eadric, take him away.

Ethelred stops Ymma from intervening as Eadric takes Silence away.

(*his arms tightly around her*) My love, in a few minutes we'll be wed. Priest, prepare an altar. Let us be joined, one flesh, one blood. Let me melt in your deep depths . . .

Agnés She cannot marry you, I'm sorry.

Ethelred Did you address me?

Agnés I beg your pardon, Sire, but she hasn't got a dress. You can't expect the daughter of a saint to marry a king in her shift. It's not dignified.

Ethelred She hasn't got a dress?

Agnés No. Forgive me, but you must delay the wedding until she finds one.

Ethelred A dress. You are right . . . she must have a dress.

Agnés And a veil. And footwear. And all the garments for underneath. It's only proper.

Ethelred Yes, even though we are all naked before God, my wife shall have a dress. It will be my first gift to her. Silk, fur, jewels; she shall have everything . . . . Priest, we shall marry at midnight and consummate our union in the new dawn. Be ready. I go on a quest for your garments.

Ethelred kisses Ymma's hand. He leaves.

Agnés She cannot marry you, I'm sorry.

Agnés Why didn't you tell me? Why didn't you trust me?

Roger Sorry?

Agnés Follow them. For God's sake, save her!

Comprehension dawns on Roger's face. He exits hurriedly after Silence and Eadric.

TWENTY-SIX

The tower.
Eadric is walking up flights of stone stairs with Silence in his arms. A high wind blows.

Silence When I awoke, I was in his arms. The afternoon had fled and everything was dark. Even the snow was invisible . . . Eadric?

Eadric I will not hurt you.

Silence Are you going to let me go?

Eadric No. But I will cause you no pain.

Silence You'll kill me without pain?

Eadric The rocks you fall on will cause the pain, not me.

Silence You're going to throw me from the tower?

Eadric Without touching you.

Silence How will you do that?

Eadric With my mind. (*He releases Silence.*) Stand up.

Silence You will never make me jump.

Eadric Go to the edge.

Silence I'll leap of my own accord and fly forever.

Eadric Tell me what is down there.

Silence Darkness.

Eadric Then prepare to meet it.

Roger appears. He is clutching Ymma's sword, afraid.

Silence I am full of colour. I love –

Roger Stand back, Eadric, or I will be forced to act!

Silence wavers. Roger tries to assist her.

Silence, child –

Silence NO!

Silence jumps.

Roger Silence! SILENCE, NO! God forgive me. God forgive me. Silence!

Roger exits.

Eadric Suicide.

He spits.

TWENTY-SEVEN

A bedchamber.
Agnés is dressing Ymma in an elaborate wedding gown.

Agnés As the hour of midnight approached, I was told to take her to a chamber and dress her in the clothes and jewels that the king had provided. It was unbearable. Ymma, there was nothing anyone could do.

Ymma (*pause*) Tighter. Make it hurt.

Agnés The only comfort I can offer is to say that for those who have faith, death is not –

Ymma Shut up. Don't you dare.

Agnés continues to dress Ymma. She is about to put on a necklace. She looks at it. Steals it.

Agnés (*pause*) Ymma, I'm going to leave you. I know this isn't a good time, but really, we've never been any good for one another and I have to go.

Ymma Pardon?

Agnés I'm sorry.

Ymma You're leaving me?

Agnés The priest and I are going to run away. We want to start a new life together.

Ymma The priest wants you for his wife?

Agnés Well he hasn't actually asked the question yet, but –

Ymma He won't marry you.

Agnés Why not?

Ymma How stupid are you, Agnés? He's going to be a bishop.

Agnés Yes, but –

Ymma The king is making him royal confessor – the most powerful cleric in the land. Do you think he'd throw all that away to go off into the dawn with you? Because what are you? What exactly are you, Agnés? A penniless maid with bedchamber skills.

Agnés Since I was ten years old, I've been living off crumbs from your life! No wonder I'm nothing! You've never cared –

Ymma Neither have you!

Agnés turns to go.

Agnés!

She grabs Agnés's hand. Neither speaks. Agnés pulls her hand away. She goes to the door.

Agnés You have it in you to rule this land. You know that, don't you? (*Pause.*) I'm sorry.

Agnés leaves. Ymma sits for a moment. She picks up a knife. She examines it. She walks into the centre of the space. She feels for her heart. She raises the knife. Eadric enters.

Eadric (*gently*) There is no need to do that, lady. I am here.

Ymma (*falters*) Eadric . . .

Pause. Eadric approaches her. He kneels.

Eadric I will do it. As you ask.

Ymma As I ask?

Eadric I hear you.

Ymma How? I've said nothing.

Eadric With your mind. The thought comes in like God-light. Help me.

Ymma I speak to you then, with my mind?

Eadric Yes.

Ymma I see . . . What am I saying now?

Eadric You're thanking me for killing Silence without pain. He fell from the tower, without pain.

Ymma (*pause. Swallows her grief*) Yes. I thank you.

Eadric You're thanking me also for this.

Ymma For what?

Eadric For what I am about to do. Treason. He will come in. And I will kill him.

Ymma I see. I thank you. And afterwards, when the treason is done; what then?

Eadric Then . . . you will open yourself, like an iris. And I will make sure you are sacred.

Ymma (*pause.*) Come to me, Eadric.

Eadric embraces Ymma's legs.

There . . .

She strokes him. She still has the knife. She raises it.

Eadric You're saying something else.

Ymma What? What else am I saying, my love?

Eadric Dog. You're calling me a dog.

Ymma Good dog . . .

Eadric (*standing, pulling her violently*) I AM NOT YOUR DOG!

Ymma stabs him with a scream. Eadric, wounded, won't let her go.

I am not . . . your dog!

Ymma Agnés, AGNÉS!

Eadric pulls Ymma on to the floor. He holds her as violently as he can, staring intently at her.

Eadric What am I?

Ymma screams.

BELOVED! Say it!

Ymma Brother . . . BROTHER!

Eadric Make her appear again.

Ymma What?

Eadric The shining lady. Make her appear . . .

Ymma There.

Ymma stabs him again. He slowly dies. Ymma is beneath him. She tries to move him. She can't.

Oh God . . . God help me!

Roger enters, dressed as a bishop in bright red robes.

Roger (*formally*) His Majesty the King.

Ethelred enters, sumptuously attired.

Ethelred Lady, the hour of midnight is almost upon us. I'm so emotional I can barely –

Roger Ymma! Sire! –

Ethelred Eadric, you BASTARD! What are you doing?

Roger and Ethelred run to Ymma's help. They lift Eadric away.

He's dead . . . My God, she's killed him. Ymma, why?

Ymma Take him away. Please.

Ethelred You, Bishop, get him out of here. Angel . . . what happened?

Roger Um. Forgive me, Sire. I'm not sure I can move him on my own.

Ethelred NOW!

Roger Of course, of course.

Roger drags Eadric away.

Ethelred Speak . . . what did he do?

Ymma He was going to hide in here and murder you.

Ethelred The son of a Kentish whore! He was my right hand! . . . Ymma, you saved me. You saved my life. Priest! She loves me and this proves it!

Roger (*off*) Marvellous, Sire.

Ethelred Oh my avenging angel, we shall be married at once.

Ymma I can't.

Ethelred Why not?

Ymma I'm a murderess. How can a murderess be a queen?

Ethelred My mother was a murderess and she was queen. Where is the problem?

Roger My lady is saying that she needs to confess. In order to be married, she must stand pure before God and as royal confessor, I must insist on hearing her sins.

Ethelred Yes . . . you are right. Bishop, she is yours. Inform me when she's redeemed and I'll return to make her my wife. (*He leaves.*)

Ymma Bless me, Father, for I have sinned.

Roger Lady –

Ymma I promised I would kill myself and I lied. I thought I wanted death, but I fought murder. I could have let him kill me, but I killed him! It means this: I would rather be alive than dead. I have chosen life without love, without freedom, with nothing to sustain me. Here is my sin: I have betrayed Silence and become life's whore.

Roger Lady, forgive me. I cannot take your confession. (*He takes off his mitre.*)

Ymma Why not?

Roger I'm no longer a priest. I have renounced the priesthood and all my vows. I am a man, this simple man you see before you. These clothes are but a costume from the king's canonical wardrobe. There is nothing sanctifying in them or in me. I feel like Adam, new created.

Ymma So, you are leaving me too?

Roger I am walking into Eden with my Eve . . . Agnés awaits me in the forest. I am hers. Oh lady, we have made miraculous plans.

Ymma Well, I'm glad. I'm truly glad . . .

Roger But we are worried at the thought of leaving you without a companion. Agnés has asked me to find someone to take her place. Not an easy task in these wild parts, but I met a young person by the walls this night, a person I think will suffice. She's a little rough, but in time you might teach her the ways of, well, womanish things.

Ymma Can she loosen a dress?

Roger I imagine that task would not be beyond her.

Ymma Then get her in.

Roger I shall leave you to prepare.

Ymma Priest –

Roger My name is Roger.

Ymma Thank you.

> *Roger shows Silence into the chamber. She is dressed in Agnés's clothes. He exits.*

Ymma (*without looking round*) Undo this, would you? It's so tight, it's making me sick. Nuns made it. Bitches.

Silence begins to undo the dress.

(*Ymma sighs.*) What's your name, girl? Speak up.

Silence I don't have one.

Ymma Then what shall I call you?

Silence makes no reply.

Silence.

She turns, she realises. They embrace.

Silence . . . Oh Silence, look at you. Please let me never wake.

Silence Ymma, it's amazing how quickly thoughts fly through your mind at the moment of your death. When I fell, my arms went out wide and for all the time it takes a mouse's heart to beat I gloried in my flying. I braced myself to hit the ground and finish – but my death was painless. There was simply nothing, nothing but cold. When I opened my eyes, I was lying in an underworld of ice. And then I heard the voice of the priest! He was trying to find me, begging God's forgiveness, really in a terrible state, wailing, crying . . . I was in snow! Feet and feet of snow! He picked me up, thanked his God for the miracle, and took me in to Agnés.

Ymma You strange creature. Strange, strange creature . . .

Silence We made a vow to be flesh and bone together. We should love and protect each other, don't you think?

Roger (*enters.*) His Majesty the King.

Ymma and Silence part. Ethelred enters. Silence begins to pin on Ymma's veil.

Ethelred My bishop says you are prepared. My love –

Ymma Your Majesty, dearly betrothed, kind king . . .
I have some small requests to make before we are wed.
May I beg your indulgence?

Ethelred You may beg anything.

Ymma When I am queen, I would like my own rooms.

Ethelred Your own rooms?

Ymma Where I receive you as a guest at my discretion.
This way, you'll never tire of me. I wish to sit in all
meetings of state, with my . . . companion, just to
observe the world of men. I want to learn how a nation
should be run.

Ethelred Bishop, why does she make these requests?

Roger She is a powerful woman, Sire, and they do come
with certain drawbacks. But these seem like small
enough requests. She saved your life, after all –

Ethelred Yes, Saviour, you shall have all you ask for.
Now take my hand and with it my life, my crown, my
England.

> *Ethelred and Ymma stand before Roger. Silence makes
> Ymma's veil fall around her. As Ymma marries
> Ethelred, she puts out a hand to Silence. Silence clasps
> it, tight.*

Roger And the Lord caused a deep sleep to fall on Adam
and he took one of his ribs and closed up the flesh
thereof. And the rib, which the Lord God had taken
from man, made he into a woman . . .

> *As the service continues, Agnés enters.*

Agnés After the wedding, we fled. We never saw either
of them again. Ymma remained consecrated queen for
sixteen years and I believe that hardly ever, during all

that time, was she parted from her companion, who was always silent in the company of the king but was often heard talking and laughing when alone with the queen. They seemed to speak a language no one else knew or understood. In the end, the king lost his throne to the Vikings and, when he died, Ymma married his Danish successor, Canute. She became one of the most powerful women of her age. The world didn't end.

Roger (*joins Agnés*) My theological ex-brothers are still convinced that Doomsday is looming. At any time an angel will open the bottomless pit and out of it will come pestilence, locusts and scorpions – and a great Beast who will wage war upon mankind! And the seas will boil and the streets will be littered with unburied dead and – forgive me; I have upset myself.

Agnés My husband is still troubled by apocalyptic dreams. I try to comfort him as best I can, but in my heart, I understand him.

She and Roger are gazing at one another.

They are the inevitable fears of our times, living as we do . . .

They move closer.

On the edge of destruction.

They kiss. Angelic music.

The End.

LOVEPLAY

For Martin

Loveplay was first performed by the Royal Shakespeare Company in the Pit Theatre, London, on 28 February 2001. The cast was as follows:

Herek/Trevelyn/Mr Quilley/Buttermere/Dieter
  Simon Coates
Marcus/Deric/Man/De Vere/Gwyn/Peter Ian Dunn
Woman/Matilda/Roxanne/Lynne/Brigitta
  Niamh Linehan
Eric/Llewellyn/Boy/Quinn Neil Warhurst
Dorcas/Hilda/Marianne/Miss Tilly/Joy/Anita
  Alison Newman
Gilda/Helen/Millie/Flynn/Rita Jody Watson

Directed by Anthony Clark
Designed by Rachel Blues
Lighting designed by Richard Beaton
Music by Conor Linehan
Fights by Malcolm Ranson
Sound by Steff Langley

Characters

Marcus, a Roman
Dorcas, a businesswoman

Herek, a Saxon
Eric, a Saxon
Deric, a Saxon
Woman

Gilda, a novice
Hilda, a nun
Matilda, the mother

Trevelyn, an actor
Llewellyn, a playwright
Helen, a malcontent

Roxanne, a scientist
Marianne, a servant
Man, an artisan

Miss Tilly, a governess
Mr Quilley, her employer
Millie, his wife

De Vere, an artist
Buttermere, a vicar

Joy, a prostitute
Boy, a virgin

Quinn, a revolutionary
Flynn, his girlfriend
Gwyn, an adventurer
Lynne, an adventurer

Brigitta, a single woman
Anita, a matchmaker
Rita, a secretary
Dieter, an alcoholic
Peter, a doctor

The play can be performed with as few as six actors.

Setting

*The action takes place on the same small square
of land, which moves through time from the past
to the present.*

The title of each scene should be shown.

Scene One

AD 79. *Open land. A half-built structure of wood and stone. Dorcas runs on. She lifts her skirts at someone following her, laughs and runs off. Marcus, a Roman soldier, enters in pursuit. He exits. We hear Dorcas shrieking and giggling. Marcus enters, pulling her by the arm.*

Marcus (*pulling Dorcas down*) Here. You. Now. This.

Dorcas Hang on; I got something in my back. (*She pushes something out from underneath her.*) What're you building here then? What's that?

Marcus Going to be latrines for the garrison.

Dorcas What's a latrine?

Marcus It's a structure of wood and stone, designed for us to shit in.

Dorcas You're building a building to shit in?

Marcus It's what we do. We have latrines.

Dorcas You can't shit in a building.

Marcus Why not?

Dorcas It's not natural. Why don't you shit in the woods like human beings?

Marcus Because we're civilised. Can we talk after?

Dorcas Don't have to talk at all if you like.

Marcus Great.

Dorcas Hang on. Isn't there something you're forgetting?

Marcus Oh yes, sorry. (*He gives her a coin.*) Here.

Dorcas (*looking at it blankly*) What's this?

Marcus A coin.

Dorcas What's a coin?

Marcus It's money. You can buy yourself something with it.

Dorcas (*uncomprehending*) What?

Marcus You can exchange this money for goods. Take it to market and buy something.

Dorcas I have to go all the way to market to get my payment?

Marcus No, that's your payment. You go to market to *spend* it.

Dorcas So all you're giving me is this?

Marcus (*trying to begin*) It's plenty; it's loads.

Dorcas (*stopping him*) It's usually a chicken.

Marcus Pardon?

Dorcas I usually get at least a chicken.

Marcus But that coin is worth more than a chicken.

Dorcas No it ain't.

Marcus In exchange for that coin you'd probably get a chicken, a bag of grain and some fruit. You might even get a piglet. Come on.

Dorcas I want a chicken.

Marcus I haven't got a chicken. I've got that. It's *money*.

Dorcas I don't wannit.

Dorcas drops the coin. She turns her face from Marcus. Pause.

Marcus Can I owe you a chicken?

Dorcas Do I look stupid?

Marcus Look, the coin means chicken. Take it to a vendor of chickens and he'll say: 'That is *currency*. I accept it. Here is a large chicken.'

Dorcas No one in their right mind would swap a chicken for that.

Marcus Not swap! It's *legal tender,* an entire system, the basis for the whole structure of civilised – Look, please . . . I've been on the road for weeks. I'm aching for this.

Dorcas Aching?

Marcus Yes.

Dorcas (*sympathetically*) Ahhh . . . (*She feels his cloak.*) Tell you what; this is nice. Isn't it soft?

Marcus My cloak?

Dorcas You can gimme that, if you like.

Marcus You can't have my cloak.

Dorcas Why not?

Marcus It's regulation issue. You only get one, and if you lose it you freeze. It's bloody cold here.

Dorcas It's a lovely colour.

Marcus Thanks.

Dorcas What d'you call that fabric then?

Marcus Wool.

Dorcas Wool? Really?

Marcus I think so.

Dorcas It's a fabulous weave. How did they get it like that?

Marcus I don't know. Look –

Dorcas Do you have different sheep down there in Rome or something?

Marcus You can't have it.

Dorcas Go on.

Marcus No! . . . Frankly, it's worth more than we agreed on.

Dorcas More than a chicken?

Marcus Yes.

Dorcas You're saying it's worth more than me.

Marcus I'm saying it would be foolish of me to give up my cloak for one shag.

Dorcas Two shags. One now and one later.

Marcus No!

Dorcas Right. (*shoving him off*) Off you get.

Marcus Look. You're lucky I'm offering to pay you at all. I could just take you.

Dorcas Oh, could you?

Marcus (*becoming violent*) Right now!

Dorcas Take me and I BITE! If you enter me without my will, the pain of it will make you think you dipped it in poison. You'll piss acid.

Marcus Are you a witch?

Dorcas Force me and I will make you shrink. You're shrivelling now; I can feel it . . . like a slug on salt.

Marcus (*getting up*) Right. Forget it.

Dorcas Oh, have I upset you? I'm so sorry. Come on, Roman, show us the might of your empire. You're very welcome if you just give me a chicken or your cloak.

Marcus spits on her. She laughs.

Scared you, have I?

Marcus We will crush you. You will fall under the foundations of our city like dust. When we've finished here, creatures like you won't exist! (*Marcus exits.*)

Dorcas Course we will. Creatures like me will always exist.

Dorcas picks up the coin. She examines it.

Money.

She throws the coin into the air and catches it.

Money for nothing.

Scene Two

THE DARK AGE

544. The space has become a clearing in a wood. The Roman latrines are in ruins. The grunts of a man having sex can be heard from within. Two grimy Saxons, Eric and Herek, are sitting in front, at a fire.

Eric What d'you reckon it was, that place?

Herek (*looking behind him*) Some sort o' temple, I s'pose. Can't see why they'd build anything else out of stone. It's got a shelf of wood. About that high. Big, round holes in it. An altar, I reckon. I threw her down on it but it was rotted. She went right through. Did it on the floor in the end.

Eric I don't like the idea of doing it in a temple.

Herek Why not? It's not a temple any more, is it? It's nothing now.

Eric What about their gods?

Herek Their gods are dead, aren't they? Dead, along with all o' them. That city we walked through back there; ruins tall as trees and not a sod in sight. A dead nation. Hundreds of years' worth of dead.

Eric What makes you think their gods are dead?

Herek Well, they must be. They're no longer worshipped.

Eric A god is immortal. The presence of a god endures, 'specially in a sacred place, even when his name is long forgot.

Herek Well . . .

Eric I'm not doing it in there.

Herek Why not?

Eric I might invoke a curse.

Herek Look, I done it in there and I'm fine.

Eric How do you know?

Herek Cause my dick hasn't fallen off.

Eric Yet.

Herek Look, if you don't wanna do it in the hut, do it in the woods.

Eric I'll do it here. By the light.

Herek Not in front of me you won't. Take her in the woods like a human being.

Eric I'll do it here.

Herek Why?

Eric I don't like the woods. A wood has spirits.

Herek Fuck's sake.

Eric Didn't you feel them as we brought her through? The same eyes that were watching us in that city were watching us in the wood.

The grunts are reaching a crescendo.

Herek It's always something with you, isn't it? Eyes, spirits, omens – always some fucking thing looking at you.

Eric The eyes of the dead.

Herek Oh, please.

Eric They don't like us.

Herek Eric –

Eric I've been on my guard against them all day long. I can feel them, here, in this place. They want to suck our lives out.

They pause uncomfortably while the man in the ruin comes to a climax.

Herek Eric, can I tell you something, for the sake of your own, you know, sanity?

Eric What?

Herek The dead are dead; finish. And this place is just a place.

Eric A place is never just a place. Everywhere you go, you have a crux – like a joining – of time, flesh, spirit – of *stuff*; past events, future portents all crowding in, visible only to the mind. It causes pressure.

Herek Well, if you don't like it here, maybe we should go. Let's just go.

Eric What about my release?

Herek What about it?

Eric I want it and I'm having it here, by the light. How can I have peace until I've had my release?

Herek You find peace in it, do you? In a rape, you find peace?

Eric Rape or not rape; makes no difference. Power, then peace . . . Why, what do you find?

Herek I don't look for anything. I just do it.

Deric (*entering from the hut*) All yours, mate.

Eric Bring her out here.

Deric What for?

Eric I want her out here.

Deric She's in there.

Herek He doesn't like the hut.

Deric What's wrong with it?

Eric Bring her out!

Deric Fuck's sake . . . (*He exits.*)

Herek You should calm down, Eric. All this shit about spirits and dead gods; it fucks you up. As if there's some great meaning to everything we're doing, as if some higher power cares. It's pathetic really, 'cause there is no higher power, there is nothing apart from this – what we do and what we see. That is the meaning. To exist here, now, and follow every desire we have. Like if I want to eat, I eat. If I want a shit, I have one. If I want to shag, I find something to shag and I shag it. That's it. As soon as something's happened, it's gone, dead, over – and as to things that haven't happened yet, as to the future, as to omens and portents and curses; well it's such a lot of shit I can't even bring myself to speak on the subject.

Eric You'll discover you're wrong when it's too late.

Deric enters with a Woman over his shoulder.

Deric Shall I dump her in the woods, then?

Eric Here.

Deric What, right here?

Eric By the light.

Deric You're not expecting us to watch, are you?

Eric You can do what you like.

Deric I'm not watching.

Eric Then go elsewhere.

Herek Oh, let him get on with it. It'll only take five seconds anyway.

Deric I don't believe it . . .

Deric dumps the Woman by Eric and stands as far apart as he can. Herek joins him. Eric prepares himself by praying.

You see, there's something about doing it which is fine, and something about watching some other bloke do it which is not fine – know what I mean?

Herek I know exactly what you mean.

Deric (*intimately*) Because it's not about watching or looking at all, is it? The whole thing. It's about . . . I mean, even having your eyes open is not a good idea. There was one point, when I had my eyes open, right, and this, between you and me – I mean strictly – is why it took me a while to finish. 'Cause I could see that she was looking at me. I could see her eyes in the dark like . . . like marsh lights shining out of her skull, you know? And her face in some kind of . . . contortion. And I thought, shall I hit her and blot it out? But I'd already hit her pretty hard, so I just thought no, I'll close my eyes. So I shut 'em and I thought of nothing, and then, at last, I found myself in that place which is the favourite place of all men since the world began.

Herek sniggers.

Deric Not that place! – I was already there! I'm talking about the, the *place* inside you that opens up – the . . . the mind. More than the mind . . . the, the spirit, the –

Herek Self.

Deric The being, yeh. Am I making sense?

Herek Yep.

Deric When I'm doing it, I am most myself –

Herek Right.

Deric I am most fully me –

Herek Yeh.

Deric In that place of closed eyes and darkness –

Herek Right.

Deric Of boundless freedom and limitless . . .

Herek Present.

Deric Yeh, the mysterious – I don't know –

Herek Moment of self.

Deric Timeless . . . Time disappears, don't it. And for that moment, you are everything, everywhere. You are Beyond.

Eric (*examining the Woman*) Deric, would you come here for a moment, please?

Deric What?

Eric Could you tell me what I'm supposed to do with this?

Deric and Herek approach Eric.

Eric Should I bury it, or burn it?

Deric What d'you mean? (*He lifts the Woman and lets her drop.*)

Eric It's dead.

Deric No, she just fainted, mate.

Eric Look at it.

Deric She ain't dead.

Eric It's nothing but a thing. Dead!

Deric She can't be dead.

Eric (*furious*) You careless fucking bastard! What about my release?

Deric Look, I only hit her. There's no way she's dead; she was looking at me!

Eric (*backing away*) There's no release in that, no power to be gained from it, nothing. I'm not touching it. It's gone.

Deric You mean, while I was – She was –

Eric The gods have taken her, not you! (*He turns towards the hut.*) I haven't set foot in it! I haven't defiled it! Whatever god you are, LEAVE ME BE! (*Eric runs off.*)

Deric What's he talking about? What god?

Herek He gives me the fucking jitters, that bloke. (*He gathers his things.*) Get your stuff. We're going.

Deric What god?

Herek He thinks that some great supernatural force actually cares about what we've done here. It's dogshit.

He follows Eric. Deric stares at the Woman. The darkness grows.

Deric You shouldn't have looked at me.

He goes. At last the Woman stirs. She slowly gets to her knees. She retches. She stands. She makes a sound of anguish – and rage. Theres is nothing weak about it. It is replaced by . . .

Scene Three

THE NEW MILLENNIUM

1099. Gilda, a novice, singing. Eerie, otherworldly, ecstatic. The space has become a house of prayer. Hilda, a nun, is kneeling over a covered corpse.

Hilda Goodbye my love, my love, my love, my love, goodbye.

Hilda kisses the dead nun's hand. Gilda ends her song. She and Matilda, the Mother Superior, join Hilda at the corpse.

Matilda When did it happen?

Hilda Half an hour ago.

Matilda God rest her soul.

Gilda Amen. I know I'm only new here but I've heard you say she was the best among us.

Matilda There was none more loving in her duty to the Lord.

Hilda I have a request, Mother.

Matilda Then speak.

Hilda May I lay her out alone?

Matilda It's not our way. This girl must learn how these things should be done. And special friendships, Sister; you know I can't approve.

Hilda reluctantly acquiesces. Matilda moves away. She kneels and prays in a low voice. Hilda and Gilda begin to wash and lay out the corpse.

315

Hilda You start down there. Wash her as if she were Christ.

Gilda begins to wash the corpse's feet. They work. Matilda continues to pray.

Gilda (*whispering to Hilda*) When she died . . . were there any signs?

Hilda Signs?

Gilda I mean what happened? Our sister was so saintly. She spent such a lot of time in prayer. Well, both of you, so often cloistered here in close communion with God. Your bold ideas about the loving Christ . . . I don't understand them, but they've put this abbey on the map. And when the bishops came she'd never see them. We thought that was great! They were always so insulted but they couldn't say a thing! She'd never see a man no matter who he was, when most of us would climb the orchard walls and graze our hands and knees to even get a peek at a retreating friar's back. She held herself above such things. And she showed us all great kindness and compassion.Her feet are big.

Hilda Keep your eyes off her flesh.

Gilda I was wondering how God received her. Was there a shimmering of incandescence? When St Bridget died, twenty-five eye witnesses saw her room shine with the light of divine splendour.

Hilda I didn't notice any light

Gilda Not even a momentary sunbeam? Perhaps her eyes were fixed on a vision of paradise reserved for her alone. Perhaps, as her soul took flight –

Hilda She rattled with death.

Gilda Oh dear.

Hilda Can we work in silence please?

They work on. Gilda is washing the corpse's thighs.
Silence but for Matilda's prayer.

Hilda Don't touch her there.

Gilda Where?

Suddenly Gilda involuntarily shrieks and reels from
the corpse.

Matilda What is it?

Gilda Sorry, Mother. There's a thing, a growth.

Matilda A what?

Gilda I felt a lump; a fleshy growth. (*She points.*) There,
on her secret place.

Matilda approaches the corpse. She lifts the sheet. She
is utterly stunned.

Matilda Novice, leave the room.

Gilda Is it a canker? Is that what killed her?

Matilda Say nothing of this.

Gilda Our dog had a canker / a big, hairy lump –

Matilda Do not ever speak of it!

Gilda Why not?

Matilda Get out I said, you stupid girl!

Gilda leaves. Matilda looks again. She is so shocked
she cannot speak.

You knew.

The shock sinks in.

You shared a cell. You shared everything . . . I trusted you. I believed in her. In him. How you must have pitied us.

Hilda continues to work.

We have lived side by side for fifteen years! Tell me Sister, before I throw you from this place, why would a man, a man who could do anything, a man who is free, why would a man choose such a life as this?

Hilda lifts the corpse's hand and holds it to her face.

Hilda Goodbye my love. My love, my love, goodbye.

Scene Four

THE RENAISSANCE

1584. A ruined abbey. Helen is joined by Trevelyn. He takes her hand. Hilda looks on.

Trevelyn
Angel.

Helen
  My love.

Trevelyn
    At last, tell me I may.

Helen
You may. You could before. Your noble strength
Alone has kept this woman's body frail
And slight, from that which always it desired.

Trevelyn kisses Helen's hand.

Why cease? These unpluck'd lips of mine
Are wasted in mere speech. You are my life
And soon as dawn ascends with light sublime,
I'll be your loving, ever faithful wife.

Trevelyn
But angel, wait –

Helen   Why wait?

Helen kisses Trevelyn full on the lips. Helen reaches for his body and pulls him towards her. He breaks away, shocked at her passion.

Trevelyn
    What is't you do?

Helen

What both of us desire.

Trevelyn

We can't, my love!
My dear betroth'd, my alabaster queen,
Forbear a few more hours. Our trusty priest
Arrives at dawn to join us; man and wife.
'Til then, inflame my loins no more –

Helen

'Tis love
Alone that urges me; now kiss!

Trevelyn

O bride
Of virgin snow, believe me when I say
There is a difference great as dark and day
Between a lover's lawless, wanton kiss
And one God-given, sweet in nuptial bliss.

Helen

My kiss tonight is different from the morn?
But why, when both are freely, gladly borne?

Trevelyn

The difference lies not in the kiss alone
But in what you bestow and what I own.

Helen

I do not understand.

Trevelyn

Once man and wife –

Helen

You do not wish to kiss me!

Trevelyn

'Pon my life

I do, with lips as red as wine, but darling
Only wait, 'til I am yours and you are mine.

Enter Llewellyn, a malcontent.

Llewellyn (*aside*)
I am a bastard. I have come
In black and ruinous mood, with festering mind
To see what chaos and corruption I can find.
Where I find none, in this sweet lovers' scene,
I'll make my own, with sulphurous, sickly spleen.
Llewellyn, jade of Fortune and her wheel,
Will smash their love, like glass beneath his heel.
For I, who watched this pockish mouse Trevelyn
Woo the beauteous, amorous Lady Helen,
Am so pent up with envy that to see them wed
Will send me green and frenzied to my bed.
So here, amid the ruins of this place,
Where brides of Christ once walked in lowly grace,
Here, where ne'er a violent act was done,
I've plotted rape and murder. I've begun –

Helen (*to Llewellyn*) Sorry, my love.

Llewellyn (*stopping, annoyed*) What?

Helen Forgive me but I'm not sure what we're supposed to be doing.

Llewellyn You're waiting for the priest.

Helen Yes. But while you're making your speech, what are we doing?

Llewellyn You're in a tableau of love.

Helen Oh. It's just that we're halfway through an argument, quite an important argument, and it seems a little strange that we should stop, that's all.

Llewellyn You stop because I make my entrance.

Helen Yes, but I'm asking my betrothed, the classics tutor I've given up everything for, why his perception of me will change after we're married – aren't I? Why he somehow finds it more desirable to kiss me as his wife than as his lover – and then we just stop, while you do your speech. Forgive me, but it doesn't make sense.

Llewellyn My speech is an 'aside'. I enter, I do an 'aside', and the action on stage stops.

Helen Yes, but –

Llewellyn It's called a convention. It makes perfect sense.

Helen But this kiss is never referred to again. And what does she think? Is she quite content that he doesn't want to kiss her? She's torn herself from her family and thrown away her wealth. She needs reassurance – and he won't kiss her!

Llewellyn Well?

Helen I think it might make her worry.

Llewellyn Worry what?

Helen That he's not the man she thought.

Llewellyn is shocked.

Trevelyn Look, to tell you the truth, my friend, I don't think it makes sense either.

Llewellyn Excellent.

Trevelyn You see, my problem is, why is he saying it in the first place? You've got to admit it's rather insipid. I mean here they are, two lovers, alone in the moonlit ruins of an ancient abbey – and any average, hot-blooded fellow would just . . . kiss her.

Llewellyn Yes, but he's nobler than that. We have to get the contrast between him and the villain. He wants to kiss her, more than anything – but he restrains himself.

Trevelyn Why?

Llewellyn Because his intentions are impeccable. He's seeking to ennoble their love by the example of his virtue. By not kissing her, we can see that he's worthy of her, that he's upright, pure in heart!

Trevelyn I don't think the audience will get that. He just comes over as a sissy milksop. And, er – that's not what I play.

Llewellyn Fine.

Trevelyn I play the hero. I'm an expert in heroes; I've been playing them since my voice broke and I can tell you my friend, the hero would kiss her.

Llewellyn Well. You'd better kiss her then. (*He turns away.*)

Helen My dearest love . . . nobody meant to offend you. We were just saying –

Llewellyn No, no, no, you're right. It doesn't make sense. Erase it.

Trevelyn What?

Llewellyn Erase the whole scene. Forget it existed.

Helen We're not saying –

Llewellyn Yes you are! It doesn't work and that's fine. It's what we've come here to find out; to play the scene in its real environment – a ruined abbey by moonlight – to see if it works. It clearly doesn't. So. Scrub out the lines from where Lady Helen says 'I'll be your loving, ever faithful wife' all the way down to my entrance.

Helen So . . . what are we doing when you come in, my love?

Llewellyn You're kissing him.

Helen Right.

Llewellyn Like you wanted to.

Helen (*pause*) What do you mean by that?

Llewellyn I mean I can sense the general feeling. And there's no point opposing the general *feeling*, is there? They're only lines, after all. When I wrote them I thought they had some power and beauty, some universal truth, but now I see I was wrong.

Helen You asked us to say what we thought.

Llewellyn Throw them away! They're ephemeral. (*bitterly*) Like love. (*He goes to the entrance and turns.*) Right. From the start. (*to Trevelyn*) This time, when I enter, you're giving her a big, hot-blooded, manly kiss.

Llewellyn exits. Helen and Trevelyn arrange themselves for the opening of the scene.

Trevelyn Well, sorry, but if it doesn't work, it doesn't work.

Helen We've hurt him.

Trevelyn He shouldn't be so sensitive. Like he says, they're only lines – and between you and me, they're not very good.

Helen It's autobiographical.

Trevelyn What?

Helen This scene. It's about us. He was my tutor in classics and philosophy. He told me about his struggles to be a poet and his plight opened my heart. He said

I was his only muse. He used to write sonnets and push them into my hand as I conjugated verbs. It was so *forbidden* . . . I thought he had a perfect understanding of love but –

Trevelyn (*amazed*) Helen.

Helen – the night before I married him, when we ran away from my father's, we got lost on the road. I wanted to kiss him, well, more than kiss him, and he pushed me away, literally held me at arm's length.

Trevelyn How could he?

Helen He was being noble. I think.

Trevelyn My God . . . I've just called him a sissy.

Llewellyn (*off*) What are we waiting for?

Trevelyn Yes. (*Shouts.*) Just seen another problem, my friend!

Llewellyn (*enters, frustrated*) What?

Trevelyn Well, your lovely wife is rehearsing the part because you wanted everything to be real, which is a marvellous idea, really innovative – but when we return to the theatre, she'll be back in the purgatory of wardrobe and I'll have to kiss a little, adolescent boy. With onion breath, probably. Right the way through your speech.

Llewellyn Well?

Trevelyn I don't like the idea.

Llewellyn (*with controlled impatience*) Are you an actor?

Trevelyn Yes, I am an actor.

Llewellyn Then act.

He exits. Trevelyn smarts under the insult. He takes Helen's hand.

Trevelyn You sacrificed wealth and family for him?

Helen (*with great sadness*) I would have sacrificed anything.

Trevelyn
　Angel.

Helen
　　　My love.

Trevelyn
　　　　　At last, tell me I may.

Helen
　You may. You could before. Your noble strength
　Alone has kept this woman's body frail
　And slight, from that which always it desired.

Trevelyn kisses her hand.

　Why cease? These unpluck'd lips of mine
　Are wasted in mere speech. You are my life
　And soon as dawn ascends with light sublime,
　I'll be your loving, ever faithful –

*They kiss. It's overpowering. The passion of it takes
them both aback. It continues while:*

Llewellyn (*enters, aside*)
　I am a bastard. I have come
　In black and ruinous mood, with festering mind
　To see what chaos and corruption I can find.
　Where I find none, in this sweet lovers' scene –

*His glance falls upon Helen and Trevelyn. He falters.
Helen and Trevelyn continue to kiss for just a moment
too long. They part.*

Trevelyn Is something wrong? We were acting. Like you said. You said act, and we acted.

Llewellyn It's a strange place, this ruin, don't you think? Built by ancient hands and stuffed with the plunder of ages. And now, five hundred years of holy history, gone. Generations of clasped hands, rustling sackcloth, mumbled prayers – dust. When it was built they must have thought it a permanent monument to God. But it proves to be ephemeral as a whore's love.

Helen What's the matter, husband?

Llewellyn Nothing. The scales fall and the blind man sees. It's all as clear as day.

Helen What is?

Llewellyn The death of love.

Helen Pardon?

Llewellyn I said, *The Death of Love*, the title of my play. Helen . . . you are a whore.

Trevelyn You can't call her that!

Llewellyn Keep out of this, you dog!

Trevelyn How dare you!

Llewellyn You great, lumpen, talentless, deceitful bastard!

Trevelyn Take that back; I am not talentless!

Llewellyn (*drawing his dagger*) This is how I'll take it back.

Trevelyn (*scrambling to his feet*) Ah ha! I see we're leaping forward to the dreary denouement, where the two-dimensional malcontent makes a hackneyed attempt on the life of the hero and is foiled by the hero's vastly superior strength!

Llewellyn Do you want her?

327

Trevelyn Pardon?

Llewellyn Do you want my wife?

Trevelyn What?

Llewellyn Take her! Let her destroy your peace. Let her be your millstone. I'll have her as mine no longer! (*He turns away.*)

Trevelyn (*pause*) Look, I only kissed her. It was one kiss – scripted by your own hand!

Helen . . . Was there nothing else there?

Trevelyn Helen, there's always something there but it's – well, I get carried away. It's difficult, you know, when you're feeling the moment, not to . . . give it your all, especially when it's a real lady. But I kiss all the time. It's part of my job! . . . It's why I hate the adolescents. They make me feel strange.

Helen (*to herself*) What's to be done? What can I do? . . . My marriage is over. I've kissed an idiot and everything has gone. (*to Llewellyn*) God help me! You don't even see the injustice! You don't see how you have driven me –

Llewellyn Driven you?

Helen *Driven!*

Llewellyn You threw yourself at him!

Helen I was reeling from the shock of someone who kissed me as if I was *real*! To you, I've always been a forbidden delight, a virginal alabaster thing – and now I'm a whore! There's nothing in the middle, is there? No place for a real woman at all! You're a wordsmith; you make words – Tell me, what's he? What is a man-whore?

Trevelyn Pardon?

Helen And you, what can I call you that would damage you as much?

Llewellyn Helen.

Helen Drooping, sissy, milksop sap! . . .

Llewellyn Helen!

Helen Impotent bastard prig!

Llewellyn This is demented!

Helen (*calmer*) No. You are an anti-lover.

Llewellyn A what?

Helen An anti-lover. I am married to an anti-lover. Someone who has no conception of love.

Llewellyn I'm an expert on love, Helen; I write about it all the time.

Helen But you don't know how to feel it. I've been married to you for a whole year and all that time I've never felt your love.

Llewellyn Then what is it? Relieve my ignorance and tell me: what is love?

Helen How am I to know, when all I've experienced is disappointment? . . . It's in a face across a table. It's as earthly as eating a meal. It's as common as laughter, and rare as a phoenix egg. It's both transcendent and mundane – and as hard to bind and hold as a moving second of time.

Trevelyn (*to Llewellyn*) Oh that's very good; you should use that.

Llewellyn I thought you formed of the finest stuff. I thought your very breath was made of heaven.

329

Trevelyn Now, why don't I wait in the cart while you two kiss and make up?

Helen Give me the knife.

Llewellyn (*handing it to her*) Are you contemplating suicide, dear wife?

Helen No. Murder.

She stabs him. He gasps. He begins to die. Before Trevelyn can react, she stabs him too. He shrieks, clutching himself. Then both men sheepishly realise they are not wounded. Helen shows them the workings of the theatrical knife.

Helen It's a pretence. (*to Trevelyn*) Like you. (*to Llewellyn*) And you. (*She stabs herself.*) The death of love.

Scene Five

THE ENLIGHTENMENT

1735. The space has become a town house. Roxanne, a lady, is reading a newspaper. Marianne, a servant, enters.

Roxanne (*without looking up*) Yes?

Marianne The man is here, my lady.

Roxanne lets the newspaper fall to the floor. She takes off her spectacles.

Marianne Would you like me to show him in?

Roxanne He's early. I said not until noon had struck.

Marianne That's what I told him. (*with a slight smirk*) He must be eager, my lady.

Roxanne Are the servants gone?

Marianne Yes, my lady.

Roxanne And my father is asleep?

Marianne Yes, my lady.

Roxanne I want you to sit outside his door. If he so much as stirs, come down immediately.

Marianne He won't stir. I gave him the draught with his breakfast. My lady, (shall I fetch the man in . . .)

There is the faintest echo: a sound of anguish.

Roxanne Shhh. (*She listens.*) That noise.

Marianne I can't hear –

Roxanne There! Listen . . .

The sound fades.

Marianne I'm sorry, I couldn't –

Roxanne It's gone.

Marianne Have you heard it before, my lady?

Roxanne Yes. The more I strain my ears, the less I catch of it; it's strange . . . Well. Send him in.

Marianne makes to go. She turns.

Marianne Do you think the place might be haunted, my lady?

Roxanne Ghosts are relics of an age of ignorance, Marianne.

Marianne Only, there's a feeling downstairs that . . .

Roxanne That what?

Marianne That it might be.

Roxanne How can it be haunted? It's brand new!

Marianne Yes / but –

Roxanne We're the first family here!

Marianne But sometimes it goes cold / for no reason and –

Roxanne I want to see the man!

Marianne Yes, my lady. (*Marianne goes to pick up the newspaper.*)

Roxanne Leave it. It's for him.

Marianne makes to leave.

Marianne. Thank you for your help in this matter.

Marianne (*with a slight smirk*) It's a pleasure, my lady.

Roxanne If anyone should hear of it, I shall throw you from this house and drag your name through the mud for as long as I draw breath. Do you understand?

Marianne Yes, my lady.

She exits. Roxanne surveys the room.

Roxanne I know what you are . . . And one day I shall find out how to reach you.

Marianne enters.

Marianne The gentleman, my lady.

Marianne shows a Man into the room. He is an artisan, plainly dressed. She leaves. Roxanne locks the door.

Roxanne (*pause*) Good afternoon.

Man Yes, ma'am.

Roxanne Would you stand over there please? On the paper.

The Man walks over to the newspaper. He decides not to stand on it. He looks at Roxanne. She decides not to pursue the matter.

What's your name?

Man Daniel Smith.

Roxanne Do you know who I am, Daniel Smith?

Man I have been told you are a lady who will pay.

Roxanne Have you been told what I want?

Man Yes.

Roxanne Are you prepared to do it?

Man Yes.

Roxanne Then do it.

The Man slowly undresses, casting his clothes on the floor. He gets down to his breeches.

Stop.

The Man stops. Roxanne walks around him. She stands in front of him.

Would you raise your arms above your head, please?

The Man does so. Roxanne puts on her spectacles, studies his under-arm hair, then takes them off again.

I thought so. (*Pause.*) Continue.

The Man continues to undress. At last, he is naked. He looks at Roxanne.

There's no need for you to look at me.

The Man slowly averts his eyes.

God's own image. The mystery, revealed.

She giggles. The Man looks at her.

Do you object to me laughing?

Man You can do what you like.

Roxanne I have never seen a naked man. I'm thirty-three years old, and I've never seen a naked man.

Man The sight is funny then?

Roxanne giggles.

I have never found the sight of a naked woman funny.

Roxanne Don't be offended, please. Laughter doesn't always signify mirth.

The Man looks away. Pause.

I've seen you working across the street. I stand at the window and . . . I see you working, from time to time.

Man I've been here since the building started. I worked on this house too.

Roxanne Did you?

Man There was a ruin here, before.

Roxanne A ruin of what?

Man Dunno. Some kind of a church.

Roxanne A church?

Man Or a prison, something like that. Thick walls; old style. The bricks are part of your foundations.

Roxanne It's strange to think that ten years ago there were fields all around, and now streets, streets and fine houses, as far as you can see. They say there is work here, for generations.

Man Yes.

Roxanne Building a city for the future.

Man Yes.

> *Roxanne puts out a hand to touch him. She removes it. She moves away.*

Roxanne Have you any learning, Daniel?

Man No.

Roxanne I have . . . nothing else but. (*She smiles.*) I am currently acquainting myself with scientific fact, with the mechanical workings of the world, with the mathematics of the spheres, the chemistry of the elements and the dimensions of space. One of the dimensions of space is time. Were you aware of that?

Man No, lady.

Roxanne It is the element of change. Do you ever wish you could change time?

Man I do not know.

Roxanne You never feel that time is an ungovernable tyranny over which we have no control?

Man I'm not sure.

Roxanne It ploughs onwards in an invincible line from past to future and our whole lives, from mewling to infirmity, are mere breaths upon its way. I'd say that was tyrannous. Would you not agree?

Man I have never thought about it.

Roxanne But if you were to think about it, what would you think? Would you come to question time, as I have, to question the justice of its nature? Would you perhaps come to think, as I do, that in a world of such change, time cannot be unchangeable?

Man I do not know.

Roxanne Supposing that time was not a line, but a sphere in which we could envisage a flow in both directions? Supposing it were possible to empirically investigate the structure of time and . . . and to change it?

Man To change time?

Roxanne Yes. We perceive time as a series of apparently indivisible moments, but supposing one could divide each moment and move between them? One would find oneself in a plenitude of ages, different worlds of endless possibility, a landscape of time that was nebulous and not definite, so that one was not confined to a particular

336

age or sphere or set of circumstances so that . . . that one, in a way, could be free?

Man (*pause*) God makes us free, lady.

Roxanne realises he has not understood.

The next world is timeless, they say.

Roxanne I'm sorry . . .

Man A heavenly paradise without time. Is that what you mean?

Roxanne Yes. (*She smiles, hurt.*) That's it exactly.

Pause.

Are you cold?

Man Not very.

Roxanne You're very clean.

Man I washed.

Roxanne I didn't ask you here to listen to me speak.

Man No.

Roxanne Would you turn your back to me?

The Man turns his back. Roxanne slowly approaches him.

I wish . . . to touch you.

Man All right.

Roxanne touches the Man's back. She closes her eyes and turns her face away. Her hand moves over his skin, eventually coming to rest. She removes it.

Roxanne I want to do something.

337

Man You may do what you like.

Roxanne embraces the back of the Man. She holds him closely, resting her head on him. It moves her. She is crying, silently. At last, she releases him. She stands apart, trying to compose herself. The Man turns round. He sees the consternation on Roxanne's face. She still has her eyes shut. He gently tries to kiss her.

Roxanne (*recoiling in shock*) Who told you to do that?

Man You are upset –

Roxanne Who said you could?

Man No one.

Roxanne Turn your back!

The Man turns from Roxanne. Roxanne recovers herself.

Dress.

Man Lady –

Roxanne I said dress. I've seen enough.

Man (*beginning to dress*) Forgive me. I thought / you wanted –

Roxanne It's not your place to think; you have no learning.

Man I thought you wanted love.

Roxanne Love? (*laughing*) Love? Is this what you call love?

Man Then what?

Roxanne To empirically investigate the nature of man.

Man And have you?

Roxanne Dress.

Man (*pause*) Are you afraid, lady? Is that why you cry?

Roxanne I said *dress*!

The Man puts on his shirt. He approaches Roxanne.

Man You think us different. But if you were naked too, we would be the same.

Roxanne We would not.

Man Our clothes make us different, that's all. But in the simple way of things we are the same.

Roxanne There is no simple way of things! If there was a simple way of anything, do you think I'd be here? With you? And how can we ever, ever be the same?

Man We are the same before God.

Roxanne God is not present here! God has not been witness to anything that's passed between us.

Man Nothing has passed between us, lady.

Roxanne throws a purse of money. It lands at the Man's feet.

Roxanne It has now.

Scene Six

1823. The attic of the town house. Miss Tilly, a governess, and Mr Quilley, her employer, are having sexual intercourse.

Miss Tilly And so he struggles as hard as he can against the effects of the drug, but it has rendered him dumb and too weak to fight. Then the governess, with almost preternatural strength, drags him upstairs to the attic, where she proceeds to tie him in chains.

Mr Quilley Yes –

Miss Tilly She leaves him lying on a bed of straw with a bowl of rank water, cruelly placed too far away for him to reach.

Mr Quilley Oh –

Miss Tilly Too late has he come to see that there is evil in her heart –

Mr Quilley Oh yes –

Miss Tilly – evil that will wreak havoc with all that he holds dear. That night, when he finally recovers the strength to cry out –

Mr Quilley Yes –

Miss Tilly – the governess springs up the stairs, her tresses loose, her nightgown shimmering in candlelight –

Mr Quilley Uh –

Miss Tilly She slaps him –

Mr Quilley Oh –

Miss Tilly And stuffs a gag in his mouth.

Mr Quilley Ah –

Miss Tilly She kicks him brutally –

Mr Quilley AH!

Miss Tilly – and burns his facial hair with her candle.

Mr Quilley reaches a climax.

'You fool,' says the governess with an icy smile, 'I've told your wife you're dead, consumed by a disease so contagious that even to view your corpse would render her in danger. She leaves for Derbyshire at dawn, never to return, for I have bribed the coachman to see that calamity befalls her.'

Mr Quilley Miss Tilley?

Miss Tilly 'I am to stay here alone, chief beneficiary of your last will and testament.'

Mr Quilley I am done.

Miss Tilly 'You shall be locked in this attic for ever, chained and beaten like a beast until slowly, the terror and the isolation send you howling mad.' And then she laughs. Like this. (*She laughs.*)

Mr Quilley (*extricating himself*) Well, that's a jolly good story . . .

Miss Tilly Yes. It's one of several that I'm working on. There's a tremendous market for them.

Mr Quilley I'm sure.

Miss Tilly I know I have a talent, Mr Quilley, but I have no contacts in the publishing world. I wonder if I could impose upon you a small request? I know you have friends –

Mr Quilley Well, not really friends –

Miss Tilly Acquaintances, colleagues –

Mr Quilley Not really in the publishing world –

Miss Tilly Mr Quilley, please would you help me with my book?

Mr Quilley My dear, as your employer, the best help I can give you is to listen to your stories.

Millie enters, heavily pregnant. Miss Tilley turns away.

Millie Oh, here you are . . .

Mr Quilley Darling, you shouldn't come up the stairs. It's far too dangerous!

Millie I missed you. And I half wondered if we had a ghost. I thought I heard strange laughing.

Mr Quilley Ah, that was Miss Tilly.

Miss Tilly Mr Quilley was telling me a most amusing story.

Mr Quilley Yes, I was helping Miss Tilley to put away some old toys and I was relating to her how little Billy ruined my jacket by vomiting all over it, just as I was due to give my first speech in the House.

Millie Oh yes, poor fellow . . . He had colic. (*Pause.*) The children are asking for you, Miss Tilly.

Miss Tilly (*making to leave*) Thank you for helping me with the toys, sir.

Miss Tilly exits.

Mr Quilley I'm very cross with you for coming up here. What if you'd fallen?

Millie Oh my love, you'd always be there to catch me, if I fell.

Millie embraces him. She is radiant.

Mr Quilley Millie . . .

Millie Do you know, I was sitting downstairs thinking of every way in which my life is blessed and I was suddenly overcome with a feeling so strong that I had to find you and share it. It's happiness, my darling. I'm so happy.

Mr Quilley Millie, you sweet thing . . .

Millie Here I am in my beautiful home, with the best of all men. I'm so, so happy . . . it makes me want to cry.

Mr Quilley holds her closer, guiltlessly cherishing her. They continue to embrace while De Vere enters and the space becomes . . .

Scene Seven

1898. A shabby, bohemian studio. De Vere, a gentleman, is gazing at an unpainted canvas, which stands on an easel. Evening.

De Vere (*examining the easel*) Yes . . . Like a darkness, shining in the light.

> *There is a knock at his door. He answers it. Buttermere, a vicar, is on the threshold.*

Buttermere! I was beginning to give up hope.

Buttermere I've had the most awful trouble finding you.

De Vere Not a part of town one often comes to, I know.

Buttermere I wasn't sure I'd got the right address. It's awfully rough out there, De Vere. All sorts of unrepeatable things said to me as I passed.

De Vere Consign them to oblivion, my friend, and have a drink.

Buttermere I think I need one. I have just heard the word for a man's organ come from the mouth of a woman.

De Vere (*amused*) Goodness . . . (*Hands Buttermere a drink.*) Well, here's to you. Your good health.

Buttermere And yours. It's wonderful to see you again.

De Vere Yes.

Buttermere After all this time.

De Vere Wonderful.

Buttermere You haven't changed at all, you know.

De Vere Oh, I have. Deeply. Nothing changes a man like travel.

Buttermere Well –

De Vere I've seen dawn over a thousand different horizons, from Cairo to the Southern Cape. How can one eat lotus by the banks of the Nile and not return a different man?

Buttermere I don't know . . . (*Pause.*) Well, interesting sort of place you've got.

De Vere My studio. It's in a dreadful state; the roof leaks, the area's a slum, but I like it. Sometimes I work here until late and the idea of going home is more than I can bear. So I have everything I need, right here. This is my empire, Buttermere, and in it I lay out the canvas of humanity.

Buttermere Gosh.

De Vere I returned home when I discovered that a man with an easel needs only his imagination to travel. He can be both hermit and explorer in one small room.

Buttermere Well, yes . . .

De Vere Days have gone by when I have been so lost in the forgetfulness of the creative mind that the outside world ceases to have any meaning and I exist only in the reality of art.

Buttermere I can't tell you how thrilled I was to hear you'd become a painter. I knew you'd do something brilliant with your life. Even at school you were . . . well, you shone. I always thought so, anyway. I was hoping you'd show me some of your work.

De Vere I'd love to. But the light's terrible. At this late hour you wouldn't get a proper impression.

Buttermere I'm sure I would.

De Vere Besides, I fear you might find my art a little shocking.

Buttermere Why?

De Vere I paint ladies of the night.

Buttermere Oh! I thought you painted scenes from antiquity.

De Vere I do. But my sitters are ladies of the night.

Buttermere Well, I – Gracious. What are they like?

De Vere Much the same as ladies of the day, only they don't mind sharing their secrets. In fact, for a coin or two, they'll share anything. (*He smiles.*) I'd forgotten that expression. Do you know, sometimes I used to bait you, just so you'd gaze at me like that.

Buttermere lowers his gaze.

I knew you'd join the church.

Buttermere I almost didn't.

De Vere I knew you would.

Buttermere Well. It seemed . . . the best thing. And frankly, I don't know what else I would have done. I was never bright, like you.

De Vere Was it the right choice? Are you happy?

Buttermere Oh yes. Of course I am. Why are you looking at me in that way?

De Vere In what way?

Buttermere In that infernal way. As if you want me to tell you I'm miserable.

De Vere Are you miserable?

Buttermere No. I have a thriving parish and a lovely wife . . .

De Vere You're married?

Buttermere Yes, yes, of course. Aren't you?

De Vere No.

Buttermere Oh, you ought to marry, you know.

De Vere Why?

Buttermere Well . . . it's what a man does. A wife makes a man complete.

De Vere Am I incomplete?

Buttermere No, but De Vere, if you were to, to meet the right girl and settle down, then . . . I suppose what I'm thinking is . . . that our wives could be friends.

De Vere You want me to marry so that our wives could be friends?

Buttermere Lavinia could do with a friend – I mean a friend like you've always been to me.

De Vere Are you not Lavinia's friend?

Buttermere Well, yes, but she doesn't talk to me, you know? In fact, she rarely talks at all. She has the curtains closed most of the time and she just –

De Vere Just what?

Buttermere Oh, you don't want to hear all this.

De Vere Of course I do. You used to tell me everything.

Buttermere Well, Lavinia is just a little quiet, that's all.

De Vere A little quiet?

Buttermere But she takes tincture of opium for her health and they say it can be quite a dampener on the spirits. She's very sensitive.

De Vere Poor Lavinia.

Buttermere And she's –

De Vere She's what?

Buttermere (*pause*) I haven't seen you for the best part of ten years. I'm with you less than five minutes and I find myself telling you things I wouldn't tell anyone.

De Vere You haven't told me anything. My friend, why don't we have another drink?

Buttermere I shouldn't have had that one.

De Vere Let me fill your glass. (*De Vere takes Buttermere's glass and fills it.*) This is the water of Lethe, which flows like a ribbon of light through the land of the dark. Those who drink it shall forget all pain and be reborn. Such is the power of liquor; it makes innocents of us all. (*handing Buttermere his glass*) To our friendship.

Buttermere Yes. To us.

They drink a toast.

De Vere There is a reason I asked you to meet me here and not at the club. It's your face.

Buttermere My face?

De Vere I've got into the habit of searching people's faces. It's what one does as an artist. When I ran into you, after all this time, your face – the light you had in your eyes, the openness of your expression – it inspired me. I want to paint you.

Buttermere To *paint* me?

De Vere I'd be honoured if you'd let me.

Buttermere (*bashfully*) Well . . . I'm profoundly moved. You really think I'm worth a portrait?

De Vere I most certainly do. You have singular qualities, my friend.

Buttermere I wouldn't have thought vicars were a very inspiring subject.

De Vere I don't wish to paint you as a vicar.

Buttermere Oh?

De Vere This isn't an ordinary portrait. I don't wish to paint you as you, at all.

Buttermere Am I to be a figure from antiquity?

De Vere In a way. Don't get me wrong here, old friend. I want to paint you as Satan.

Buttermere *What?*

De Vere Or should I say Lucifer. Lucifer, before he fell.

Buttermere That's not funny, De Vere.

De Vere I don't intend it to be. When I saw you, an image leapt into my mind, so suddenly. I thought, 'The Son of the Morning, First Archangel of the Heavenly Host, Lucifer, Prince of this World!' I saw you like a dazzling darkness shining in the light. (*Pause.*) Does the idea appeal?

Buttermere Look at me. How is it possible that I make you think of Lucifer?

De Vere Before he fell. My dear fellow, you're as beautiful as an angel.

Buttermere Don't be ridiculous –

De Vere And there's something in you, stirring in the heart of you, that wishes to rebel, to throw in God and all of his works –

Buttermere What?

De Vere Something that desires freedom. I can see it in your face.

Buttermere Nonsense.

De Vere Put down your drink.

Buttermere Why should I?

De Vere I want you to take your clothes off.

Buttermere What for?

De Vere I want you in a pose of innocence, as if receiving benediction from your maker.

Buttermere Absolutely not!

De Vere And at the moment of blessing, you realise a basic truth: your maker didn't make you at all. You are as fundamental a part of the universe as he is. You are the father of desire and one cannot have life without desire.

Buttermere You can't ask me to blaspheme!

De Vere I want to capture the moment when you realise the nature of the thing that you are; when you understand your potential. I want to paint your first free thought. It's not blasphemous, it's profound. (*Pause.*) The title is *The Birth of Love*.

Buttermere The birth of evil –

De Vere The birth of love – because love is nobler than worship, love cannot be kept in ignorant submission; love is only holy when it's free. Real love requires knowledge and free will. Lucifer gave us both. And if those things represent evil to you then I really don't know what to say.

Buttermere (*pause*) You know, if anyone looks like Satan here, it's you.

De Vere I'm sure my life is in my face, just as yours is. If you let me paint you, I shall tell you. Let me paint you and I shall tell you my whole journey down the primrose path. Then afterwards, if you wish to, you can save my soul.

Buttermere (*pause*) Get me another drink . . .

De Vere We shall paint the truth. It will be you and I together!

Buttermere Get me a drink.

De Vere pours Buttermere a drink. He downs it in one. He takes off his jacket.

You could always make me do anything for you.

De Vere I have never made you do anything that you didn't want to do.

Buttermere begins to take his collar off. De Vere helps. He throws it on the floor.

Buttermere My shackles. That's what you think, isn't it? You think I'm in shackles.

De Vere slides his arms around Buttermere and holds him, with compassion.

I hate my life, De Vere. What am I to do?

De Vere I don't know.

They are still.

Buttermere turns and embraces De Vere. They hold each other tightly. They kiss.

Buttermere walks to a position by the canvas. He takes off his shirt.

Buttermere You wish to capture . . . (*He lets the shirt fall to the ground.*) . . . my first free thought.

Scene Eight

1932. A dingy bedsit. A Boy is standing in his underwear. Joy, a prostitute, lies barely clad on a bed. The Boy looks devastated. He picks up his shirt from the floor – the position where Buttermere dropped his. He begins to dress. Joy watches. As the Boy does up his shirt, he goes to the window. He looks out. Pause.

Joy What's it like out there?

Boy Fog.

Joy Still foggy is it?

Boy Yes.

Joy Everything disappears when it's like that. Just this room and nothing else.

> *The Boy looks at her, disturbed by what she has said. He continues to dress. Joy lights herself a cigarette. She holds it up.*

D'you want one o' these?

Boy No thank you.

Joy You know you got another ten minutes yet. (*Pause.*) You don't have to go for another ten minutes. You paid for half an hour. So you don't have to go yet.

Boy (*doing up his school tie*) I have to.

Joy You gonna find your way in all that fog?

Boy Yes.

Joy (*pause*) This your first time?

Boy No.

Joy D'you mind me asking?

Boy No.

Joy You don't have to go. You got another ten minutes. You can try again if you like. There's no shame in it.

Boy (*rapidly pulling on a school blazer*) No.

Joy Might make you feel better.

Boy No!

Joy Was it me? . . .

The Boy goes to the door. He tries it. It appears to be locked. He pulls and pulls it, in a rapidly growing panic. He becomes frantic. He is almost at the point of shrieking when he stops and attempts to control himself.

I put the bolt in. Up at the top. Sometimes the other girls walk in.

The Boy looks up. He draws back the bolt. He bursts into tears. He sobs, with his head against the door. Joy puts out her cigarette. She sits. She despairs.
   Flynn enters. She takes the blankets off Joy's bed and wraps them round her, as the space becomes . . .

Scene Nine

1969. A squat. Flynn starts to take her clothes off under the blankets. She is shivering, trying to keep herself warm. The room has a screen with badly painted murals across it.

Flynn Any progress in there?

Quinn (*behind the screen*) No.

Flynn How long's it gonna take? 'Cause we said turn up from ten.

Quinn I can't get the connection! The electric's about a million years old.

Flynn Well, maybe we should just put some money in the meter.

Quinn (*appearing*) This is about free love, isn't it?

Flynn (*starting to stuff her clothes into a binbag*) Yes.

Quinn So if it's free, why should we put money in the meter?

Flynn 'Cause it's freezing. No one's gonna even take their jumpers off if it's like this – never mind getting naked.

Quinn Have you got any money?

Flynn No.

Quinn Well, I haven't either.

Flynn Oh.

Quinn So let's do it my way, OK? (*Flynn nods.*) Give us a peek.

Flynn briefly opens her blankets.

Take your socks off.

Flynn I'm too cold.

Quinn Sissy. (*Quinn goes behind the screens.*)

Flynn Quinn?

Quinn Yeh?

Flynn Are you really going to, you know, like go all the way?

Quinn Well, that's sort of the point, isn't it?

Flynn Yeh, I know, only –

Quinn What?

Flynn Now we've come to it . . .

Quinn (*appearing again, irritated*) What?

Flynn I'm a bit nervous. That's all.

Quinn Why are you nervous?

Flynn Well, I know we'll all be blindfold and everything –

Quinn Yeh –

Flynn – which is a great idea, really innovative – so it's all about touch and feeling rather than the aesthetic, yeh, but suppose your blindfold slips, right, and you find yourself doing it with someone, you know, like fat or repulsive –

Quinn It's not about that, is it?

Flynn Yeh I know, but supposing it's like a dirty old man or something.

Quinn We haven't invited any dirty old men! Jesus, Flynn, you're very good at lapping up all the theory, being all keen and eager, but then, when it actually comes to the point of action, you're like a little nun.

Flynn Don't say that.

Quinn This is important for us. It's about the emancipation of love. People we dig, coming together to share the miracle of sex, turning all that amazing energy into a positive force for change, a force for peace. It's about revolutionising the whole way we are with one another, creating something completely new for the future.

Flynn I know –

Quinn Getting rid of the ownership, the possession, the jealousy. It's about freedom, freedom of love. And a lot of people have lost their lives for that.

Flynn But we have freedom of love, don't we? I mean, just you and me?

Quinn We have a beautiful thing. That's why we have to share it with others, baby. It's selfish to keep it to ourselves. I don't wanna possess you. It's bourgeois.

Flynn So we have to be generous even to spotty, pongy, bad-breath people?

Quinn Look, if my blindfold slips, and I find I'm doing it with some less than dazzling chick, I'm not gonna stop, am I? She'd be hurt. (*Pause.*) I'm going in the loft. (*He disappears behind the screen. As he exits:*) It's weird, this place. There's stuff up there that gives me the creeps; freaky paintings and pigeon bones.

> *Lynne and Gwyn enter. Flynn rushes behind the screen, hiding from them.*

Lynne Is this it?

Gwyn It can't be.

Flynn Hello. Hi!

Gwyn Is this the Love-In?

Lynne We found your invite yeh? Thought it would be a bit more happening . . .

Flynn Yeh, but we're not ready yet, OK?

Lynne Oh.

Flynn Um, you're a bit early. 'Cause we're trying to tap into the mains yeh, so that the corporate pigs can pay for it, but Quinn, that's my boyfriend – like in a non-ownership way? – hasn't actually got it together. He can't get a connection.

Gwyn Why are you hiding?

Flynn 'Cause I um – look, there's some pillowcases out there, yeh? And some labels? And some blindfolds, so take your clothes off, put them in a pillowcase, stick a label on it with your name on, yeh, and then put a blindfold on and come behind here and this is where it's all gonna be happening. Only it's a bit cold 'til we get the heating on.

Gwyn Are we the first here?

Flynn Um, yeh, but don't let that bother you.

Lynne 'Cause we don't wanna end up just doing it with each other.

Gwyn We do that all the time.

Lynne And we're sick of it. Actually.

Gwyn That's why we've come.

Lynne I mean we love each other, yeh, but the spark's gone.

Flynn Right –

Gwyn You know, it always does. You always end up thinking this is really mundane, man.

Lynne So we're still a couple but we need Dr Illicit Sex to keep us, you know . . .

Gwyn Hot.

Flynn Well, d'you wanna come back later when it's all like a bit warmer even?

Gwyn Not really, no.

Flynn Or you could start with Quinn, I s'pose.

Lynne What, both of us?

Flynn He's definitely up for it. Shall I shout him?

Gwyn I don't wanna shag another bloke.

Lynne He's sick of that as well. He's sick of everything.

Gwyn No I'm not.

Lynne Yes you are; you've glutted yourself on pornography.

Gwyn So?

Lynne It's boring.

Gwyn (*to Flynn*) What about you, babe? Why don't you and me start it?

Flynn Um . . .

Gwyn You got three tits or something? That why you're hiding?

Flynn We're not supposed to see each other, 'cause we're all blindfold, so the intensity of touch is like, much more?

Lynne Oh great. It'll be a relief not to have to see anyone's face. 'Specially his.

Gwyn Let's start then, babe. And your boyfriend can join in.

Flynn Um, I can't. Sorry.

Lynne Why not?

Flynn Well actually, I got my period. So I'm just sort of here doing the snacks and drinks and that.

Gwyn I don't care about your period.

Lynne Neither do I, sister.

Flynn Yeh, but I got a rash. As well. So I can't. Well I could, but I wouldn't if I were you. You'd be better off waiting for someone else.

Gwyn Jesus.

Lynne She's a scared kid . . .

Gwyn Oh for fuck's sake. I thought this was adults only.

Lynne Come on. We can pick someone up in the pub more easily than this.

Gwyn Why don't we just go home? I'll make myself pretend you're someone else.

Lynne Yeh well. You can pretend I'm someone who's bloody well asleep. 'Cause I will be.

Gwyn What a waste o' time.

They leave. Flynn reappears. She ties her blindfold on. She is close to tears.

Flynn I *will* do it. I *can* do it. I will emancipate love. I have to liberate myself. Freedom of love. Freedom of love . . .

Scene Ten

THE AGE OF EXCESS

The present. The space has become a brand new office building: a dating agency. A video plays. We see a logo for 'Hearts International, the exclusive place to find love' and then an image of Brigitta.

Brigitta Um, hello, my name's Brigitta . . . and I've never done anything like this. Um, I'm thirty (-three), I'm single and . . . I mean a lot of you will probably be fast-forwarding already but for those of you who are still here . . . I'm a really decent person and you'd be lucky to get me, so if you're a *proper* man – (*She sighs.*) why on earth would you be looking at this? (*a moment of static*) Hi, I'm Brigitta. I'm thirty, I'm single and I'm looking for . . . Anything.

Rita enters. She picks up a remote control and watches, her feet on Anita's desk.

Anything . . . (*brightly*) So if you're shallow and sleazy and you'd like a meaningless, depressing encounter, why don't you – (*static*) Hi, I'm Brigitta. (*Pause.*) I can't do this.

Rita fast-forwards.

It's like there's this chasm – Oh, I don't know. I feel as if I'm standing on some kind of an ice floe and the rest of humanity is just drifting further and further away. I feel *so alone* . . . And it's not just me; all of us. We're – we don't have enough – I don't know – whatever it is . . . whatever it is that makes swans stay together.

Rita Oh my God.

Brigitta They never part. Once they meet, that's it, for life. Would you say that was love or just some kind of instinct? Blackbirds do it too.

Rita Fuck's sake.

Brigitta Sorry. I'm really sorry. (*Static. Much more brightly*) Hi, I'm Brigitta. I'm twenty-nine, I'm a Gemini, I like music, travel, dining out and life's simple pleasures. So, if you're aged between thirty and forty, if you're looking for friendship, fun and a bit of sunshine in your life, why don't you give me a call?

Rita (*spelling it out*) S-a-d-d-o.

Anita enters, hurried. Rita flicks the video off.

Anita Hi, sorry, some ball-less little no-dick tried to clamp me. I had to spend twenty minutes trying to convince him that I was thick and he was gorgeous before he'd let me go – cunt. Any messages?

Rita Don't you think you should knock before you come in?

Anita Rita, / are there any –

Rita I don't like your tone. You should address me as Miss Clark. And knock before you come in. I could have been doing anything in here.

Anita (*amused*) Really?

Rita Anything.

Anita Sorry, Miss Clark, but the saddos are going to be here in about five minutes. I need to check everything's ready.

Rita Everything's fine. Take your jacket off.

Anita Rita –

Rita Miss Clark. Get it off.

Anita undoes her jacket.

Throw it on the floor.

Anita is tempted.

Anita I haven't got time . . .

Rita Unbutton your shirt and come here.

Anita Baby, I haven't got / time.

Rita I'm not your baby.

Pause.

Anita Sorry.

Rita You never have time.

Anita Can't we do something later? After the saddos.

Rita I'm busy later.

Anita Doing what?

Rita says nothing. She removes her feet from the desk.

God, I've only just walked in the door and already I'm in the doghouse.

Rita You don't give a shit about me, do you?

Anita Oh come on.

Rita Say it then.

Anita Say what?

Rita Say it.

Anita I won't be forced. (*She starts checking that everything is ready.*)

Rita You know it amazes me that someone who spends her whole life shoving romance down people's throats is so terrified of the whole idea of love that she can't even bring herself to say the word.

Anita Rita, if you're going to be a pain in the arse, can you just go home?

Rita Oh, I wouldn't dream of it. Let me give you your messages and while I'm at it why don't I suck your cock?

Anita You are so childish.

Rita (*leafing through a notepad*) The photocopier bloke can't get here until Monday. *Home and Garden* are doing a deal on advertising space, half a page for the price of a quarter. And sticky-out-chin-woman isn't coming.

Anita What?

Rita Yep. She's found love on a chat-page.

Anita She *what*?

Rita I told her she'd never get our kind of exclusive clientele on a website but she said she didn't care. She's been communicating with some bloke from Ramsgate who understands her pain.

Anita You're joking!

Rita I said have you sent him a photo yet? But she didn't deign to reply.

Anita You told me everything was ready!

Rita It is. I put the nibbles out; the champagne's in a bucket.

Anita Have you tried to get someone else?

Rita At an hour's notice?

Anita Well, what are we going to do?

Rita (*unconcerned*) I don't know.

Anita I've got two blokes and only one woman!

Rita Lucky old her.

Anita This is the kind of thing that brings down my name! They're all new – new clients, and I've set them up in a fucking threesome.

Rita They might enjoy it.

There is the faintest echo, a sound of anguish.

Anita I needed sticky-out-chin-woman for weird-doctor. She's the only one I could rely on to make him feel he wasn't (the ugliest person in the room) –

Rita Shhh!

Anita What?

Rita That noise.

Anita What noise?

Rita There.

Anita I can't hear anything.

Rita Shhh!

The sound stops.

Anita . . . I think this place is haunted.

Anita Don't be stupid. It's brand new; we're the first people to lease it.

Rita I know it's new, but it's built on top of old stuff.

Anita Of course it is. We're right in the middle of the city.

Rita So there might be an Inca burial ground underneath, or a pet cemetery; something unrestful. I'm not being funny. The place goes cold sometimes.

Anita You think my office is haunted by a dead pet?

Rita You know what I mean!

Anita Frankly, Rita, I'm more concerned with what to do when the saddos get here.

Rita It's probably my juvenile dementia, that's what you're thinking, isn't it?

Anita (*coldly*) I don't think you can ever assume to know what I'm thinking.

Rita Do you know what I'm thinking?

Anita No.

Rita (*icily*) Good.

There's a buzz on the intercom.

Anita Shit.

Rita I'm going home, OK?

Anita Don't!

Rita I've got to pluck my toenails.

Anita Don't. Please Reet, you can't. (*into the intercom*) Hello? (*to Rita*) Wait! (*into the intercom*) Hi, Dieter! (*She buzzes him in. To Rita*) I'm sorry. I've been an absolute cow since the moment I got in and I'm really sorry. I'll make it up to you any way I can – but right now you have to be the other woman.

Rita What?

Anita Pretend to be the other saddo. Please. I'd do it myself, only they've all met me.

Rita Are you serious?

Anita You don't have to go on a date with them or anything. You just have to meet them for half an hour, make an excuse and leave.

Rita I don't believe it.

Anita Please, *please*, Rita; I'll meet you later, we'll go out, I'll buy you dinner –

Rita You pimp!

Dieter enters.

Dieter Hello.

Anita Dieter, so glad you could make it.

Dieter Am I the first?

Anita No, this is . . . Lolita.

Rita looks at her aghast.

She's a new client too.

Dieter Hello.

Rita Hi.

Dieter holds out his hand. Rita shakes it.

Anita So, would you guys like a glass of champagne?

Dieter I'll just have a mineral water, thanks.

Rita I'll have champagne. Lots of it.

Anita Cool. Back in two nanoseconds. (*She exits.*)

Rita So you don't drink?

Dieter No.

Rita Are you pregnant or something?

Dieter Er no . . . I'm a recovering alcoholic.

Rita Oh. How long have you been sober?

Dieter Two years.

Rita What made you give up?

Dieter The realisation of what had made me drink.

Rita What had made you drink?

Dieter Terror.

Rita Terror?

Dieter Yes, I think so. (*attempting to change the subject*) So how / about you?

Rita What made you realise that? Only I'm thinking of becoming an alcoholic myself and I thought maybe you could tell me if it was worthwhile.

Dieter I can't be glib about it, I'm sorry.

Rita No, I'm sorry . . . I'm really glib and sorry.

Dieter That's OK.

Rita What were you terrified of?

Dieter Well, if you want the whole story, I was reaching for the Scotch one night –

Anita enters, with a bottle of champagne.

Anita Just opening this; I haven't gone away!

Rita We're fine.

Dieter And I was suddenly convulsed with pain and I was violently sick – it was quite horrible – and what had come up was somewhere between blood and treacle.

Rita Eurrr.

Dieter I thought my God, that's my whole liver.

The buzzer goes. Anita goes to answer it.

And I blacked out as usual and remembered nothing, but next morning, I was racked with shocking pain. I couldn't move. I nearly died.

Anita (*into the buzzer*) Hi, sweetheart, come on up!

Dieter So I lay in bed and thought long and hard.

Anita Yep – oh!

Dieter I thought, I've been trying to die for years; this must be what I want.

Anita Cool, great! (*She exits.*)

Dieter And then at some point in the afternoon I had a kind of a well, I suppose a – I've never really known how to describe it. It was like an incredible sense of calm, and I realised that I was no longer afraid. Because what had always terrified me more than death . . . was life. I was terrified of life. And I thought that if I chose, I could stop being afraid. I could decide to live. So, two years later, here I am . . . trying to live.

Rita is moved. Anita returns, followed by Brigitta and Peter.

Anita Now that's what I call handy, meeting on the stairs! Who'd like a glass / of bubbly?

Brigitta Please.

Peter Thanks.

Dieter So anyway, now I'm terribly embarrassed, so –

Rita Don't be. I think you're very brave. And honest.

Anita pops the bottle.

Anita That's the sound I like to hear!

Rita You make me feel ashamed.

Dieter What of?

Brigitta (*looking nervously at the furnishings*) This is nice . . .

Rita My name isn't Lolita.

Dieter Oh?

Rita It's Rita Clark. My last relationship was with a woman.

Peter (*to Brigitta*) Very soft . . .

Rita I'm confused, you see.

Dieter Well, a lot of us are.

Anita (*handing the glasses round*) Brigitta.

Brigitta Thanks.

Anita Peter.

Peter Jolly good.

Rita I shouldn't be here.

Anita (*handing her a drink*) Of course you should! And an aqua-fizzy for Dieter.

Dieter Thanks.

Anita Here we go. Cheers, folks. Welcome to Hearts International.

They awkwardly clink glasses.

Now, I call evenings like this 'Icebreakers' and they're all about you breaking the ice with one another, having a friendly, open chat with no strings attached, before embarking on the hazardous business of choosing a date. I never invite more than four specially selected clients, so you don't feel crowded out and you can all get an idea of the kind of exclusive people we have on our books. So, I'm going to take a back seat, sort out the canapés, and leave you to say hello. OK? (*Anita moves to one side. She keeps one ear on Dieter and Rita.*)

Peter It sounds like organs for transplant, doesn't it?

Brigitta Pardon?

Peter Hearts International.

Brigitta Oh. Right . . .

Peter You know, one of those dodgy agencies that buy bodily organs from the poor and disadvantaged.

Rita (*to Dieter*) This woman I was seeing . . .

Brigitta Mmm.

Peter Kidneys and the odd lung / and what-have-you.

Rita I've decided. I'm gonna dump her completely.

Dieter Oh?

Rita 'Cause sometimes I just think she's out to twist me up inside. She thinks I act like a kid but actually, / she's the childish one.

Peter I'm a doctor.

Brigitta That's / nice.

Dieter Oh dear.

Rita You know, she plays manipulative games.

Brigitta Do you specialise in anything?

Rita Sometimes she'll dump me in awkward situations –

Peter Yes I do.

Rita Just to watch me sink or swim –

Peter I'm a urologist.

Brigitta Oh.

Peter That's waterworks –

Brigitta Yes, I know.

Rita / She holds back affection to punish me for her own stupid past –

Peter Well, not waterworks actually –

Rita And she's never ever, not even once, said she loves me.

Peter That's just a stupid / expression I use –

Rita Do you know what that's like?

Dieter I can imagine.

Peter Because for some reason people seem to be embarrassed / talking about their urinary tracts.

Rita / It's why I want to change.

Brigitta I'm not.

Rita I'm gonna kick her out of my life.

Peter Yes, you see? Where would we be without them? Certainly not drinking champagne! (*He is laughing.*)

Rita I want to know what it's like being with a man.

Peter We'd all be carrying catheters about, wouldn't we?

Rita A good, nice man.

Dieter Oh, right. Well, good luck . . .

Anita (*relieved at Dieter's reply*) Is anybody ready for a top-up? Lolita?

Rita holds out her glass. Anita tops it up.

Goodness, aren't you thirsty.

Peter (*moving across*) Is your name Lolita?

Rita No.

Peter Our hostess just called you Lolita.

Rita It's a *nom de plume*.

Brigitta (*to Anita*) Could I trouble you?

Anita No problem, sweetheart. (*Anita pours Brigitta some champagne.*)

Peter Are you a writer?

Rita No.

Peter Then why have you got a *nom de plume*?

Rita I don't know. Why do you care?

Peter Well, my cat's called Lolita.

Anita No! (*She laughs uproariously.*)

Peter I've got two cats and a terrapin.

Anita Great. (*She exits.*)

Brigitta (*shyly, to Dieter*) Hi, I'm Brigitta.

Dieter Hi. Dieter.

Brigitta Have you been to one of these things before?

Dieter No.

Brigitta Me neither.

Dieter Oh.

Brigitta It's very . . .

Dieter and Brigitta are tongue-tied. The attraction between them is obvious.

Peter My cats are called Lolita and Lucrezia and the terrapin's a male. He's called Severin.

Rita Severin the terrapin?

Peter Yes.

Rita I hate cats.

Brigitta I'm . . . I'm divorced. With two kids.

Peter So, if your name's not Lolita, what is it?

Rita Rita Clark.

Peter Why did you lie?

Rita I didn't.

Peter You obviously did.

Rita A *nom de plume* isn't a lie, it's a *nom de plume*.

Dieter I'm a recovering alcoholic.

Brigitta Oh?

Peter It's a false name, a falsehood. Why did you come here with a false name?

Rita I didn't. Who are you anyway, the Spanish Inquisition?

Peter No, I'm just an ordinary, fee-paying client and I got given strict instructions not to lie on my form.

Brigitta . . . Would you like to go?

Rita I don't remember that instruction.

Dieter What, just leave?

Rita Perhaps I ignored it.

Brigitta Yes . . .

Peter So you admit to lying?

Dieter You want to leave . . . with me?

Brigitta nods.

Rita As a matter of fact, my entire form is a web of deceit.

Anita (*entering with canapés*) Now then, who'd like a nibble? Peter?

Peter helps himself. Dieter and Brigitta are gazing at one another.

Peter So, what did you lie about?

Rita I said my favourite colour was blue when really it's green. I said I was a lapdancer when really I'm a temp.

Peter I don't believe you.

Rita I said I could breathe underwater when really I can't. And that sometimes I get stigmata, when I don't.

Dieter and Brigitta are deeply moved. Anita approaches them.

Anita Would you like a little dip?

Dieter We're going to go.

Anita What?

Brigitta Sorry.

Peter You're going?

Brigitta Yes.

Anita Is something the matter?

Dieter No.

Brigitta We just . . .

Anita Do you two know each other?

Dieter No.

Brigitta Not yet.

Dieter (*intimately*) When you find out about me . . .

Brigitta I'll accept everything. Everything you are.

He draws closer.

Please be true.

They kiss. They prepare to leave. The others are staring at them, flabbergasted.

(*to Anita*) Thank you.

Peter Wait! You can't just go!

Dieter Why not?

Peter It's not fair!

They leave.

Why wasn't she like that with me?!

Rita Because you're a creep.

Anita Now, let's not have any nasties, OK? If you don't get on, that's fine. It's best just to call it a day and start again with someone else.

Peter (*to Rita*) Don't you dare speak to me like that.

Rita What's the matter? I thought we were getting on great.

Peter You just called me a creep!

Rita I like creeps. I feel a strong attraction towards them.

Peter What?

Anita Peter, why don't you go home and I'll find you someone more suitable in the morning?

Rita Seriously, I'm fascinated. I want to know more about your terrapin.

Peter (*taking the challenge*) I lied about the terrapin. It's a female.

Rita Does it have a name?

Peter Wanda.

Rita Do you mistreat it?

Peter Sometimes.

Rita How?

Peter I put my ex-wife's hairdryer on it.

Rita That's disgusting.

Anita Would you two knock it off?

Peter What else do you find disgusting about me?

Rita Where do you want me to start?

Peter I think you should buy me dinner. I think it's the least you could do after all your lies and insults.

Rita I'll buy the first round of drinks. You buy the dinner.

Anita Rita!

Rita And if you're lucky, I'll throw it over you.

Peter That's exactly what I'd expect.

Anita Rita, stop it.

Rita Why should I?

Anita Peter, I'm really sorry. I had serious doubts about inviting her here tonight. She's extremely unstable and we've had trouble with her before.

Peter That's fine.

Anita She's not what you're looking for, believe me.

Peter I'm looking for an unstable, lapdancing stigmatic.

Rita And I'm looking for a creep with pets.

Anita (*to Rita*) You're going too far!

Rita (*to Peter*) Get out. Now. And dinner's going to be expensive.

Peter You'll pay. One way or the other, you'll pay.

Peter goes. Rita is putting on her coat.

Anita Are you serious?

Rita You know how to stop me.

Anita You're going to go with him, just to get back at me?

Rita Say it.

Anita (*pause*) You can't blackmail me into saying something like that.

Rita Right. See you then.

Anita He's a nut! What if he tries to kill you?

Rita On your head be it. (*She's almost gone.*)

Anita Rita! (*Rita stops. Hopes.*) They fell for each other, right before our eyes. Two people just fell . . . I've never seen that before in my life.

Rita (*bitterly disappointed*) It won't last, will it?

Rita goes. Anita is alone.

Anita They fell in l . . . l-l-l-l . . . Rita, I l-l-l – I l-l-l-l-l –
I l-l-l –

*Anita is in tears. The office disappears. Open land.
Dieter and Brigitta enter.*

Dieter Here.

Brigitta You.

Dieter Now.

Brigitta This . . .

They kiss.

Blackout.